CAPITAL CONTROLS AND INTERNATIONAL ECONOMIC LAW

Focusing on capital controls, this study provides rigorous legal analysis to establish whether the mandate of the International Monetary Fund (IMF) extends to the capital account; that is, whether the IMF has the authority to control and/or regulate the use of capital controls by its member states. The book then analyses whether a country's use of capital controls is consistent with the obligations and commitments undertaken in various multilateral and bilateral trade and investment agreements. Finally, it analyses the tension within international economic law, as the IMF now encourages the use of capital controls under certain circumstances, while most trade/investment agreements prohibit or limit their use. Proposing a way forward to alleviate the tension and construct a more harmonious relationship between the norms and standards of finance, trade and investment, this study will be essential reading for academics, practitioners and policymakers.

BRYAN MERCURIO is the Simon F. S. Li Professor of Law at the Chinese University of Hong Kong. He is co-author of World Trade Law: Text, Materials and Commentary (third edition, 2018), co-editor of International Economic Law after the Global Crisis: A Tale of Fragmented Disciplines (Cambridge, 2015) and author of Drugs, Patents and Policy: A Contextual Study of Hong Kong (Cambridge, 2018).

CAMBRIDGE INTERNATIONAL TRADE AND ECONOMIC LAW

Series editors

Professor Lorand Bartels, *University of Cambridge*
Professor Thomas Cottier, *University of Berne*
Professor Tomer Broude, *Hebrew University of Jerusalem*
Professor Andrea K. Bjorklund, *McGill University, Montréal*

Processes of economic regionalisation and globalisation have intensified over the last decades, accompanied by increases in the regulation of international trade and economics at the levels of international, regional and national laws. At the same time, significant challenges have arisen with respect to economic liberalization, rule-based systems of trade and investment, and their political and social impacts. The subject matter of this series is international economic law, in this contemporary context. Its core is the regulation of international trade, investment, finance and cognate areas such as intellectual property and competition policy. The series publishes books on related regulatory areas, in particular human rights, labour, environment and culture, as well as sustainable development. These areas are horizontally interconnected and vertically linked at the international, regional and national levels. The series also includes works on governance, dealing with the structure and operation of international organisations related to the field of international economic law, and the way they interact with other subjects of international and national law. The series aims to include excellent legal doctrinal treatises, as well as cutting-edge interdisciplinary works that engage law and the social sciences and humanities.

Books in the series

Capital Controls and International Economic Law
Bryan Mercurio

The Law and Practice of Global ICT Standardization
Olia Kanevskaia Whitaker

Between Market Economy and State Capitalism: China's State-Owned Enterprises and the World Trading System
Henry S. Gao and Weihuan Zhou

New Asian Regionalism in International Economic Law
Pasha L. Hsieh

Essential Interoperability Standards: Interfacing Intellectual Property and Competition in International Economic Law
Simon Brinsmead

Digital Services in International Trade Law
Ines Willemyns

Law and Politics on Export Restrictions: WTO and Beyond
Chien-Huei Wu

Energy in International Trade Law: Concepts, Regulation and Changing Markets
Anna-Alexandra Marhold

Shareholders' Claims for Reflective Loss in International Investment Law
Lukas Vanhonnaeker

Transparency in the WTO SPS and TBT Agreements: The Real Jewel in the Crown
Marianna B. Karttunen

Preferential Services Liberalization: The Case of the European Union and Federal States
Johanna Jacobsson

Emerging Powers in International Economic Law: Cooperation, Competition and Transformation
Sonia E. Rolland and David M. Trubek

Commitments and Flexibilities in the WTO Agreement on Subsidies and Countervailing Measures
José Guilherme Moreno Caiado

The Return of the Home State to Investor-State Disputes: Bringing Back Diplomatic Protection?
Rodrigo Polanco

Industrial Policy and the World Trade Organization: Between Legal Constraints and Flexibilities
Sherzod Shadikhodjaev

The Public International Law of Trade in Legal Services
David Collins

The Prudential Carve-Out for Financial Services: Rationale and Practice in the GATS and Preferential Trade Agreements
Carlo Maria Cantore

Preferential Services Liberalization: The Case of the European Union and Federal States
Johanna Jacobsson

Judicial Acts and Investment Treaty Arbitration
Berk Demirkol

Distributive Justice and World Trade Law: A Political Theory of International Trade Regulation
Oisin Suttle

Freedom of Transit and Access to Gas Pipeline Networks under WTO Law
Vitalily Pogoretskyy

Reclaiming Development in the World Trading System, 2nd edition
Yong-Shik Lee

Developing Countries and Preferential Services Trade
Charlotte Sieber-Gasser

Establishing Judicial Authority in International Economic Law
Edited by Joanna Jemielniak, Laura Nielsen and Henrik Palmer Olsen

WTO Dispute Settlement and the TRIPS Agreement: Applying Intellectual Property Standards in a Trade Law Framework
Matthew Kennedy

Trade, Investment, Innovation and their Impact on Access to Medicines: An Asian Perspective
Locknie Hsu

The WTO and International Investment Law: Converging Systems
Jürgen Kurtz

The Law, Economics and Politics of International Standardisation
Edited by Panagiotis Delimatsis

Export Restrictions on Critical Minerals and Metals: Testing the Adequacy of WTO Disciplines
Ilaria Espa

Optimal Regulation and the Law of International Trade: The Interface between the Right to Regulate and WTO Law
Boris Rigod

The Social Foundations of World Trade: Norms, Community, and Constitution
Sungjoon Cho

Public Participation and Legitimacy in the WTO
Yves Bonzon

The Challenge of Safeguards in the WTO
Fernando Piérola

General Interests of Host States in International Investment Law
Edited by Giorgio Sacerdoti, with Pia Acconci, Mara Valenti and Anna De Luca

WTO Disciplines on Subsidies and Countervailing Measures: Balancing Policy Space and Legal Constraints
Dominic Coppens

The Law of Development Cooperation: A Comparative Analysis of the World Bank, the EU and Germany
Philipp Dann

Liberalizing International Trade after Doha: Multilateral, Plurilateral, Regional, and Unilateral Initiatives
David A. Gantz

Domestic Judicial Review of Trade Remedies: Experiences of the Most Active WTO Members
Edited by Müslüm Yilmaz

The Relevant Market in International Economic Law: A Comparative Antitrust and GATT Analysis
Christian A. Melischek

International Organizations in WTO Dispute Settlement: How Much Institutional Sensitivity?
Marina Foltea

Public Services and International Trade Liberalization: Human Rights and Gender Implications
Barnali Choudhury

The Law and Politics of WTO Waivers: Stability and Flexibility in Public International Law
Isabel Feichtner

African Regional Trade Agreements as Legal Regimes
James Thuo Gathii

Processes and Production Methods (PPMs) in WTO Law: Interfacing Trade and Social Goals
Christiane R. Conrad

Non-Discrimination in International Trade in Services: 'Likeness' in WTO/GATS
Nicolas F. Diebold

The Law, Economics and Politics of Retaliation in WTO Dispute Settlement
Edited by Chad P. Bown and Joost Pauwelyn

The Multilateralization of International Investment Law
Stephan W. Schill

Trade Policy Flexibility and Enforcement in the WTO: A Law and Economics Analysis
Simon A. B. Schropp

CAPITAL CONTROLS AND INTERNATIONAL ECONOMIC LAW

BRYAN MERCURIO

The Chinese University of Hong Kong

Shaftesbury Road, Cambridge CB2 8EA, United Kingdom

One Liberty Plaza, 20th Floor, New York, NY 10006, USA

477 Williamstown Road, Port Melbourne, VIC 3207, Australia

314–321, 3rd Floor, Plot 3, Splendor Forum, Jasola District Centre, New Delhi – 110025, India

103 Penang Road, #05-06/07, Visioncrest Commercial, Singapore 238467

Cambridge University Press is part of Cambridge University Press & Assessment, a department of the University of Cambridge.

We share the University's mission to contribute to society through the pursuit of education, learning and research at the highest international levels of excellence.

www.cambridge.org
Information on this title: www.cambridge.org/9781009045452

DOI: 10.1017/9781009042215

© Bryan Mercurio 2023

This publication is in copyright. Subject to statutory exception and to the provisions of relevant collective licensing agreements, no reproduction of any part may take place without the written permission of Cambridge University Press & Assessment.

First published 2023
First paperback edition 2024

A catalogue record for this publication is available from the British Library

Library of Congress Cataloging-in-Publication data
Names: Mercurio, Bryan, author.
Title: Capital controls and international economic law / Bryan Mercurio, The Chinese University of Hong Kong.
Description: Cambridge, United Kingdom ; New York, NY : Cambridge University Press, 2023. | Includes bibliographical references and index.
Identifiers: LCCN 2022057079 (print) | LCCN 2022057080 (ebook) | ISBN 9781316517437 (hardback) | ISBN 9781009042215 (ebook)
Subjects: LCSH: Capital movements – Law and legislation.
Classification: LCC K4444 .M47 2023 (print) | LCC K4444 (ebook) | DDC 343/.03–dc23/eng/20230403
LC record available at https://lccn.loc.gov/2022057079
LC ebook record available at https://lccn.loc.gov/2022057080

ISBN 978-1-316-51743-7 Hardback
ISBN 978-1-009-04545-2 Paperback

Cambridge University Press & Assessment has no responsibility for the persistence or accuracy of URLs for external or third-party internet websites referred to in this publication and does not guarantee that any content on such websites is, or will remain, accurate or appropriate.

CONTENTS

Foreword page xi
   Jesús Seade
Preface xv
Acknowledgements xxv
List of Abbreviations xxvii

PART I   **Key Concepts: Capital Flows and Controls**

1   The Liberalisation of Capital Flows   3
2   Capital Flow Management Measures   25

PART II   **The IMF, Capital Flows and Controls**

3   Shifting the IMF Mandate   49
4   The Legality of the IMF's Mandate Expansion   76

PART III   **Legal Frameworks, Rules and Conflicts**

5   The Multilateral Trade Framework   97
6   Bilateral and Regional Trade Agreements   122
7   International Investment Agreements   142
8   Conclusions   184

Bibliography 196
Index 207

FOREWORD

Capital controls have for many decades been a source of controversy, disagreement and forceful policy debates. Previously thought of as simply part of the domestic policymakers' toolkit, this gradually changed as the world became more interconnected – and as global trade and finance blurred the once clear divide between the current and capital accounts. Capital controls fell out of fashion as countries of all kinds and for different reasons felt the need to walk away from them in the 1960s–1980s, and countries using them increasingly came under extreme pressure from other governments as well as international organisations. Economists continued engaging in a contentious policy debate over the value, role and effectiveness of capital controls, but for all intents and purposes by the 1990s the policy debate was all but settled – the dominant view becoming that capital controls should not be part of the policy toolkit to maintain stability and forestall crises.

But of course problems continued to exist all along, and equally policy debates, which I was part of, both in the formation and in the early years of the World Trade Organization (WTO) – where it fell on me to negotiate a *cooperation agreement* with the International Monetary Fund (IMF) to provide information flows to best inform decisions on trade-finance linkages – as well as at the IMF where I was involved in crisis management in the aftermath of the 1997 Asian Meltdown, when financial 'contagion' was born. This crisis led to many calls among outside experts and staff for sand to be placed in the wheels of capital movements in appropriate circumstances and form.

That string of financial crises hitting East and South-East Asia, then Russia, Brazil and Argentina, Turkey and many others in the late 1990s and early 2000s was a traumatic episode for developing and emerging markets, as dire for them if not worse than the subsequent Global Financial Crisis (GFC) of 2008 – even if on a global scale its sparing the major economies made it look relatively tame compared to the larger successor crisis. But a lot of thinking and reflection took place during and in the aftermath of those crises, and increasingly intellectuals and policymakers questioned the extreme liberal order with no place in it for capital account measures.

The IMF thus learned a lot from these crises and gradually underwent a shift in its thinking, as well as changes in how it approaches advice to countries needing support in times of crisis. Officially since 2012, and in practice since the Emerging Markets' crises at the turn of the century and then with the GFC, the IMF eschewed its former dogmatic position against the imposition of capital controls. This is reflected in its advice, which now includes advocating the imposition or maintenance of capital controls in certain circumstances.

Nevertheless, while economists and policymakers have focused their attention on public discussion and debates on the impact and effectiveness of financial liberalisation and capital controls, the legal framework to navigate these complex waters has been much understudied and underappreciated, as much in the academic literature as in practice. With no international framework governing capital movements, the 'rules of the game' can be unclear. While the right of a government to take action to prevent or forestall a crisis is paramount, this right is always tempered through the voluntary entrance into agreements with other governments, whether bilaterally, regionally or multilaterally. Such is the case with capital controls: governments enter agreements with one or more partners in free trade agreements (FTAs), in bilateral investment treaties (BITs) and in multilateral institutions such as the IMF and WTO. Such fragmentation in the results, or diverse incidence of legal commitments on the same issues, in differing and sometimes confusing structures and rules, as well as gaps in the rules, can contain contradictions and potential for conflicting rights and obligations. While governments and inter-governmental organisations attempt to fill the gaps with dialogue, this usually happens on an ad hoc basis, informal and unstructured, often yielding only marginal or partial results. And while numerous countries have negotiated a range of international agreements that liberalise capital movements, most seemingly fail to have macroeconomic stability at the core of the negotiation.

To most observers, the existence of exceptions to liberalisation commitments and other safeguards is confusing, and again, fully dependent on the relevant treaty at issue. The possibility of conflicting commitments grows with each new agreement, and of course the potential for conflict between these treaties and an IMF recommendation or commitment is also present. I therefore welcome wholeheartedly this valuable and penetrating monograph from Bryan Mercurio – the first study to expertly and systematically engage with and analyse such issues.

I met Bryan shortly after I arrived in Hong Kong fresh from the IMF in 2007. He was then the very active associate dean (research) of the Chinese

University of Hong Kong's (CUHK) Faculty of Law, and a major force on issues pertaining to WTO as much as international finance. He is a respected international economic law scholar with a distinct gift to see both the larger picture where countries engage and the intricacies of specific problems and issues, and to see and appreciate as much the trade and the financial dimensions.

Mercurio's acumen and penchant for precise legal analysis and insightful policy-based commentary is on full display throughout the eight chapters of this book. Importantly, he has done so in a way that can be read and digested by a non-expert. In this regard, the first two chapters introduce the key concepts, background information and historical developments that set the stage for the analysis to come. Part II of the book features a ground-breaking legal analysis of the IMF's oversight and control over capital movements. In so doing, Mercurio deftly explains how the IMF used legal means to slowly and steadily shift its mandate to cover the capital account through what he has termed a 'byroad' to avoid the historical distinction between 'capital movements' and 'current international transactions'. Thus, as the book makes clear, by the time the IMF issued its Institutional View in 2012, the result was not a massive change but more so an announcement of the direction that the Fund had pursued in the GFC. Another key component of the analysis is Mercurio's conclusion that the Fund's expansion in mandate is legally valid and legitimate. Referencing both hard and soft law, the conclusion may not be welcome by the Fund's critics, but it is well grounded, legally sound and persuasive. Often neglected in the literature, the addition of solid analysis on the legal authority of the Fund to expand its mandate is critical to its legitimacy to continue operating in this space.

Having set out the Fund's mandate and widening authority over capital movements, the book then shifts focus to analyse whether the Fund's emerging approach to capital controls could possibly conflict with obligations under international economic law: in particular whether a country imposing capital controls with the IMF's blessing would be inconsistent with the disciplines of trade and investment law. Mercurio's legal expertise and acute awareness of broader policy issues are on display when reviewing, analysing and balancing market commitments and exception clauses for such matters as balance of payment difficulties and prudential measures. Here again, the conclusions are carefully reasoned and technically sound. One of the most significant, and perhaps most surprising, findings is that it is larger, developed countries that now include the most exceptions and safeguards in their trade and investment agreements, whereas in agreements between developing countries such safeguards and exceptions can be entirely absent. This is an important finding for many reasons, and one would hope that at least developing countries will take note of it and act.

While Mercurio's analysis persuasively demonstrates that most trade and investment agreements offer sufficient flexibilities to prevent direct conflict with an IMF bailout package that includes the implementation or maintenance of capital controls, one has to understand the author's point that each agreement may be subtly different, and therefore the risk for each country varies by agreement. Governments should listen to Mercurio's advice and ensure future agreements allow for the imposition and maintenance of capital controls in order to prevent or forestall crises.

This book advances the literature on IMF governance of capital movements and the relationship between various strains of international economic law. It provides researchers and policymakers with detailed and informed analysis and clear policy advice. The book also provides confirmation that governments are on the correct path in balancing commitments and obligations with safeguards and exceptions, while also reminding us that work remains to be done and offering a pathway to proceed.

Jesús Seade
Founding WTO negotiator and deputy director-general;
former IMF senior advisor; and Mexico's USMCA chief negotiator

PREFACE

There may never again be a period so prosperous as the fifty years following the conclusion of the Second World War. The livelihoods of millions were improved, and the dream of a middle-class life with all its luxuries became the reality for much of the developed world. In the developing world, abject poverty remained but the growing middle class prospered and the elites became some of the richest humans on the planet. During this time, liberal and neo-liberal doctrines and ideologies dominated international policymaking and economic integration and cross-border trade in goods flourished. With the rise in trade came the need for cross-border payment methods, which correspondingly have also become easier and cheaper over the years. Trade in services also substantially increased in the past few decades, progressively transforming cross-border payments into cross-border brick and mortar investments and, more recently, financial investments. All in all, the world became more globalised than ever and some began to see the free movement of people, goods and capital as an ideal which for the first time seemed on the cusp of reality rather than mere fiction. The increased interdependence of countries combined with a free market ethos created opportunities and was making the world rich.

The past quarter-century, however, has stirred if not shaken the global order from an economic, policy and ideological perspective. Globalisation not only brought about peace and prosperity but also exacerbated economic crises, most notably the Asian financial crisis in the late 1990s, Argentina's financial crisis in 2001 and the Global Financial Crisis (GFC) of 2008. These crises have caused a variety of voices to question the validity of the liberal economic model, both from a financial governance perspective at the International Monetary Fund (IMF) and from a trade governance perspective at the World Trade Organization (WTO). At the same time, those same voices began questioning the financial stability of the liberal model at the domestic level.

While the world has not experienced much of a decline or reversal of trade liberalisation, the same cannot be said of finance. Over the past two decades – and undoubtedly as a result of the repeated economic crises – there has been a slow and steady reversal of the longstanding movement towards the free flow of capital. A diverse range of economies – including Brazil, Chile, China, Greece, Iceland, Malaysia, Taiwan and Thailand – have done so by effectively limiting the free flow of capital by putting in place capital controls (also commonly referred to as Capital Flow Management measures (CFMs) or Capital Account Regulations (CARs)) as a way to re-assert control over their economic systems and preserve their financial stability.

The trend towards preserving policy space to limit the flow of capital is worth emphasising for two reasons. First, it is an indication that unrestricted financial liberalisation is not a 'one size fits all' proposition, and that numerous countries will seek to maintain a form of independence against the excesses of the 'all-in' economic and financial ideal. Second, and perhaps more importantly, this development suggests that the rules of the game have somehow changed. Whilst economic and financial liberalism has always faced some criticism, they have remained the dominant doctrine. The repeated financial crises seen in the last two decades have led to a slow but sustained evolution in thinking and government policy. The first part of this book will explore and document the 'slow but sustained' shifts in the economic, doctrinal, ideological, policy and legal paradigm.

The idea of researching and writing a book that focuses on financial liberalisation and the constraints built into the international economic law system relating to capital controls seems an obvious extension of my work on regime fragmentation and overlap. Moreover, being based in Hong Kong at a time when Beijing is attempting to control outwards capital flows made the topic a natural fit for a research project. The decision to dedicate time to this project was cemented when reading an article published in the *Financial Times* in early 2016 which documented a conversation between Chinese president Xi Jinping, Japanese Central Bank governor Haruhiko Kuroda and managing director of the IMF, Christine Lagarde.[1] The article quotes the Japanese Central Bank's governor as saying that '[c]apital controls could be useful to manage [China's] exchange rate as well as domestic monetary policy in a constructive way', which contrasts sharply with the liberal doctrine historically promoted by Japan and more broadly the IMF. What is more, in a seemingly surprised tone the article observes that 'Kuroda's suggestion of temporary controls to help restore confidence was not rejected by Christine Lagarde … [who] dodged the question'.

---

[1] Chris Giles, 'Kuroda Calls for China to Tighten Capital Controls' (*Financial Times*, 23 January 2016) www.ft.com/content/03395bdc-c1c4-11e5-808f-8231cd71622e.

From my perspective, the most interesting aspect of the article was not Kuroda's suggestion or Lagarde's dodge, but the tone of surprise at the conversation. While liberalisation remains the dominant paradigm, by the time of the GFC the idea of controlling capital should not have been surprising. In fact, as early as the 1990s reasonable and qualified economists began discussing the usefulness (and drawbacks) of capital controls. For instance, in the midst of the Asian financial crisis the Nobel Laureate Paul Krugman briefly (but effectively) illustrated the complexity of implementing capital restrictions:

> Asia is stuck: Its economies are dead in the water, but trying to do anything major to get them moving risks provoking another wave of capital flight and a worse crisis. In effect, the region's economic policy has become hostage to skittish investors. Is there any way out? Yes, there is, but it is a solution so unfashionable, so stigmatised, that hardly anyone has dared suggest it. The unsayable words are 'exchange controls.' ... If this sounds too easy to you, you're right. Exchange controls present lots of problems in practice.[2]

By the time of the conversation between Kuroda and Lagarde, regulators and policymakers increasingly considered restrictions on capital to be one of the components of the regulatory toolbox necessary to manage the economy. The IMF had even by that time seemingly shifted its longstanding position and endorsed, to a limited extent, the use of CFMs. More specifically, in 2012 the IMF published an 'Institutional View' which cautiously embraced CFMs as part of the policy 'toolkit', thereby allowing countries to regulate cross-border capital flows. For the first time, the IMF explicitly: (i) recognised that financial sector regulation/reform must be tailored to the socio-political components of each member; (ii) confirmed CFMs are part of the available regulatory toolkit; (iii) signalled that CFMs may be included in IMF programmes as part of more comprehensive efforts to provide stability; and (iv) did not preclude the long-term maintenance of such measures.[3] To some onlookers, the Institutional View represented a radical shift from its traditional position towards open capital accounts. To those who believe the IMF has no mandate over capital movements,

---

[2] Paul Krugman, 'Saving Asia: It's Time to Get Radical. The IMF Plan Not Only Has Failed to Revive Asia's Troubled Economies but Has Worsened the Situation; It's Now Time for Some Painful Medicine.' (*Fortune Magazine*, 7 September 1998) https://archive.fortune.com/magazines/fortune/fortune_archive/1998/09/07/247884/index.htm.

[3] IMF, 'The Liberalization and Management of Capital Flows: An Institutional View' (International Monetary Fund 2012) www.imf.org/external/np/pp/eng/2012/111412.pdf.

the Institutional View was a usurpation of authority and undue limitation on members' ability to regulate capital movements.

Economists and political scientists have discussed and debated the worthiness of CFMs and the IMF positional shift, but analysis of the legal dimension to CFMs and the IMF position remains scarce. This insight led to the conclusion that more research was necessary to (i) clarify whether CFMs ought to be considered as legitimate regulatory tools to maintain financial stability and forestall economic crises; (ii) determine the extent to which the IMF supports reliance on such tools, and whether it has the authority to even weigh in on the issue; and (iii) understand whether governments have the legal and policy space to take such measures or whether the existing international economic law landscape might prevent such measures from being utilised.

The research conducted for this book has provided the opportunity to widen the scope of the debate on CFMs. To date, academic and policy research has focused on two questions. First, commentators have considered but not fully decided whether capital account liberalisation leads to economic growth, as the empirical literature on capital account liberalisation and growth is both voluminous and contradictory. Even research papers produced by the IMF fail to come to a consensus; some are supportive of the traditional liberalisation approach,[4] while others find no evidence of direct or indirect benefits on growth.[5] Second, commentators have explored whether and how host governments could rely on CFMs to preserve economic stability. The related literature is essentially economic in nature, but again largely equivocal. At best, CFMs seem effective in countries with existing restrictions on capital flows but ineffective in countries where the capital account has been more fully liberalised.[6] Moreover, the evidence generally finds that CFMs are more successful in changing the composition of capital flows rather than in reducing aggregate volume. More surprisingly, however, economists remain divided

---

[4] See i.e. Giovanni Dell'Ariccia and others, *Reaping the Benefits of Financial Globalization* (International Monetary Fund 2008); M. Ayhan Kose and others, 'Financial Globalization: A Reappraisal' (2009) 56 (1) IMF Staff Papers 8; IEO IMF, 'IMF's Approach to Capital Account Liberalization 2005' (International Monetary Fund) 24–29 www.imf.org/en/Publications/Independent-Evaluation-Office-Reports/Issues/2016/12/31/IEO-Evaluation-Report-on-the-IMF-s-Approach-to-Capital-Account-Liberalization-2005-18289.
[5] See Olivier Jeanne, Arvind Subramanian and John Williamson, *Who Needs to Open the Capital Account* (Peterson Institute 2012) 56–58.
[6] IEO IMF, *IMF Response to the Financial and Economic Crisis* (International Monetary Fund 2015) www.imf.org/en/Publications/Independent-Evaluation-Office-Reports/Issues/2016/12/31/The-IMF-and-the-Crises-in-Greece-Ireland-and-Portugal-An-IEO-Assessment-42404.

on the main objectives of the measures – that is, just what capital controls measures are designed to accomplish.[7] Simply stated – the impact of CFMs 'in crisis and non-crisis periods' remains unestablished.[8] The GFC may have brought about a major rethink among the economic elite, but economists remain 'widely divided about the interpretation of the crisis and especially their interpretation of capital controls and the governance of the international financial system'.[9]

Thus while it is clear that the crisis 'shattered' the consensus which had built around financial openness and governments resurrected and legitimatised CFMs during and after the crisis subsided, it is less clear which CFMs were prudent and justifiable in the circumstances and which did little or nothing to bring stability to the ailing host nation. For instance, Otto Hieronymi wrote that the subprime bubble burst was only the 'detonator' of the GFC but the root 'was the profound metamorphosis' of the global financial and monetary landscape over the years leading to the 'gradual elimination of systemic checks and balances [caused by] … the absence of a common international monetary order' following the collapse of the Bretton Woods system and the replacement of 'external discipline' with 'monetary nationalism'.[10] Similarly, Brummer opined that international financial regulation has mainly come from the ability of a select few domestic financial authorities to impose and export their regulatory preferences, not in relation to financial stability but in relation to their own expectations, thus making international financial regulation (*lex financiaria*) a 'fragmented' system.[11] Referring to what he calls 'productive incoherence', Grabel is more blunt in questioning the 'proliferation of responses to the crisis by national governments, multi-lateral institutions, rating agencies and the economics profession that have not yet congealed into a consistent approach to capital controls'.[12]

Indeed, in the absence of precise policy objectives, governments are faced with an innumerate range of potential policy actions to maintain financial

---

[7] Jean Tirole, *Financial Crises, Liquidity, and the International Monetary System* (Princeton University Press 2002) 31–32.
[8] Adrian Blundell-Wignall and Caroline Roulet, 'Macro-Prudential Policy, Bank Systemic Risk and Capital Controls' (2014) 2013 *OECD Journal: Financial Market Trends* 7.
[9] Tirole (n 7) x.
[10] Otto Hieronymi, 'From "Global Finance" to the Crisis of Globalization', *Globalization and the Reform of the International Banking and Monetary System* (Palgrave Macmillan 2009) 11–16.
[11] Chris Brummer, *Soft Law and the Global Financial System: Rule Making in the 21st Century* (Cambridge University Press 2015) 22.
[12] Ilene Grabel, 'The Rebranding of Capital Controls in an Era of Productive Incoherence' (2015) 22 *Review of International Political Economy* 7.

stability and often apply a myriad of inadequate and incongruent measures in their attempt to prevent financial crisis. The inconsistent policy recommendations over capital controls turned almost comical, since, depending on whom one was listening to, CFMs were either critically necessary to forestall crisis or a misguided tool that would hasten and deepen financial crisis. There is not even a consistent opinion or approach as to whether CFMs should be employed as temporary stopgap measures or necessary efficiency tools and/or safeguards to be applied on a long-term basis. Hence, critics view CFMs as nothing more than a red herring, with Hieronymi even facetiously describing CFMs as 'a self-propelling phenomenon [and] the only major activity that could create value out of thin air'.[13]

The economic discussion remains ongoing and contentious, but what seems clear is that the majority of economists believe that in some cases, particularly those involving developing countries with weak regulatory structures and immature markets, regulation of cross-border finance can be essential for maintaining financial stability. The underexplored aspect of regulation is the legal perspective. Other than a document compiled by a group made up predominantly of economists and political scientists who argued that the current web of investment and trade agreements embed liberalism and prevent regulators from restricting capital flows,[14] there is very little sustained discussion on the legal aspects of CFMs in the literature. The second part of this book seeks to add a legal voice to the debate and focuses on the international regulatory framework.

The financial framework applicable to global capital flows – or the lack thereof – is vitally important to study and understand, if only because the lack of oversight in global finance constitutes a veritable source of legal and political uncertainty. The prevailing view of most commentators is that the world lacks a forum for governing global capital flows, and that the Bretton Woods conference did not create such a framework.[15] Thus, the world community has tended to 'allow capital controls as long as they do not have large negative externalities on other countries, [an idea] anchored on the principle that a country's sovereign right to implement policies that they deem best for national welfare should

---

[13] Hieronymi (n 10).
[14] Kevin P Gallagher and others, 'Capital Account Regulations and the Trading System: A Compatibility Review' (2013) Pardee Center Task Force Report, Frederick S. Pardee Centre for the Study of the Longer-Range Future, Boston University.
[15] Kevin P Gallagher, *Ruling Capital: Emerging Markets and the Reregulation of Cross-Border Finance* (Cornell University Press 2015) 30.

be respected as long as there are no substantial negative externalities on other countries'.[16]

What is missing, however, is a single legal framework designed specifically to regulate or coordinate capital movements and restrictions. In practice, capital movements are in fact regulated, but in a piecemeal manner in accordance with the various international economic law regimes developed over the past several decades. First and foremost, of course, is the IMF, which has tirelessly worked for decades to liberalise the cross-border flow of capital and ensure that the financing of trade is not only possible but also stable and secure. Another important source of law is the WTO and free trade agreements (FTAs), which regulate and aim to progressively liberalise trade in goods and services between members and signatories, respectively. The final source of legal obligations are bilateral investment agreements (BITs) and investment chapters contained in FTAs – collectively referred to as International Investment Agreements (IIAs) – which can also contain legal obligations regarding the financial services sector and capital flows. Among other things, IIAs aim to protect foreign investors from political pressure and regulatory uncertainty by placing them under the protection of international standards of treatment – which typically guarantee the absence of restrictions on investment capital repatriation – while facilitating the free exchange of capital from one treaty partner to another.[17]

An IMF working paper published in 2010 lamented the absence of a formal framework for capital flow management, describing the applicable framework for financial regulation as a 'patchwork' of bilateral, regional and other arrangements with contradictory, differing and discriminatory provisions.[18] The working paper also noted that '[m]any Fund members have assumed legal obligations to liberalise capital movements under a broad range of international agreements with varying objectives and

---

[16] Maria Socorro Gochoco-Bautista and Changyong Rhee, 'Capital Controls: A Pragmatic Proposal' (2013) No. 337 ADB Economics Working Paper Series.

[17] As Broomfield notes, those agreements 'typically do not allow for the imposition of restrictions on capital outflows associated with foreign investments for balance-of-payments reasons'. See Elizabeth Broomfield, 'Reconciling IMF Rules and International Investment Agreements: An Innovative Derogation for Capital Controls' (2012) Columbia FDI Perspectives. See also Kevin P. Gallagher, 'Policy Space to Prevent and Mitigate Financial Crises in Trade and Investment Agreements', *G-24 Discussion Paper Series Research papers for the Intergovernmental Group of Twenty-Four on International Monetary Affairs and Development* (United Nations Conference on Trade and Development 2010).

[18] IMF, 'The Fund's Role Regarding Cross-Border Capital Flows' (International Monetary Fund 2010) 22 www.imf.org/en/Publications/Policy-Papers/Issues/2016/12/31/The-Fund-s-Role-Regarding-Cross-Border-Capital-Flows-PP4516.

scope ... [but] most of them do not approach capital account issues from the perspective of macroeconomic stability, or consider the effects their provisions may have on global stability'.[19] A document produced in 2015 by the Fund's Independent Evaluation Office (IEO) similarly noted that international policy coordination relating to capital flows 'is an ongoing challenge ... There is currently a patchwork of bilateral, regional, and international agreements regulating cross-border capital flows among different groups of countries, but there are no universally agreed "rules of the game"'.[20]

Overall, there is a shared feeling among most commentators that the current system is incoherent as cross-border financial flows are regulated by the independent policymaking priorities and needs of countries that seek to develop and preserve their own markets,[21] yet these efforts are constrained by a variable assortment of international legal standards. In this regard, international bodies and inter-governmental dialogues ranging from the United Nations, United Nations Conference on Trade and Development (UNCTAD) and G20 have expressed concern regarding the extent to which constraints on capital controls can limit policy choices.[22]

What is somewhat surprising, however, is that governments and scholars have generally overlooked or treated in a cursory manner the key issue of to what extent the various rules and sources of international economic law permit or prevent CFMs. The IMF's Institutional View essentially acknowledged the void in legal analysis – and the potential problems unleashed by its new embrace of CFMs – by stating that 'liberalization obligations [in FTAs and IIAs] may create challenges for the management of capital flows ... institutions and members should take [the Fund's] view into account' when drafting new agreements.[23] The IMF thus identifies that its position and recommendation to members in loan/stabilisation

---

[19] Ibid 17.
[20] IMF, *IMF Response to the Financial and Economic Crisis* (n 6).
[21] For a similar argument, see for instance Adam Feibelman, 'The IMF and Regulation of Cross-Border Capital Flows' (2015) 15 *Chicago Journal of International Law* 409; Broomfield (n 17); Annamaria Viterbo, *International Economic Law and Monetary Measures: Limitations to States' Sovereignty and Dispute Settlement* (Edward Elgar Publishing 2012).
[22] See United Nations Report on Reform of International Monetary and Financial System (2009), at 104; UNCTAD, Trade and Development Report (2011), at 100; Macro prudential policy tools and frameworks – Update to G20 Finance Ministers and Central Bank Governors (FSB, IMF, BIS, February 2011), at 13.
[23] IMF, 'The Liberalization and Management of Capital Flows: An Institutional View' (n 3).

programmes could perhaps lead to violations of other international agreements yet does nothing to resolve the coming clash.[24]

The framework for the legal regulation of cross-border capital flows is critically important yet remains vastly unexplored and undeveloped. This book aims to fill the void and contribute detailed legal analysis to the ongoing discussion and debate. In contrast with existing literature, this book does not focus on the utility of CFMs but on legal issues of fragmentation and associated problems. As mentioned, only a handful of political scientists have studied this issue[25] and the existing literature starts with the premise that members should have an absolute right to maintain CFMs – as a result, over-reading and misinterpreting provisions is rife. My approach to the issue came with no pre-conceived ideological viewpoint but instead sought to provide solid analysis on the consistency of CFMs with the trade and investment regimes and to develop a framework to manage and avoid regime conflict in existing and future treaties.

The book is structured in three parts: Part I sets out and defines the key concepts and debates concerning capital account liberalisation and capital controls. More specifically, Chapter 1 provides a general overview of the global financial landscape by introducing the IMF and other key components of the traditional approach to capital flows and demonstrating how and why this traditional approach to free capital flows has shifted over time. Chapter 2 then defines and explores the role, impact and legitimacy of capital controls/CFMs.

Part II focuses on the IMF's oversight and control over the use and legitimacy of capital controls. Chapter 3 explores the legal foundation for the IMF's mandate over capital controls, finding that while the Fund grounded its mandate shift and expansion on the text and wording of the

---

[24] Former IMF legal counsel Deborah Siegel bluntly states that FTA/IIAs 'are potentially on a collision course with the [IMF] because of how [they] deal with capital transactions'. See Deborah E Siegel, 'Using Free Trade Agreements to Control Capital Account Restrictions: Summary of Remarks on the Relationship to the Mandate of the IMF' (2003) 10 *ILSA Journal of International and Comparative Law* 297.

[25] See Jeffrey M Chwieroth, 'Normative Change from Within: The International Monetary Fund's Approach to Capital Account Liberalization' (2008) 52 *International Studies Quarterly* 129; Jeffrey M Chwieroth, *Capital Ideas: The IMF and the Rise of Financial Liberalization* (Princeton University Press 2009); Jeffrey M. Chwieroth, 'Controlling Capital: The International Monetary Fund and Transformative Incremental Change from within International Organisations' (2014) 19 *New Political Economy* 445; Jeffrey M Chwieroth, 'Managing and Transforming Policy Stigmas in International Finance: Emerging Markets and Controlling Capital Inflows after the Crisis' (2015) 22 *Review of International Political Economy* 44; Gallagher and others (n 14); Gallagher (n 15).

Articles of Agreement, it did so by using a 'byroad' which allowed the Fund to interpret its constitutive instrument and creatively use its legal instruments to escape the historical distinction between 'capital movements' and 'current international transactions'. The chapter also makes clear that while the Fund's Institutional View of 2012 was important, it does not represent a radical break from tradition but merely a formalisation and crystallisation of the ideas and direction it has pursued since 2008, and did not create any new rights; nor did it change the Fund's legal mandate. Chapter 4 then explores whether the Fund's expansion in mandate is legally valid and legitimate. By looking at hard and soft law, the chapter concludes that the mandate expansion was in line with the standards of international law applicable to international organisations and thus the Fund can legally monitor and discipline capital movements.

Part III seeks to determine whether the Fund's approach to capital controls conflicts with international economic law, namely the disciplines of trade and investment law. Through the negotiation of trade and investment agreements, countries agree to certain obligations and make specific market access commitments. While such agreements contain safeguards and exception clauses, the scope and depth of such clauses vary between agreements. For this reason, the Fund's approach to capital controls may very well run afoul of the obligations and commitments undertaken in certain agreements. Chapter 5 assesses the issue under the multilateral trade regime, most notably the WTO's General Agreement on Trade in Services (GATS), while Chapter 6 focuses on bilateral and regional trade agreements. Chapter 7 analyses the situation with regards to investment treaties. Chapter 8 ties together the analysis of the preceding three chapters and offers concluding analysis.

ACKNOWLEDGEMENTS

This book is the product of over six years of studying, examining and questioning the linkages between finance, trade and investment law. It took me out of my comfort zone and led me down paths I never expected to travel. It has been frustrating at times, and if I had realised the depths to which I would have to go to understand exactly how and why the International Monetary Fund operates as it does, I am unsure if I would have ever started on this journey. But now that it is over, I look back fondly and am proud to have contributed to the literature.

Along the way, I have benefitted from numerous conversations with friends and colleagues. I am grateful to those that generously agreed to be interviewed and to those that read draft chapters of the manuscript. All errors and omissions, of course, remain my own. I would also like to thank emeritus professor and former dean of the Faculty of Law at the Chinese University of Hong Kong, Christopher Gane, for his years of support, friendship and leadership. As with my previous book, this book benefitted tremendously as our many social meetings at the Tin Tin Bar inevitably turned into casual but productive work-related meetings. I miss you, boss!

As always, I thank my former dean at the Faculty of Law at the University of New South Wales, Leon Trakman, and George Williams, for their unwavering belief and support since day one. Without them, I would not be in academia. I owe them both a debt of gratitude. I also thank Cambridge University Press, with whom I have cultivated a deep relationship for well over a decade. Finola O'Sullivan and Kim Hughes have been supportive, good-natured and professional throughout our many projects, and Joe Ng has again been incredibly helpful and encouraging in the production of this book. Happy retirement, Finola! I look forward to working with Kim and Joe again in the not too distant future, and hopefully meeting all again before too long. I would also like this thank Ruth Martin for compiling the index with accuracy and in a compressed period of time.

A debt of gratitude goes to those research associates and students who worked on the book during this journey. A huge thank you goes to Antoine P. Martin, who was by my side for several years as a senior research associate. We had a productive few years, and Antoine has been instrumental in helping me understand the technicalities and peculiarities of finance law. Antoine played a significant role in this project, keeping it on track and contributing to the final product. It is not an exaggeration to say that its shape and direction would have been very different but for his astute understanding of key concepts, issues and concerns. Academia suffers from your decision to go in a different direction, but I am glad to see you so happy. See you at Scarlett soon! I would also like to thank Maggie YuanYuan Zhang, my former research assistant and recent PhD graduate from the Chinese University of Hong Kong, for her research and help in coding international investment agreements.

Finally, while the idea to write such a book came long ago, it would not have been possible if not for the support of the Hong Kong University Grants Committee. I gratefully acknowledge the financial support received by Hong Kong General Research Fund (GRF) for Project No. 14613717, entitled 'When Regimes Clash on Capital Controls: Managing the Conflicting Norms and Standards of the IMF, WTO and International Investment Agreements'. Thank you for providing funds to make this book possible.

ABBREVIATIONS

ASEAN	Association of Southeast Asian Nations
AUSFTA	Australia-United States Free Trade Agreement
BIT	Bilateral Investment Treaty
BoP	Balance of Payment
CAR	Capital Account Regulations
CETA	Comprehensive Economic and Trade Agreement
CFM	Capital Flow Management
CPTPP	Comprehensive and Progressive Trans-Pacific Partnership
EEA	European Economic Area
EFTA	European Free Trade Association
EU	European Union
GFC	Global Financial Crisis
FDI	Foreign Direct Investment
FET	Fair and Equitable Treatment
FTA	Free Trade Agreement
FX	Foreign Exchange
GATS	General Agreement on Trade in Services
GATT	General Agreement on Tariffs and Trade
IBRD	International Bank for Reconstruction and Development
ICJ	International Court of Justice
IEO	Independent Evaluation Office
IIA	International Investment Agreement
ILO	International Labour Organization
IMF	International Monetary Fund
IMFC	International Monetary and Financial Committee
KAFTA	Korea-Australia Free Trade Agreement
KORUS	United States and the Republic of Korea Free Trade Agreement
MA	Market Access
MAI	Multilateral Agreement on Investment
MFN	Most-favoured Nation
NAFTA	North American Free Trade Agreement
NT	National Treatment
NPM	Non-precluded Measures

OECD	Organisation for Economic Co-operation and Development
PCIJ	Permanent Court of International Justice
QE	Quantitative Easing
RCEP	Regional Comprehensive Economic Partnership
TPP	Trans-Pacific Partnership
UK	United Kingdom
UN	United Nations
UNCTAD	United Nations Conference on Trade and Development
US	United States of America
USD	United States Dollar
USMCA	United States-Mexico-Canada Agreement
WTO	World Trade Organization

PART I

Key Concepts: Capital Flows and Controls

Part I of this monograph introduces, sets out and defines the key concepts and debates concerning capital account liberalisation and capital controls. This part contains two chapters. Chapter 1 provides necessary context by offering an overview the global financial landscape and introducing the IMF and other key components of the traditional approach to capital flows. The chapter also outlines how and why the traditional approach to capital flows has evolved and shifted over time. Having set out the basic framework, Chapter 2 then introduces in more detail the concept of capital controls/CFMs. More specifically, the chapter defines and explores the role, impact and legitimacy of capital controls/CFMs in the global financial system. In this regard, Part I establishes the background and foundational knowledge from which the analysis in the remainder of the book draws and builds upon.

1

The Liberalisation of Capital Flows

Cross-border capital flows have long played an important role in the world economy and as such have been described as the 'connective tissue of the international financial system'.[1] Yet foreign capital brings both benefits and risks to host countries. On the one hand, the progressive development of global trade and the related increase in financial transactions have permitted market expansions and created wealth in both industrialised and emerging economies. On the other hand, cross-border capital flows and freer capital movements can worsen economic conditions and deepen monetary instability.

Several financial crises over the past two decades have made numerous countries acutely aware of such risks. In particular, the Asian Financial Crisis of the late 1990s served as a wake-up call for many economists, policymakers and academics, but this crisis was quickly followed by another financial crisis in Argentina and elsewhere. Being the largest crisis, the GFC in 2008 generated such concern among policymakers that a variety of countries proactively attempted to stave off economic decline and preserve the soundness of their financial systems by regulating cross-border financial flows.

As a result, while capital account liberalisation and the free flow of capital were once almost universally praised as the solution to foster global economic growth, they have now come under serious scrutiny for stability and security reasons. In effect, there is an emerging consensus among policymakers and academics that a more careful and balanced approach to the management of cross-border capital flows is warranted, especially

---

[1] Rawi Abdelal, *Capital Rules: The Construction of Global Finance* (Harvard University Press 2007); Annamaria Viterbo, *International Economic Law and Monetary Measures: Limitations to States' Sovereignty and Dispute Settlement* (Edward Elgar Publishing 2012); Adam Feibelman, 'The IMF and Regulation of Cross-Border Capital Flows' (2015) 15 *Chicago Journal of International Law* 409.

for the health and stability of the international monetary and financial system.[2] Stated differently, while financial liberalism in the form of free financial flows has long been the dominant doctrine for the international community, some restraints are now being put into place to limit the excesses of the system.

Before we explore these restraints and the legal and policy framework in which they have evolved, it is necessary to first provide a general overview of the current global financial landscape. This chapter thus begins by introducing the key pillars of the system – capital flows, the IMF and financial liberalisation – before elaborating on why this traditional approach to free capital flows has slowly but consistently shifted over time.

1.1 The Three Pillars: Capital Flows, the IMF and Financial Liberalisation

Before delving into the substance of this book, we must first introduce and explain the three pillars of the current economic and financial landscape. We begin with an explanation of the concept of capital flows before introducing the most relevant and important international actor in the field, the IMF. Finally, we discuss the IMF's traditional approach to issues relating to financial liberalisation and capital flow management.

1.1.1 *Pillar One: Cross-Border Capital Flows*

Capital flows are at the heart of the policy debate on financial stability; thus it is necessary to define and understand the term. Simply put, capital owners tend to make inward and outward transactions on either a short- or long-term basis to suit a variety of purposes. The term is therefore often used in a very generic way to describe the movements of capital from one economy to another, but what is often lost is that there are various types of capital flows.

The main considerations when it comes to defining capital flows are their geographical dimension, time dimension and nature. Inward flows describe the capital flows entering a domestic market and originating

---

[2] Martin Wolf, *Why Globalization Works* (Yale University Press 2004); Dani Rodrik, *The Globalization Paradox: Democracy and the Future of the World Economy* (WW Norton & Company 2011); Adrian Blundell-Wignall and Caroline Roulet, 'Macro-Prudential Policy, Bank Systemic Risk and Capital Controls' (2014) 2013 *OECD Journal: Financial Market Trends* 7.

from a foreign economy, whereas outward flows refer to capital leaving a domestic economy to be invested abroad.

In regard to the time dimension, capital flows can be regarded as short or long term depending on the type of operational transaction, investment and transfer. Examples of short-term capital transactions are debt or portfolio investments – encompassing trade in securities such as stocks, bonds, bank loans, derivatives and various forms of credit.[3] Due to their 'stop and go' nature, short-term capital flows tend to be considered as speculative and volatile liquidities.[4] As such, they are risky as 'hot money' may enter or exit markets rapidly when high return or risky positions are identified (i.e. currency valuation or devaluation opportunities and changes in monetary and fiscal policymaking). In contrast, long-term capital flows correspond to flows of foreign direct investment (FDI), which are generally more sought after for their ability to finance development through the financing of joint ventures, local businesses and infrastructure projects.[5] Long-term capital flows significantly differ from the short-term flows, as they tend to have a much longer life span and can accommodate and mitigate short-term variations and developments.

Hence, not only do short- and long-term capital flows differ in terms of operational functions, they also tend to have a different impact and influence on economic development. Due to their speculative nature, short-term capital flows can have negative impacts because inflows can quickly turn to outflows – and vice versa – when the market conditions deem such a positional change to be required. Such a reversal typically occurs when the situation in the host economy degrades, or when a situation improves in another country which economically justifies an investment pivot.[6] For instance, sudden or progressive exchange rate depreciation tends to

---

[3] Christopher J Neely, 'An Introduction to Capital Controls' (1999) 81 *Federal Reserve Bank of St. Louis Review* 14.
[4] IMF, 'Pursuing Equitable and Balanced Growth' (International Monetary Fund 2011) 9 www.imf.org/en/Publications/AREB/Issues/2016/12/31/Pursuing-Equitable-and-Balanced-Growth; IMF, 'The Fund's Role Regarding Cross-Border Capital Flows' (International Monetary Fund 2010) 3, 7 www.imf.org/en/Publications/Policy-Papers/Issues/2016/12/31/The-Fund-s-Role-Regarding-Cross-Border-Capital-Flows-PP4516.
[5] OECD, 'Foreign Direct Investment for Development: Maximising Benefits, Minimising Costs' (OECD 2002) www.oecd.org/investment/investmentfordevelopment/1959815.pdf.
[6] See for instance Philip J MacFarlane, 'The IMF's Reassessment of Capital Controls after the 2008 Financial Crisis: Heresy or Orthodoxy?' (2015) 19 *UCLA Journal of International Law and Foreign Affairs* 167; L Kaminsky Graciela, 'International Capital Flows, Financial Stability and Growth' (United Nations, Department of Economic and Social Affairs 2005) DESA Working Paper ST/ESA/2005/DWP/10, www.un-ilibrary.org/economic-and-social-development/international-capital-flows-financial-stability-and-growth_6f7080e3-en.

increase outflows for two reasons – depreciations both reduce the value of assets on international markets and tend to limit the capital owners' access to credit because, with money being devaluated, the lender's investment (the collateral) loses its value. The limitation of credit availability also brings negative impacts, such as reducing investment in domestic firms which depend on external funding for development, deterring foreign investors from investing locally or, in a worst-case scenario, providing the same foreign investors incentives and encouragement to cash out of the economy by taking their gains or mitigating their losses and re-investing the funds in more favourable economies.[7]

Long-term capital flows also have drawbacks. In particular, and especially in FDI-seeking countries, long-term capital flows may create imbalances on the country's capital account (which measures the country's balance of physical and financial assets), especially when domestic capital leaves the economy in significant amounts.[8] Long-term capital flows may also generate deficits to the current account (which measures the country's balance of trade, weights the net income originating from abroad and assesses net current transfers) when the profits generated by foreign capital exit the economy due to foreign investors altering their positions. This is most often the case where political tensions or exchange rate depreciations threaten the foreign investors' positions on the domestic market.[9]

1.1.2 Pillar Two: International Monetary Fund

In 1944, with the Second World War nearing its end, forty-four nations met at Bretton Woods in order to begin reconstruction. Among their key roles was to avoid the reappearance of the economic and financial instability which characterised the period and led to economic and physical destruction.[10] Hence, included in the reconstruction was a blueprint for international financial and monetary relations,[11] and for the creation of what was by then described as a liberal 'postwar

---

[7] On balance sheet effects and falling aggregate demand loops, see Anton Korinek, 'The New Economics of Prudential Capital Controls: A Research Agenda' (2011) 59 *IMF Economic Review* 523, 53. See also Neely (n 3).

[8] Ajit Singh, 'Capital Account Liberalization, Free Long-Term Capital Flows, Financial Crises and Economic Development' (2003) 29 *Eastern Economic Journal* 191.

[9] See for instance MacFarlane (n 6) 172. See also Stijn Claessens, 'Portfolio Capital Flows: Hot or Cold?' (1995) *The World Bank Economic Review* 172.

[10] Joseph P Joyce, *The IMF and Global Financial Crises: Phoenix Rising?* (Cambridge University Press 2012) 20.

[11] Ibid.

economic order ... designed to prevent economic nationalism by fostering free trade and a high level of international interaction' capable of guaranteeing peace.[12]

Practically speaking, the Bretton Woods conference led to the creation of the International Bank for Reconstruction and Development (IBRD), more commonly known as the World Bank, and the IMF. The two institutions were designed to function in different and distinct ways. The Bank was charged with financing reconstruction in Europe and fostering development through the promotion of foreign investment,[13] while the IMF's mandate focused on promoting international monetary cooperation, facilitating a balanced growth of international trade, ensuring exchange stability and supporting the facilitation of global transactions while eliminating exchange restrictions. In this regard, Article I of the Fund's Articles of Agreement provides:

> The purposes of the International Monetary Fund are: (i) To promote international monetary cooperation through a permanent institution which provides the machinery for consultation and collaboration on international monetary problems; (ii) To facilitate the expansion and balanced growth of international trade, and to contribute thereby to the promotion and maintenance of high levels of employment and real income and to the development of the productive resources of all members as primary objectives of economic policy; (iii) To promote exchange stability, to maintain orderly exchange arrangements among members, and to avoid competitive exchange depreciation; (iv) To assist in the establishment of a multilateral system of payments in respect of current transactions between members and in the elimination of foreign exchange restrictions which hamper the growth of world trade.

---

[12] Jeffrey A Hart and Joan Edelman Spero, *The Politics of International Economic Relations* (6th ed., Routledge 2013) 15.

[13] Articles of Agreement of the International Monetary Fund and International Bank for Reconstruction and Development, United Nations Monetary and Financial Conference, Bretton Woods, NH 1 to 22 July 1944 at Article I. Purposes (Article I. Purposes provides that 'The purposes of the Bank are: (i) To assist in the reconstruction and development of territories of members by facilitating the investment of capital for productive purposes, including the restoration of economies destroyed or disrupted by war ...; (ii) To promote private foreign investment by means of guarantees or participations in loans ...; To promote the long-range balanced growth of international trade and the maintenance of equilibrium in balances of payments by encouraging international investment for the development of the productive resources of members, thereby assisting in raising productivity, the standard of living and conditions of labor in their territories'.), http://siteresources.worldbank.org/EXTARCHIVES/Resources/IBRD_Articles_of_Agreement.pdf.

As far as financial developments were concerned, the dominant approach – formulated by the famous British economist and government representative John Maynard Keynes – was that the coordinated regulation of capital was essential to national security interests and key to the stability of the overall framework.[14] This approach reflected the position held by many during the early stages of liberalism that nations needed the flexibility and space 'to strike their own balance between global economic integration and the democratic enhancement of national welfare'.[15]

As we will see throughout this book, the IMF has come to play an important role in building and maintaining the current financial and monetary system.[16] In so doing, the Fund has provided the international community with two major 'international public goods' – economic and financial stability.[17]

The IMF was originally conceived and designed as an international organisation capable of 'provid[ing] information and resolv[ing] problems of cooperation among its members, thus lowering the transaction costs to collective action'. Behind this position was the idea that policies with a global reach would otherwise be impossible to implement by isolated members.[18] What has changed over time, however, is the global monetary landscape within which the Fund operates.

Under the system created at Bretton Woods,[19] the value of currencies was fixed on a 'parity' basis with the Gold Standard or the United States (US) dollar (USD).[20] To ensure that the system functioned, the exchange rates of members' currencies could not differ by more than

---

[14] On Keynes' approach to monetary and financial cooperation, see also Otto Hieronymi, 'From "Global Finance" to the Crisis of Globalization', *Globalization and the Reform of the International Banking and Monetary System* (Palgrave Macmillan 2009) 47; Kevin P Gallagher, *Ruling Capital: Emerging Markets and the Reregulation of Cross-Border Finance* (Cornell University Press 2015) 32–33.
[15] Gallagher (n 14) 39.
[16] See Chapter 3.
[17] Joyce (n 10) 10.
[18] Ibid. 9.
[19] For a detailed explanation of the Bretton Woods system, see Hart and Spero (n 12) 12–20.
[20] On the role of the dollar, see for instance Hart and Spero (n 12) 12 ('After World War II, the US dollar became the key international currency. Dollars were held as reserves by central banks; the dollar became indispensable for international trade, investment and finance; and dollars were used to intervene in exchange markets to influence exchange rates'). On the Gold Standard, see also Michael Melvin, *International Money & Finance* (7th ed., Pearson/Addison-Wesley 2004) 41–47.

1 per cent from this parity requirement.[21] Hence, the IMF initially acted as an entity to monitor the exchange rate regime.[22] In the early 1960s, however, the role of the IMF began to shift. Major European countries began to implement Article VIII of the Agreement, which aimed at lowering restrictions on current payments, reducing discriminatory currency practices and ensuring the greater convertibility of foreign-held balances.[23] At the time, the goal of those members was to guarantee the convertibility and functionality of their respective currencies on the international market while reducing dependency on the USD. As a result, other IMF members similarly began to question the use of the USD as the reserve currency.[24] In 1971, and with the treasury under pressure, President Nixon abandoned the gold convertibility policy under which the US had until then committed to providing gold in exchange for dollars. As a result, members were forced for the first time to discuss ways to reorganise currency exchanges in light of increasing cross-border financial flows.[25]

With the changes in the currency regime, however, also came changes to the role and operations of the Fund. The IMF's original mandate was to act as what some have called a 'credit union'; members would contribute to a fund, which would over time be used to provide them with financial assistance when necessary.[26] This became insufficient, however; hence the Fund slowly transformed its mandate to include a supervisory role. This transformation will be considered in more depth later in this book.

1.1.3 Pillar Three: Financial Liberalisation

The third pillar of the book is the dominant approach to financial liberalisation from the 1980s onwards, that being the liberalisation of capital flows – or the facilitation of capital flows across borders through the lifting

---

[21] Articles of Agreement, Article IV, Sections 1, 3 and 5. ('The par value of the currency of each member shall be expressed in terms of gold as a common denominator or in terms of the United States dollar of the weight and fineness in effect on July 1, 1944' ... 'The maximum and the minimum rates for exchange transactions between the currencies of members taking place within their territories shall not differ from parity' ... 'A member shall not propose a change in the par value of its currency except to correct a fundamental disequilibrium'.). See also Hart and Spero (n 12) 13–15.
[22] Joyce (n 10) 2.
[23] Article VIII, Sections 2, 3 and 4.
[24] Joyce (n 10) 21.
[25] Ibid. 21, 32, 49.
[26] Ibid. 25–27.

of capital restrictions. For the past several decades, the IMF has served as the chief architect and enforcer of the liberalisation of capital flows. Before that, however, various types of restrictions on capital flows were commonly employed by countries, with the most prevalent controls being restrictive outgoing capital flow policies in relation to a balance of payments crisis and restrictive inflow policies to avoid speculative bubbles.

In the 1990s, financial liberalism became the way forward. The IMF and others positively viewed and preached that the liberalisation of financial flows and policies aimed at reducing controls on capital flows would lead to an increase in inbound capital, growth and wealth creation. As many developing economies had lost access to capital markets funding over the past two decades due to successive economic crises,[27] these countries therefore embraced the shift to financial liberalism as a way to prevent destructive rounds of financial instability. This shift in economic mindset became known as the 'Washington Consensus' – a much-discussed and misunderstood concept. At the time, the Consensus was nothing more than a term of expression created by economist John Williamson to simplify and summarise a list of ten 'good polic[ies] to help the debtor countries' (i.e. in South America) to 'overcome their debt burden'.[28] Such policies, he suggested, would indeed be more likely to be approved by Washington-based decision makers and donors. More recently, Williamson described (and commented upon) his own 'consensus' list in the following terms.

---

[27] See for instance IEO IMF, *IMF Response to the Financial and Economic Crisis* (International Monetary Fund 2015) 24, 29, www.imf.org/en/Publications/Independent-Evaluation-Office-Reports/Issues/2016/12/31/The-IMF-and-the-Crises-in-Greece-Ireland-and-Portugal-An-IEO-Assessment-42404. See also Hart and Spero (n 12) 223–27. On the theory of 'surplus' flows, see also Daniela Gabor, 'Paradigm Shift? A Critique of the IMF's New Approach to Capital Controls' (2011) 48 *Journal of Development Studies* 714; MacFarlane (n 6) 188; Neely (n 3) 15; Manuela Moschella, 'The Institutional Roots of Incremental Ideational Change: The IMF and Capital Controls after the Global Financial Crisis' (2015) 17 *The British Journal of Politics and International Relations* 442, 449; Maria Socorro Gochoco-Bautista and Changyong Rhee, 'Capital Controls: A Pragmatic Proposal' (2013) No. 337 ADB Economics Working Paper Series; Neely (n 3) 15; Feibelman (n 1) 432. But see IEO IMF, 'The IMF's Approach to Capital Account Liberalization: Revisiting the 2005 IEO Evaluation' (International Monetary Fund 2015) 10, https://ieo.imf.org/en/our-work/Evaluations/Updates/The-IMFs-Approach-to-Capital-Account-Liberalization (providing a counter-argument which emphasizes a lack of consensus as to the benefits of liberalization) [hereinafter Revisiting the 2005 IEO Evaluation].

[28] On the history of the Washington Consensus, see in particular John Williamson, 'A Short History of the Washington Consensus' (2009) 15 *Law and Business Review of the Americas* 7. See also Philip Arestis, 'Washington Consensus and Financial Liberalization' (2004) 27 *Journal of Post Keynesian Economics* 251.

1. **Fiscal Discipline.** This was in the context of a region where almost all countries had run large deficits that led to balance of payments crises and high inflation that hit mainly the poor because the rich could park their money abroad.
2. **Reordering Public Expenditure Priorities.** This suggested switching expenditure in a pro-growth and pro-poor way, from things like non-merit subsidies to basic health and education and infrastructure. It did not call for all the burden of achieving fiscal discipline to be placed on expenditure cuts; on the contrary, the intention was to be strictly neutral about the desirable size of the public sector, an issue on which even a hopeless consensus-seeker like me did not imagine that the battle had been resolved with the end of history that was being promulgated at the time.
3. **Tax Reform.** The aim was a tax system that would combine a broad tax base with moderate marginal tax rates.
4. **Liberalising Interest Rates.** In retrospect I wish I had formulated this in a broader way as financial liberalisation, stressed that views differed on how fast it should be achieved, and recognised the importance of accompanying financial liberalisation with prudential supervision.
5. **A Competitive Exchange Rate.** I fear I indulged in wishful thinking in asserting that there was a consensus in favor of ensuring that the exchange rate would be competitive, which pretty much implies an intermediate regime; in fact Washington was already beginning to edge towards the two-corner doctrine which holds that a country must either fix firmly or else it must float 'cleanly'.
6. **Trade Liberalisation.** I acknowledged that there was a difference of view about how fast trade should be liberalised, but everyone agreed that was the appropriate direction in which to move.
7. **Liberalisation of Inward Foreign Direct Investment.** I specifically did not include comprehensive capital account liberalisation, because I did not believe that did or should command a consensus in Washington.
8. **Privatisation.** As noted already, this was the one area in which what originated as a neoliberal idea had won broad acceptance. We have since been made very conscious that it matters a lot how privatisation is done: it can be a highly corrupt process that transfers assets to a privileged elite for a fraction of their true value, but the evidence is that it brings benefits (especially in terms of improved service coverage) when done properly, and the privatised enterprise either sells into a competitive market or is properly regulated.

9. **Deregulation.** This focused specifically on easing barriers to entry and exit, not on abolishing regulations designed for safety or environmental reasons, or to govern prices in a non-competitive industry.
10. **Property Rights.** This was primarily about providing the informal sector with the ability to gain property rights at acceptable cost (inspired by Hernando de Soto's analysis).[29]

The validity of the so-called Washington Consensus has been widely discussed, debated and questioned, both at the time and over time,[30] but the term has nonetheless become part of the vernacular. Indeed, and despite Williamson specifically stating that he did not include capital account liberalisation within the scope of the Washington Consensus, such policies became intertwined with the other aspects of the Consensus. Throughout the years, in fact, the Washington Consensus formed the basis of a paradigm shift whereby capital account liberalisation policies were increasingly adopted by developing economies wanting to signal their stability, openness and convertibility to foreign capital and overseas investors.[31] Progressively, the steady reduction of regulatory barriers led to an increase in financial inflows to both advanced economies and emerging markets,[32] and the Fund became involved in the process by requiring the removal of capital controls in its loan stabilisation and assistance programmes. To the IMF, the removal of financial regulatory barriers was a winning strategy. In fact, a 1997 IMF staff working paper even stated that 'countries have benefitted significantly from the global transfers of savings and technology associated with increased international capital flows [including through] inflows consisting of foreign direct investment and portfolio transactions'.[33] The working paper also noted that, when discussing capital account convertibility, the Executive Board 'underscored the beneficial effects on growth and investment of the expansion of private capital flows'[34] and that 'free capital movements facilitate a more efficient global allocation of savings

---

[29] Williamson (n 28).
[30] John Williamson, 'Democracy and the "Washington Consensus"' (1993) 21 *World Development* 1329, 1336; Moises Naim, 'Washington Consensus or Washington Confusion?' (2000) 118 *Foreign Policy* 87; Dani Rodrik, 'Goodbye Washington Consensus, Hello Washington Confusion? A Review of the World Bank's Economic Growth in the 1990s: Learning from a Decade of Reform' (2006) 44 *Journal of Economic Literature* 973.
[31] See for instance Joyce (n 10) 78. See Hart and Spero (n 12).
[32] IMF, 'The Fund's Role Regarding Cross-Border Capital Flows' (n 4) 1.
[33] IMF, 'Capital Account Convertibility and the Role of the Fund: Review of Experience and Consideration of a Possible Amendment of the Articles' (International Monetary Fund 1997) SM/97/32 7.
[34] Ibid. 8.

and contribute to the channeling of resources into their most productive uses, thus increasing economic growth and welfare'.[35]

To be fair, the working paper did briefly mention that liberalisation could have negative effects on domestic economies in certain circumstances. Yet, the focus was clearly on showing the inefficiencies of capital flow restrictions in general and the benefits of liberalisation.[36] To this end, while recognising that the removal of controls must be done in a coordinated manner, the working paper lauded the Fund's own role as an assessor of the benefits and detriments of existing capital controls and guardian of the global finance system:

> More recently, the Fund has become increasingly involved in assisting members to ensure that liberalization is undertaken in a setting of financial soundness and in conjunction with the necessary structural reforms. It has also become more active in assessing when the maintenance of controls would be counterproductive. The assessment of the merits of controls is of particular importance to the international monetary system considering that controls imposed by one country typically affect others adversely (for example, by delaying necessary exchange rate adjustments, or limiting the repatriation of invested capital or financial market access) and can, therefore, be destructive of international prosperity.[37]

Economists have commented on this point at length. As Moschella put it, the view at the time was that 'controls had negative spill-over and contagion effects that could interfere with the efficient allocation of investment across countries ... [while] on the contrary, the opening of the capital account was considered as a useful mechanism through which to increase the efficiency of the domestic financial system, by introducing competition and innovation from abroad'.[38] Alfaro concurred, arguing that the view of the Fund was that 'the imposition of capital controls can drive up the cost of capital and curb investment ... [and also] increase uncertainty while reducing the availability of external finance' and impact firms.[39] Joyce added that 'the IMF saw no conflict between encouraging capital liberalization and its mandate to promote economic stability and growth.

---

[35] Ibid.
[36] Ibid. 10–11.
[37] Ibid. 16.
[38] Moschella (n 27) 449–50.
[39] Laura Alfaro, *Global Capital and National Institutions: Crisis and Choice in the International Financial Architecture* (World Scientific 2010) 5–6 (referring to René M Stulz, 'Globalization of Equity Markets and the Cost of Capital' (National Bureau of Economic Research 1999)); Anusha Chari and Peter Blair Henry, 'Risk Sharing and Asset Prices: Evidence from a Natural Experiment' (2004) 59 *The Journal of Finance* 1295.

The fund supported the removal of regulations on capital flows in its dealings with members and sought to use its own loans as a catalytic agent to promote private financial flows'.[40]

1.2 The Changing Attitude towards Liberalisation

The perception of complete liberalisation – that is, the free flow of capital – has shifted over time. Following the Asian Financial Crisis of the late 1990s, critics of the IMF, academic commentators and governments identified several potential drawbacks and systemic risks inherent to the liberalisation of capital flows and open capital accounts. Another shift in perception occurred as a result of the asymmetry between trade and financial flows, with the realisation that the financial markets are now operating largely beyond their initial transactional and trade facilitation role. A third shift occurred as new methods of entering markets have constantly emerged over the past decades. Despite some of these factors being beyond the control of the IMF, the fact is that the Fund was blamed when things went wrong.

1.2.1 The Asian Crisis and the Pitfalls of Liberalisation

The main reason for the progressive change in perception and attitude towards free capital flows and open capital accounts has undoubtedly been the realisation that liberalisation brings not only benefits but also a real possibility of detriments. Described by Grabel as 'the roots of change',[41] the Asian Financial Crisis played a particularly important role in exposing the risks and inherent instability of financial markets.[42] During the 1980s and the 1990s, interest rates in the more advanced economies were low and investors searching for better returns created an incentive for investment into the emerging markets. Foreign capital flowed into Asian and

---

[40] Joyce (n 10) 14, 72. It should be noted that the liberal ideology was confined to the Fund but pervaded the thinking and financial policy practices of large regional and supranational organisations. This included the Organization for Economic Development and Cooperation (OECD), which aims to eliminate residency-based measures on cross-border capital movements, while the European Union (EU) more generally proscribes capital movement limitations.

[41] Ilene Grabel, 'The Rebranding of Capital Controls in an Era of Productive Incoherence' (2015) 22 *Review of International Political Economy* 7, 9.

[42] On the inherent instability of capital markets, see for instance Chris Brummer, *Soft Law and the Global Financial System: Rule Making in the 21st Century* (Cambridge University Press 2015) 8–10.

1.2 THE CHANGING ATTITUDE TOWARDS LIBERALISATION

other emerging economies, where technocrats trained in the new welfare economics school of thought implemented market-friendly economic and financial policies.[43] The 'emerging market' became the trendy darling of investors as growth prospects, appreciating currencies and rising asset prices seemed to be a panacea for return-hungry capital investors.[44]

For some time, the open world seemed to benefit both capital investors and host states – capital account deregulation worldwide enhanced capital mobility, international financial integration and market openness. Foreign investors could easily diversify and invest where the return was the greatest, while emerging economies seeking to attract capital in order to develop their own markets could always find a willing investor.[45] Certain emerging economies which traditionally ran current account deficits even began running surpluses; but the capital was unstable as the search for better investor returns never ceased. Wade seemingly predicted the bubble would burst when he made the following comment prior to the Asian Financial Crisis:

> Asia is building up huge current account surpluses. Korea's is running at an annualized rate of about 10 per cent of GDP, which is enormous. Thailand's is nearly as big. Malaysia's surplus is likely to be about 2 per cent of GDP. But foreign bankers and portfolio investors have been fleeing these economies. China has the second biggest foreign exchange reserves in the world after Japan and an enormous current account surplus, yet there are fears of a renmimbi devaluation.[46]

Eventually, the rapid inflow of capital stoked fear of unwanted bubbles and inflation – particularly in real estate markets. At some point, the IMF suggested that 'if current conditions of high external and domestic liquidity and rising credit growth persist, they [would be] conducive to over-stretched valuations arising in the medium term'.[47] The bubble burst shortly thereafter, starting with Thailand. The Thai government had progressively established liberal capital policies since the early

---

[43] See for instance Gallagher (n 14) 103.
[44] IMF, 'Resolving the Crisis Legacy and Meeting New Challenges to Financial Stability', *Global Financial Stability Report, April 2010: Meeting New Challenges to Stability and Building a Safer System* (International Monetary Fund) 3, www.elibrary.imf.org/view/IMF082/10503-9781589069169/10503-9781589069169/C1.xml?redirect=true
[45] Joyce (n 10) 73.
[46] Robert Wade and Frank Veneroso, 'The Gathering World Slump and the Battle over Capital Controls' (1998) 231 *New Left Review*.
[47] IMF, 'Resolving the Crisis Legacy and Meeting New Challenges to Financial Stability' (n 44) 3.

1990s with the goal of transforming the country into a regional financial hub.[48] In a show of stability and demonstration of good governance, the government linked the value of the currency (the baht) to the US dollar. When the value of the US dollar began increasing in 1995, the value of the baht accordingly increased but the negative impact on the country's exports and economic prospects were underestimated. Exports plummeted and the current account deficit soared.[49] Property prices and stock values plunged, and the contagion effect spread as investors began losing confidence in the market fundamentals of the economy and transferring capital out of the country. The Thai Central Bank exhausted foreign exchange reserves in an effort to maintain the link to the US dollar but eventually was forced to abandon the link and devalue the currency. In an attempt to maintain the appearance of control and steadiness, the Central Bank desperately fought (and spent) to stabilise the value of the baht, but the weight of the market proved too great. The Thai government called on the IMF for assistance.[50]

The contagion spread as the situation repeated in neighbouring countries such as the Philippines, Indonesia and Malaysia where economic levels and economic governance were rather fragile. In every case, bad situations were made worse by the 'herd effect' of investors following others in fleeing the markets lest they be the last ones remaining to hold the worthless assets. Krugman bluntly summarised the effect of this at the time – 'what turned a bad financial situation into a catastrophe was the way a loss of confidence turned into self-reinforcing panic'.[51]

The situation essentially repeated a decade later in the GFC. While this crisis began in the US as a result of over-use and reliance on complicated and dubious financial products, it quickly spread to Europe and elsewhere around the world. Yet again, capital outflows exerted pressure on domestic currencies and banks alike, and central banks were forced to intervene.

With two devastating crises within a ten-year period, a fundamental question has therefore emerged: were these crises unusual or should they

---

[48] Medhi Krongkaew, 'Capital Flows and Economic Crisis in Thailand' (1999) 37 *The Developing Economies* 395.
[49] Joyce (n 10) 107–9. See also Brummer (n 42) 13–14.
[50] Joyce (n 10) 107–9.
[51] Paul Krugman, 'Saving Asia: It's Time To Get Radical The IMF plan not only has failed to revive Asia's troubled economies but has worsened the situation. It's now time for some painful medicine.' (7 September 1998) *Fortune Magazine*, https://archive.fortune.com/magazines/fortune/fortune_archive/1998/09/07/247884/index.htm

1.2 THE CHANGING ATTITUDE TOWARDS LIBERALISATION 17

be expected as a correction of the market?[52] For most commentators, the answer is that we should expect regular periods of financial instability. For instance, Jeanne et al. found a similar pattern between both financial crises, with economic analysis 'show[ing] the same capital flows a decade earlier, starting at the time of the Asian Financial Crisis (1997–98) and continuing through the subsequent crises in Russia (1998) and Brazil (1998–99)'.[53] For Gabor, the 1997 Asian Financial Crisis introduced the idea that capital flows work in cycles and contain an inherent degree of volatility and instability.[54] For Gochoco, 'The global financial crisis provided another convincing case of the well-known critique that openness to cross-border mobility of capital can give rise to macroeconomic concerns as well an increased risk of financial crisis despite the many benefits it brings'.[55] In short, these crises not only changed the prevailing view on liberalisation, but they continue to impact the historic and traditional perception towards free capital flows to such an extent that literature has emerged that questions the correlation between capital account liberalisation and growth.[56]

At the same time, research on the determinants and effects of sudden stops in capital inflows and outflows is becoming more robust and pointing towards a correlation between free flows and instability risks. In this regard, the IMF notes that 'there are two types of sudden stops: inflow driven, when foreign investors sharply reduce, discontinue, or withdraw their investments; and outflow driven, when residents invest heavily abroad. … External factors, such as increased investor risk aversion, higher global growth, and higher interest rates in the advanced economies, increase the probability of sudden stops [in capital flows, which] may lead to excessive exchange rate depreciation, credit busts, and asset price deflation, and thus may destabilise the domestic economy'.[57] Similarly,

---

[52] Olivier Jeanne, Arvind Subramanian and John Williamson, *Who Needs to Open the Capital Account* (Peterson Institute 2012) 9.
[53] There are several similarities between the crises of the 1990s and the recent crisis. Ibid. 9.
[54] Gabor (n 27) 5.
[55] Gochoco-Bautista and Rhee (n 27) 1.
[56] See also Kevin P Gallagher and Jose Antonio Ocampo, 'IMF's New View on Capital Controls' (2013) 48 *Economic and Political Weekly* 10 (referring to IMF economists (JEANNE) concluding in 2012 that 'the inter-national community should not seek to promote totally free trade in assets – even over the long run – because … free capital mobility seems to have little benefit in terms of long-run growth'); Jeanne, Subramanian and Williamson (n 52) 11.
[57] IMF, 'Annual Report on Exchange Arrangements and Exchange Restrictions 2014' (International Monetary Fund) 60, www.imf.org/external/pubs/nft/2014/areaers/ar2014.pdf2

Neely notes that 'large international capital inflows, especially short-term foreign borrowing can exacerbate these perverse incentives and pose a real danger to banking systems'.[58] In any case, it has become clear that 'heavy capital inflows can fuel asset value bubbles and exchange rate appreciation, overwhelm regulatory and supervisory capacity, and make an economy vulnerable to capital flow reversals'.[59] In the same vein, it is now also clear that capital outflows can impact exchange rate policies, weaken foreign reserves, 'imperil domestic financial systems and exacerbate or spur an acute financial crisis with likely spillover effects' because anticipation somehow remains a complex and inexact science.[60]

1.2.2 *The Asymmetry between Trade and Capital Flows*

In addition to the realisation that free capital flows can impact financial stability and volatility, another element that helps explain the changing attitude towards capital account liberalisation is the growing asymmetry between trade and capital flows. From the 1970s, the distinction between capital and trade exchanges among countries progressively became blurred as the idea of capital controls to maintain control lost popularity and fell out of fashion. Despite the inherent risk of volatility, free capital movements were then associated with faster economic growth and in line with the overall trend towards increased liberalism. Indeed, the financial services industry at the time mainly consisted of domestic actors taking local deposits and loaning money to local investors.[61] Hence, the idea of free cross-border capital flows was praised for creating easier access to capital at a lesser cost to the society (in comparison to public capitals and public debt), for improving the structure and liquidity of financial markets and for improving standards of living in the emerging economies. Free capital movements were also seen as a means to allow trade from a purely transactional and operational perspective because they were the

---

[58] Neely (n 3) 20.
[59] 'The external effects of domestic policies designed to manage capital flows in or out of an economy are often unanticipated or broader than intended. Policies that cause outward capital flows generally create inflows elsewhere and vice versa. They can also indirectly impact similarly situated countries by raising concerns among market participants that those other countries will adopt similar policies. Thus, managing cross-border capital flows requires international, multilateral coordination across a broad range of policies, some of which impact capital flows only indirectly', in IMF, 'Annual Report on Exchange Arrangements and Exchange Restrictions 2014' (n 57) 60.
[60] Ibid.
[61] Brummer (n 42) 10.

key to exchanging value across borders. Simply put, the objective was to increase capital flows in order to achieve better repartition of wealth and foster trade.[62] With trade becoming the main goal of the international community, countries moreover refrained from imposing restrictions on current account payments.[63] Progressively, as a result, free capital flows became a prime tool for development and a vehicle for trade.

At the same time, freer and increased financial flows also created a standalone industry, particularly with the development of financial services and significant improvements in financial technologies. In time, transaction and trade funding became just one aspect of capital flows, alongside capital market and portfolio investment.[64] In such a climate, speculative investing abounded.[65] For some, the financial industry became interested in merely creating artificial wealth and trading 'the only major activity that could create value out of thin air'.[66]

The perception towards trade and capital balances has shifted dramatically over time, but this is not to say that the tendency of governments to liberalise financial markets has abated.[67] That said, there is now more caution in doing so and the liberalisation is often accompanied by safeguards or, at a minimum, carefully reasoned explanations. Thus, while cross-border capital flows and global liquidity are commonly described as the 'connective tissue' of today's international financial system,[68] the public, governments and commentators are now acutely

---

[62] See for instance MacFarlane (n 6) 171, 181. For a counter-argument emphasizing a lack of consensus as to the benefits of liberalization, see also IMF, 'The IMF's Approach to Capital Account Liberalization' (n 27).

[63] In line with Article VIII, Section 2. See Article 1 (iv) To assist in the establishment of a multilateral system of payments in respect of current transactions between members and in the elimination of foreign exchange restrictions which hamper the growth of world trade.

[64] Antoine Martin and Bryan Mercurio, 'The IMF and Its Shifting Mandate towards Capital Movements and Capital Controls: A Legal Perspective' (2017) 44 *Legal Issues of Economic Integration* 211.

[65] See for instance Brummer (n 42) 10. See also John B Goodman and Louis W Pauly, 'The Obsolescence of Capital Controls? Economic Management in an Age of Global Markets', *International Political Economy. Perspectives on Global Power and Wealth* (4th ed., Routledge 2002) 285.

[66] Brummer (n 42).

[67] As of 2014, the IMF reports that 'Member countries moved toward greater current account openness' and observes that 'the trend toward greater overall liberalization of capital transactions continued'. See Gabor (n 27) 6.

[68] See Feibelman (n 1) 495, and Gallagher (n 14) 39, suggesting that the financial industry has become a matter of global markets.

aware that financial tension generated by sudden and unpredictable capital movements can become a liability or more worryingly snowball into a crisis.

Perhaps more importantly, the world is now also aware that the global regulatory landscape is ill-equipped to face such challenges as it lacks common financial policy objectives. Some referred to a general 'confusion and loss of orientation' translating into a general 'crisis of the dominant doctrines'.[69] Jeanne et al. similarly comment in the following manner on the lack of overarching framework:

> In reality, there is an asymmetry between the international regulation of trade in goods and trade in financial assets and capital flows. Under the World Trade Organization (WTO) and its predecessor, the General Agreement on Tariffs and Trade (GATT), international rules were promulgated to promote free trade in goods. In contrast, trade in financial assets and capital flows has been largely left to the discretion of individual countries, and this is reflected most saliently in the fact that the IMF has no jurisdiction over how its member countries manage their capital account.[70]

What is clear, therefore, is that while capital flows have replaced trade as the 'major conduit for the transmission of global shocks', governments must 'develop[] mechanisms to curb the effects of large and volatile capital inflows on growth and financial stability'.[71] It is also clear that governments are taking different paths in their unending hunt for capital and delicate balance of other interests, including that of a stable financial system. Economists likewise have not reached consensus on the way forward, or on what mistakes cause the greatest amount of damage. This is in clear contrast to the trading regime, with the WTO setting rather clear and enforceable rules and bilateral and regional trade agreements building from that solid foundation with a similar architecture and structure.[72]

1.2.3 *The Sequencing Doctrine*

The shifting attitude towards free capital flows can also be seen in policymaking, with the increasing recognition of the so-called sequencing doctrine. The potential pitfalls of financial liberalism were well known to

---

[69] Jean Tirole, *Financial Crises, Liquidity, and the International Monetary System* (Princeton University Press 2002) 31–32; Hieronymi (n 14).
[70] Jeanne, Subramanian and Williamson (n 52) 109.
[71] See Gabor (n 27) 6. See also MacFarlane (n 6) 172; Brummer (n 42) 11.
[72] Simon Lester, Bryan Mercurio and Arwel Davies, *World Trade Law: Text, Materials and Commentary* (3rd ed., Bloomsbury 2018) 334.

1.2 THE CHANGING ATTITUDE TOWARDS LIBERALISATION   21

the IMF in the 1990s,[73] but they were ignored from an ideological and doctrinal perspective. What did occur, however, was a slow but steady consensus calling for a more careful and balanced approach to the management of cross-border capital flows in order to more fully protect and preserve the health and stability of both the international monetary and global financial systems.[74]

The sequencing doctrine, in other words, attempted to limit the premature liberalisation of the capital account by first ensuring that adequate institutions and prudential regulations were in place. This safeguard has not been the norm in IMF dealings, however, and many commentators blame the Fund for organising a wave of hasty liberalisation conducted with insufficient attention to sequencing and for failing to establish the appropriate preconditions to liberalisation which could have reduced financial instability and economic distress experienced by many emerging market countries in the 1990s.[75] Most commentators, in fact, are now in agreement that removing capital control without setting up the appropriate structure is 'a recipe for disaster'.[76]

That said, there appears to be no magic formula. In practice, the needs and developmental levels of countries differ such that 'correct sequence and timing of reforms depend in part on the circumstances of the country and should begin with macroeconomic stabilization, including fiscal consolidation'.[77] Of course, there are certain *preconditions* that will certainly always be included before any reform takes place, namely the 'creation of a financial regulatory structure to monitor bank conduct, the adoption of accounting standards, and the protection of investors' rights'.[78] The terms 'precondition' and 'reform' are crucial here, because they are the cornerstones of the trend which has emerged since the late 1990s. As early as 1997 the Fund clearly recognised that liberalisation of the capital account must occur following or in tandem with other regulatory and structural shifts:

> In their July 1995 discussion Executive Directors concluded that capital account liberalization should be undertaken subsequent to, or at least

---

[73] IMF, 'The IMF's Approach to Capital Account Liberalization' (n 27) 29.
[74] See for instance Feibelman (n 1) 499. See also UNGA, 'The Commission of Experts of the President of the UN General Assembly on Reforms of the International Monetary and Financial System' (United Nations 2009), www.un.org/en/ga/president/63/pdf/calendar/20090325-economiccrisis-commission.pdf; Blundell-Wignall and Roulet (n 2).
[75] IMF, 'The IMF's Approach to Capital Account Liberalization' (n 27) 9.
[76] Joyce (n 10) 80.
[77] Ibid.
[78] Joyce (n 10) (emphasis added). See also Feibelman (n 1) 516.

broadly simultaneously with, other reforms in the domestic financial system, including the strengthening of prudential regulations, and with adequate attention to differing conditions among individual countries. Subsequently the Board has further emphasized the links between banking sector issues and the capital account.[79]

Despite recognising the importance of sequencing, the doctrine has proven difficult to put into place for many countries, and the Fund never provided newly emerging markets with what some have described as 'templates of successful decontrol'.[80] Of course, the notion of liberalisation has shifted over time, and the ideological belief that free capital flows are a panacea to growth and development has been replaced with a firm recognition that capital market liberalisation should be rigorously organised.

1.2.4 Blaming the IMF

The IMF has largely taken the blame for being the chief architect and initiator of financial market and capital account liberalisation policies. In part, the criticism is well placed since, as explained above, the Fund had for some time promoted deregulation to facilitate market access and increase capital flows (even in countries that had poor financial infrastructure). In fact, the IMF's IEO even published a report in 2005 assessing the Fund's policy noting that over the past decades and especially before the Asian Financial Crisis the IMF 'acted as a cheerleader' towards market-opening policies.[81] In practice, the Fund has often linked the obtainment of stabilisation and other loan programmes to the liberalisation of capital flows. While the recipient country would technically propose and voluntarily accept the opening of capital accounts as a condition for receiving the IMF assistance, most did so out of financial desperation and necessity rather than conviction.

More often than not, the recipient governments entered into agreements with the Fund to send a signal of stability and openness to global financial markets. These countries did not strenuously oppose financial liberalisation commitments, but their purpose was not to open markets out of a conviction that deregulated capital flows would be beneficial to the economy either. Despite the risks, what mattered was playing by the rules imposed by the Fund, with the expectation that more private capital

---

[79] IMF, 'Capital Account Convertibility and the Role of the Fund: Review of Experience and Consideration of a Possible Amendment of the Articles' (n 33).
[80] Joyce (n 10) 80 [referring to Carmen M Reinhart and Kenneth S Rogoff, 'The Aftermath of Financial Crises' (2009) 99 *American Economic Review* 466].
[81] IMF, 'The IMF's Approach to Capital Account Liberalization' (n 27) 94.

would follow.[82] In many instances, therefore, countries felt pressure and coercion on behalf of the IMF to open capital account liberalisation as a *sine qua none* condition for funding. Joseph Stiglitz, a chief critic of IMF policy, has even questioned the very existence of a recipient country's genuine 'freedom to choose' and has argued that the Fund 'vigorously pursued privatization and liberalization, at a pace and in a manner that often imposed very real costs on countries ill-equipped to incur them'.[83]

For Stiglitz, 'the IMF and the World Bank have approached the issues from a narrow ideological perspective – privatization was to be pursued rapidly'.[84] Stiglitz views the situation as desperate countries coming to the IMF for assistance and facing imbalanced negotiations where the only choice was to take the deal as proposed by the IMF or continue to suffer economic crises. In this regard, conditionality was simply an acceptable part of the process. Taking the example of South Korea, Stiglitz wrote:

> The IMF, of course, claims that it never dictates but always negotiates the terms of any loan agreement with the borrowing country. But these are one-sided negotiations in which all the power is in the hand of the IMF, largely because many countries seeking IMF help are in desperate need of funds ... Korean officials reluctantly explained that they had been scared to disagree openly. The IMF could not only cut off its own funds, but could use its bully pulpit to discourage investments from private funds by telling private sector financial institutions of the doubts the IMF had about Korea's economy. So Korea had no choice. Even implied criticism by Korea of the IMF program could have a disastrous effect: to the IMF, it would suggest that the government didn't fully understand 'IMF economics'.[85]

Not everyone agrees with Stiglitz's views, of course, and there is a large degree of the 'patient blaming the doctor' when in fact the patient could have been irreparably sick or terminal prior to asking for treatment. For instance, Indonesia, Korea, Thailand and other countries most badly hurt in the Asian crisis all had serious structural defects in their economies which needed to be reformed in order to recover in a sustainable manner.[86] Whether the IMF got it right, or to what degree it got it wrong in each case, remains a matter of

---

[82] '[F]ree capital flows were not at fault ... instead, the clear implication was that government should fix its distorted policies so that emerging economies would no longer experience crises and could enjoy the full benefits of international financial integration, that is access to foreign finance to augment their capital stock and to engage in international risk-sharing'. Korinek (n 7) 528.
[83] Joseph E Stiglitz, *Globalization and Its Discontents* (Norton 2002) 54.
[84] Ibid.
[85] Ibid. 42.
[86] Paul Blustein, *The Chastening: Inside the Crisis That Rocked the Global Financial System and Humbled the IMF* (PublicAffairs 2001).

discussion and contention today and it is not the role of this legal monograph to weigh in on the debate. Rather, the point here is simply to state that, like Stiglitz, many commentators 'widely blamed [the Fund] for indirectly contributing to the ... crises by advocating the premature removal of controls on capital flows, and then imposing harsh and inappropriate measures on the countries that were forced to borrow from it'.[87]

Some commentators take a slightly more nuanced view, blaming not the Fund but rather the influential and powerful main sources of funding and 'dominant' members of the Fund, which from the 1970s to the 1990s all had an overriding interest in increasing access to the emerging markets.[88] For instance, Joyce describes the Fund as a catalyst to capital account liberalisation, but finds 'no evidence ... to suggest that countries liberalized their capital accounts against their will'.[89] In fact, Joyce instead points to a connection between IMF funding and private funding, with the former being in many instances perceived as a precondition to obtaining the latter.[90] Stated differently, while private capital was considered during the 1980s as a non-negligible 'means of financing external sector deficits that could supplement the Fund's own efforts', this 'complementarity' transformed IMF activities into a form of 'catalytic finance' based on the idea that IMF lending – and the reforms coming with it – 'would increase the willingness of private investors to lend to a country' or invest there.[91]

Hence, although the Fund's policies could be criticised for lacking empirical rigour or even for being insufficiently tailored to the conditions of each individual recipient country, it can nonetheless be said that the reforms mandated by the IMF were necessary to create access to much-needed private capital. In recent times, however, financial policies on a large scale have moved towards the idea of controlling capital flows, and IMF policies have followed this route. In effect, the Fund nowadays considers that CFMs are a valid element in the financial policy toolbox. This point will be explored in Chapter 2.

---

[87] Joyce (n 10) 1.
[88] Ibid. 3 ('IMF's activities during the period of 1973–2008 reflected the influence of its dominant members as well as the IMF's own commitment to capital market integration').
[89] Ibid. 79.
[90] In reality, Joyce notes that the mere existence of a fund program does not guarantee any increase in private capital flows. Instead, the increase in flows and in the issuance of bonds was only witnessed 'when a country's fundamentals are in "intermediate" range', that is, 'when there is evidence that the program will be effective'. See Ibid. 82.
[91] Ibid. 81.

2

Capital Flow Management Measures

The previous chapter introduced the contentious debates on financial liberalisation which have taken place throughout the past two decades. The chapter also explained how increased capital volatility created by the 'stop and go' nature of financial cycles has led to shocks across the globe and emphasised that while the progressive liberalisation of cross-border capital flows created wealth and increased investor returns, it has also increased risks of crises and periods of instability. Increasingly, commentators and governments have therefore called for a 'brake' mechanism to the liberalisation, mainly in the form of restrictions or controls on capital flows. This chapter focuses on how such measures have progressively become part of the global financial policy toolbox.

As explained in Chapter 1, major cracks appeared in the liberalisation approach to capital flows during the Asian Financial Crisis and widened in subsequent crises in the early 2000s when policymakers and commentators began to understand that unregulated finance and cross-border flows could generate extreme financial instability. Hence, over the past years, and particularly during and in the aftermath of the GFC, restrictive capital measures were deployed in economies as diverse as Iceland, Brazil, Chile, Argentina, Cyprus, India, Thailand, Malaysia, Indonesia, Taiwan and South Korea.[1] For some, the controls were limited in nature and duration. For others, controls were widespread and remained for an extended

---

[1] On crisis controls, *see* Joseph E Stiglitz, 'Capital Market Liberalization, Economic Growth, and Instability' (2000) 28 *World Development* 1075 (discussing ideological shifts regarding financial liberalisation); Richard N Watanabe, 'Foreign Exchange and Capital Movement Controls in Taiwan' (1997) 16 *UCLA Pacific Basin Law Journal* 1, 9, 17. In the case of Taiwan, for instance, foreign exchange and capital movement controls were employed during a rapid economic growth period to preserve domestic savings, restrict foreign ownership in specific sectors and reduce instability risks generated by capital inflows. Ibid. 2. See also Philip J MacFarlane, 'The IMF's Reassessment of Capital Controls after the 2008 Financial Crisis: Heresy or Orthodoxy?' (2015) 19 *UCLA Journal of International Law and Foreign Affairs* 167, 169.

period. Iceland is an example of the latter. Having established capital controls on outflows in 2008 (with the acquiescence if not advocacy of the IMF[2]) after its three largest banks collapsed and the value of its currency fell sharply, the country completed its incremental reduction and eventual elimination of the controls only in 2017.[3] It is also becoming clear that post-crisis, the IMF has been more accepting of CFMs and in particular shifted its position on the extent to which they can be a source of instability in emerging markets.[4]

The question explored in this chapter is that of the role and legitimacy of CFMs. Section 2.1 provides a definition of CFMs and explains their role and impact in terms of capital flow management. Section 2.2 explains why CFMs are so controversial and elaborates on their operational aspects and overall desirability. Section 2.3 discusses why CFMs remain difficult to manage from a macro level in the absence of a global regulatory framework.

2.1 Defining CFMs

The terms 'capital flow management measures' and 'capital controls' are often used interchangeably, with those opposed to interventionalist policy preferring the latter while those in favour of intervention most often using the former. With the terms used so often in economic and political circles, however, it is striking – and somewhat surprising – that the definition of CFMs remains somewhat elusive. There are, however, slight differences between CFMs and capital controls in that while the latter is a form of the former, not all CFMs are capital controls.

The Fund explained this point in extremely technical language when it wrote that 'liberalization needs to consider CFMs more broadly, and not just capital controls [because while] liberalization of capital flows is generally understood as easing restrictions that discriminate based on residency ... non-discriminatory measures that are designed to affect

---

[2] See Silla Sigurgeirsdottir and Robert Wade, 'From Control by Capital to Control of Capital: Iceland's Boom and Bust, and the IMF's Unorthodox Rescue Package' (2015) 22(1) *Review of International Political Economy* 103–33.

[3] See for instance Fridrik M Baldursson and Richard Portes, 'Capital Controls and the Resolution of Failed Cross-Border Banks: The Case of Iceland' (2014) 9 *Capital Markets Law Journal* 40. See also MacFarlane (n 1) 192, 193.

[4] For econometric modeling on this point, see Kevin P Gallagher and Yuan Tian, 'Regulating Capital Flows in Emerging Markets: The IMF and the Global Financial Crisis' (2017) 7 *Review of Development Finance* 95, 104–5.

capital flows can often substitute for capital controls'.⁵ In addition, the Fund submitted that many policies and measures – such as administrative controls, 'financial sector, monetary or taxation policies, and policies implemented for public health or security reasons' – could typically create indirect CFMs without a willingness to control capitals *per se*.⁶ It thus added, rather helpfully, that 'the assessment of whether a particular measure is a CFM requires judgment as to whether the measure was *designed to influence* capital flows, and would need to take into account the overall context and circumstances in which it was adopted'.⁷ As a practical example, the IMF proposed the following idea:

> For example, certain residency based measures on capital inflows through the banking system could be replaced with measures that treat domestic and foreign currency transactions differently. The latter measures would generally still qualify as CFMs, and not entail an effective liberalization of the specific transaction. However, by avoiding residency-based limitations, they would more closely adhere to the standards of fairness that parties to a multilateral framework like the Fund would expect for their nationals. Given the Fund's multilateral framework and the approach used in respect of current payments and transfers, it would also be important to avoid measures that discriminate among Fund members.⁸

In line with this suggestion is the idea that the concept of CFMs has significantly evolved over time. Far from their current function, the first capital restrictions in modern times were adopted by countries during the First World War as a means to retain capital and finance during the war effort.⁹ By placing restrictions on capital outflows as well as on the acquisition of foreign loans and assets, governments realised that they could mechanically increase the domestic taxable base while gaining access to war-funding resources and reducing the cost of borrowing money.¹⁰

---

⁵ IMF, 'Liberalizing Capital Flows and Managing Outflows' (International Monetary Fund 2012) www.imf.org/external/np/pp/eng/2012/031312.pdf para. 27. This book, therefore, uses the term 'CFM' not to signal a position on government intervention in the markets but in line with the IMF's usage of the term.
⁶ If only because such policies and measures 'directly or indirectly inhibit cross-border capital flows [and] affect international capital flows, even if inadvertently'. Ibid. para. 27.
⁷ Ibid. paras. 25–27 (emphasis added).
⁸ Ibid. para. 27.
⁹ See Christopher J Neely, 'An Introduction to Capital Controls' (1999) 81 *Federal Reserve Bank of St. Louis Review* 15 (referring to Age FP Bakker, *The Liberalization of Capital Movements in Europe* (Kluwer Academic Publishers 1996) and R Barry Johnston and Natalia T Tamirisa, 'Why Do Countries Use Capital Controls?' (International Monetary Fund 1998) IMF Working Paper No.98/181).
¹⁰ Neely (n 9).

More recently, governments have extended the range of circumstances justifying CFMs, and the panel of applicable solutions has substantially broadened as a result of a significant increase in the variety of capital flows. Hence, in modern times the term 'capital control' tends to be used in a generic (and haphazard) way to describe policies and measures aimed at managing cross-border capital flows, whether these are inflows or outflows, and whether short or long term.[11]

Despite a good deal of variety, it nonetheless remains correct to write that CFMs are most often implemented for domestic prudential reasons, foreign exchange–related (FX) reasons, financial instability risks and other macro-economic purposes.[12] Such restrictions are frequently taken in relation to either monetary or banking difficulties that are likely to impede financial stability, when a government is attempting to preserve the value of its currency (or avoid repeated interventions from the central bank) or in order to stave off large capital outflows which may act as a signaling effect to the electronic herd of investors.[13]

Alternatively, CFMs can act as restrictions on capital movement by discriminating between residents and non-residents to the extent that the measures aim to limit the outward flow of capital from a domestic economy.[14] Importantly, however, restrictions may also be directed towards domestic rather than foreign investors. This is particularly the

---

[11] Kevin P Gallagher and Jose Antonio Ocampo, 'IMF's New View on Capital Controls' (2013) 48 *Economic and Political Weekly* 10, 13.

[12] Jonathan D Ostry and others, 'Capital Controls: When and Why?' (2011) 59 *IMF Economic Review* 562.

[13] Korinek, for instance, defines crises in which capital controls may be utilised as 'situations in which an emerging economy loses access to international financial markets and experiences a feedback loop in which declining aggregate demand, falling exchange rates and asset prices, and deteriorating balance sheets mutually reinforce each other – a common phenomenon in recent emerging market crises. Individual market participants take aggregate prices and financial conditions as given and do not internalize their contribution to financial instability when they choose their actions. As a result they impose externalities in the form of greater financial instability on each other, and the private financing decisions of individuals are distorted toward excessive risk-taking'. See Anton Korinek, 'The New Economics of Prudential Capital Controls: A Research Agenda' (2011) 59 *IMF Economic Review* 523. See also Daniela Gabor, 'Paradigm Shift? A Critique of the IMF's New Approach to Capital Controls' (Bristol Business School, University of West England 2011) Working Paper from Department of Accounting, Economics and Finance.

[14] Mahvash S Qureshi and others, 'Managing Capital Inflows: The Role of Capital Controls and Prudential Policies' (National Bureau of Economic Research 2011) Working Paper No.17363 www.nber.org/papers/w17363 ('measures that treat transactions between residents and non-residents less favourably than those amongst residents').

case in China, where restrictive policies are in place in order to limit the outflows of Chinese capital to other jurisdictions.[15]

In some ways, a parallel can therefore be drawn between the difficulty in defining CFMs (and their scope and depth) and the difficulty in defining capital flows, as discussed in Chapter 1. In that chapter, we noted the various types of capital flows, emphasised that inward capital flows differ from outwards capital flows and insisted that short-term speculative flows must be differentiated from long-term and more stable investment-related flows. Similarly, a CFM can take a multitude of forms and encompass a variety of measures, depending on the type of flows that the government seeks to control. Controls have been used as quotas and quantitative restrictions on cross-border movements – whether as credit allocation, as a tool to sanction or to reduce demand for foreign goods and services – for the purposes of limiting outflows. Inflows have also been subject to controls for, *inter alia*, preserving balance of payment surpluses (i.e. reducing the quantity of foreign products entering domestic markets), preventing subjection to volatile inflows and restricting foreign ownership of domestic assets.[16] As discussed in Part II of the book, CFMs have also been placed on and impacted long-term investments, most often ostensibly justified by a necessity to take prudential measures to preserve financial and monetary stability as part of a wider financial crisis mitigation strategy.

2.2 The Desirability of CFMs

Beyond definition issues, CFMs are also a contentious topic to the extent that economic experts are divided as to whether restrictions are desirable. In light of the various crises that have negatively affected the global economy over the past decades, supporters often point out how restrictions help create and sustain stable domestic and international financial systems – as a hedge against the unfettered nature of free and unpredictable financial flows – and in ensuring monetary and

---

[15] Bryan Mercurio, Ross Buckley and Jiangyuan Fu, 'The Legitimacy of Controlling Capital Flows under International Economic Law during a Retreat from Globalization' (2021) 70 *International and Comparative Law Quarterly* 59, 73–81; Jiangyuan Fu and Bryan Mercurio, 'Do Beijing's Capital Controls Restrict Hong Kong? Reality or Illusion' (2021) 9 *Chinese Journal of Comparative Law* 109.

[16] Neely (n 9) 16.

economic stability.[17] Yet, while this may at present be the prevailing view, and while governments are becoming increasingly reliant on CFMs in situations involving volatility in cross-border capital flows, the discussion is far from settled and CFMs remain fiercely debated. As Fratzscher accurately surmises, 'there are few policy issues that have been as controversial as the one on the desirability of capital controls'.[18]

2.2.1 The Sceptics of CFMs

Sceptics of CFMs are often free marketers who support the opening of capital markets and encourage the free flow of capital as a means to efficiently allocate available funds and facilitate economic development and progress in general. Such sceptics embraced the liberalisation of the 1980s and 1990s and thus the imposition of CFMs is viewed as inefficient, inherently distortive and avoided except in the most extreme of circumstances.[19] For some time, the IMF position embodied such sentiments. For example, in a document dating to 1997 the IMF used rather strong language to condemn the long-term use of capital controls, even while acknowledging some value in temporary control measures to counter sudden threats to the financial system:

13. *Assessing the utility of capital controls* – In their July 1995 discussion, Executive Directors concluded that controls on capital movements had proved largely ineffective in preventing outflows of savings and sustaining inconsistent macroeconomic policies because of the difficulties of enforcing them in a world of highly integrated international capital markets. They noted, however, that controls could, on occasion, provide temporary breathing room in dealing with balance of payments difficulties, although the controls could not and should not substitute for fundamental policy adjustments. Similarly, in situations where inflows

---

[17] See for instance Adam Feibelman, 'The IMF and Regulation of Cross-Border Capital Flows' (2015) 15 *Chicago Journal of International Law* 409; IEO IMF, *IMF Response to the Financial and Economic Crisis* (International Monetary Fund 2015) www.imf.org/en/Publications/Independent-Evaluation-Office-Reports/Issues/2016/12/31/The-IMF-and-the-Crises-in-Greece-Ireland-and-Portugal-An-IEO-Assessment-42404; Joseph P Joyce, *The IMF and Global Financial Crises: Phoenix Rising?* (Cambridge University Press 2012) 6.

[18] Marcel Fratzscher, 'Capital Controls and Foreign Exchange Policy' (Social Science Research Network 2012) ECB Working Paper No. 1415 2 https://papers.ssrn.com/abstract=1991084.

[19] IMF, 'Capital Account Convertibility and the Role of the Fund: Review of Experience and Consideration of a Possible Amendment of the Articles' (International Monetary Fund 1997) SM/97/32 10–16.

complicate macroeconomic management, temporary controls may provide breathing room while other policy responses take hold. In this context, Directors pointed to the potential distortionary effects of such measures as well as their growing ineffectiveness over time.

15. While it is generally accepted that controls on capital movements are inefficient, and should not be used to sustain inconsistent macroeconomic and exchange rate policies, they may nevertheless provide some protection against abrupt and sharp portfolio shifts by limiting capital mobility to the extent that it may be difficult to evade controls in the short run. Where such controls are adopted in response to sudden adverse developments, they should be undertaken as part of a comprehensive package of stabilization and structural reform, they should be temporary and, to the extent possible, market based and transparent. In addition, the use of controls should avoid defaults on debt obligations and disruptions to international commercial relations, which can have a substantial and lasting adverse impact on countries' access to international capital markets.[20]

Even in the wake of the GFC, the IMF remained largely sceptical of the value of CFMs, acknowledging that even if controls may be beneficial to the host country, they can negatively affect other countries and the global system:

> Even if capital controls prove useful for individual countries in dealing with capital inflow surges, they may lead to adverse multilateral effects. The adoption of inflow controls in one country, if effective, can divert capital flows to its peers, prompting the introduction of capital controls in those countries as well. A widespread reliance on capital controls may delay necessary macroeconomic adjustments in individual countries and, in the current environment, prevent the global rebalancing of demand and thus hinder the recovery of global growth.[21]

Likewise, in 2012, the Fund remained sceptical of controls on inflow, noting that 'only a few countries tightened controls significantly to address capital outflow surges [in the last decade and that there is] relatively little academic research that exists on the effectiveness of outflow controls

---

[20] Ibid. See also Rudiger Dornbusch, 'Capital Controls: An Idea Whose Time Is Past', in 'Should the IMF Pursue Capital-Account Convertibility?' *Princeton Essays in International Finance* No. 207, May 1998, 20–27.

[21] Annamaria Kokeyne and others, 'Global Liquidity Expansion: Effects on Receiving Economies and Policy Response Options' (International Monetary Fund 2010) IMF Global Financial Stability Report.

consists mainly of case studies', referring mainly to Argentina, Iceland and Ukraine before noting that no clear pattern could be established.[22]

The reason for so few restrictions on outflows is simple: such restrictions send a negative political message to investors and create an incentive for those in the market to rapidly change positions (i.e. liquidate and exit the market) in order to preserve capital.[23] This idea is not in isolation, and various commentators have written that CFMs could increase market uncertainty and reduce the availability of external financing necessary to domestic firms, which in turn could also lower equity investment into domestic firms.[24] For example, and emphasising the risk of poor policymaking, they argued that in Brazil CFM policies eventually replaced the need for sound policy in that they had 'become a means for the Brazilian government to control the influx of foreign capital, and the tax has repeatedly been both raised and expanded to include other forms of investments'.[25] Perhaps even more damning is the evidence that concludes CFMs have only temporary and/or limited effects in the countries where they were put into place.[26] To Jeanne et al., a 'disadvantage of capital controls is that they may leave the authorities with the illusion that they have a greater ability to determine the course of events than they actually do', while at the same time discounting the varied and ways traders and citizens can evade the controls.[27]

---

[22] IMF, 'Liberalizing Capital Flows and Managing Outflows' (n 5) 54–55.

[23] See for instance Neely (n 9) 26 [referring to Carmen Reinhart and R Todd Smith, 'Too Much of a Good Thing: The Macroeconomic Effects of Taxing Capital Inflows', in *Managing Capital Flows and Exchange Rates: Perspectives from the Pacific Basin* (Cambridge University Press 1998)]; Barry J Eichengreen, *Toward a New International Financial Architecture: A Practical Post-Asia Agenda* (Institute for International Economics 1999).

[24] Laura Alfaro, *Global Capital and National Institutions: Crisis and Choice in the International Financial Architecture* (World Scientific 2010) 26. See also MacFarlane (n 1) 201.

[25] Alfaro (n 24) 9.

[26] Maria Socorro Gochoco-Bautista and Changyong Rhee, 'Capital Controls: A Pragmatic Proposal' (2013) No. 337 ADB Economics Working Paper Series 4 ('Capital controls were only temporarily able to drive a wedge between foreign and domestic interest rates and to reduce pressures on the exchange rate in Brazil, Chile, Colombia, Malaysia, and Thailand. Some studies show that capital controls either did not have an independent effect on total net private capital flows, or only had a temporary effect on net private capital inflows without any significant effects on the real exchange rate. Some studies find that capital controls were effective in reducing net private capital inflows while others find that capital controls reduced the amount of external borrowing but did not significantly reduce the volume of non-FDI flows and also significantly increased exchange rate volatility. There is a preponderance of evidence though that capital controls can affect the composition of capital inflows and outflows over the long term').

[27] Olivier Jeanne, Arvind Subramanian and John Williamson, *Who Needs to Open the Capital Account?* (Peterson Institute 2012) 16, 18.

2.2.2 *The Proponents of CFMs*

Proponents of CFMs believe that both short- and long-term capital flows may influence – or even create 'destabilizing patterns' in[28] – exchange rates and currency fluctuations. For instance, unrestricted capital flows may generate financial instability in an economy or group of economies, transfer financial shocks from one economy to another and spread contagion on a global scale, especially in the countries where financial regulatory mechanisms are less developed.[29]

Capital volatility may also negatively affect a country's balance of payments. As a snapshot of a country's transactions with the world, the balance of payment is built upon a 'current account' (balancing the value of trade in goods and services) and a 'capital account' (balancing domestic and foreign capital flows). The balance of payment may therefore become 'unbalanced' if there is capital account disequilibrium between domestic reserves and outflows appears.[30] Unforeseen massive capital outflow may depreciate the value of a currency, which in turn can affect trade relations while forcing a central bank to sell foreign currency reserves in an attempt to stabilize or limit its own currency's depreciation on international markets. In such a scenario, the impact is twofold, and the economy can be harmed both from a currency (e.g. monetary) and a trade (e.g. GDP) perspective. China has become a master strategist in this regard, with governmental restrictions being placed on both capital inflows and outflows. The result has been a massive accumulation of international reserves that will ensure any negative impact of an economic slowdown (e.g. trade) will be compensated by a low level of currency exchange rates (e.g. monetary).[31]

Large capital inflows can alternatively lead to an excessive appreciation of exchange rates. This has been witnessed in several instances since the 1980s, mainly after foreign investors poured capital into emerging countries in search of yield and following important domestic policy reforms. This influx of capital, however, fueled massive appreciation in the value of various currencies and therefore reduced the export competitiveness

---

[28] Korinek (n 13) 524.
[29] See for instance ibid.
[30] See MacFarlane (n 1) 174. See also Michael Melvin, *International Money & Finance* (7th ed., Pearson/Addison-Wesley 2004) 27.
[31] John Williamson, Olivier Jeanne and Arvind Subramanian, 'International Rules for Capital Controls' (11 June 2012) VoxEU.org https://voxeu.org/article/international-rules-capital-controls accessed 27 February 2020.

of domestic companies in international markets,[32] thus pushing several South American and Asian countries to set up a variety of CFMs as part of comprehensive stability measures and packages.[33] The starkest example occurred in the late 1980s and early 1990s in Brazil, where inflation rates reached 80 per cent per month and up to 2400 per cent in 1993.[34] Subsequently, in 1998, capital outflows dramatically increased as the Asian Financial Crisis spilled over to other regions, and Brazil has required assistance from the IMF in order to stabilize its economy.[35] Since then, Brazil established further CFMs between 2008 and 2012 to control a currency which had appreciated by 50 per cent since 2004 as a result of successful reforms aimed at attracting foreign investors.[36] As other commentators then noted, 'In the fall of 2008, there were very large outflows of bank and portfolio flows, the impact of which on the current account and domestic demand was largely buffered by an equivalent reduction in the stock of reserves, which mitigated the repercussions of the sudden stop on the real economy'.[37]

---

[32] Neely (n 9) 18.
[33] Gochoco-Bautista and Rhee (n 26) 3–4 (stating that '[i]n the early to mid-1990s, countries such as Brazil, Chile, Colombia, Malaysia, and Thailand set limits on short-term capital inflows, largely through the use of market-based controls such as direct or indirect taxation of inflows or outflows. Brazil, Chile, and Malaysia also used administrative and direct controls (prohibition of non-resident purchases of money market securities and non-related swap transactions with non-residents), an explicit entrance tax on foreign exchange transactions (Brazil), and indirect taxation of inflows through an unremunerated reserve requirement or URR (Chile and Colombia). Some countries such as the Republic of Korea and the Philippines, on the other hand, began liberalizing inflows, but intermittently tightened their controls on capital flows, particularly during periods of high capital flow volatility in the run-up to a financial crisis ... With the exception of Argentina, a number of Latin American countries undertook capital account liberalization towards the end of the 1990s, but tightened their controls on inflows beginning in 2002–2004. De jure controls on outflows on the other hand, increased in intensity in 2007–2008, in reaction to the instability caused by the US mortgage crisis in 2007 and the global financial crisis in 2008–2009').
[34] Edmund Amann, Carlos Azzoni and Werner Baer, *The Oxford Handbook of the Brazilian Economy* (Oxford University Press 2018) 106. See also Elias C Grivoyannis (ed), *The New Brazilian Economy: Dynamic Transitions into the Future* (Palgrave Macmillan 2016) 181–82.
[35] Joyce (n 17) 125–26.
[36] Laura Alfaro, Anusha Chari and Fabio Kanczuk, 'The Real Effects of Capital Controls: Financial Constraints, Exporters, and Firm Investment' (Harvard Business School 2014) Working Paper No.15-016 8–9. See also Kevin P Gallagher, *Ruling Capital: Emerging Markets and the Reregulation of Cross-Border Finance* (Cornell University Press 2015) 84–90.
[37] Jeanne, Subramanian and Williamson (n 27) 9.

Other examples include Colombia, which established restrictive measures in 2007 as a means to limit currency appreciation in the face of surging capital inflows (motivated following an increase in the interest rates),[38] and Indonesia and South Korea, which both preventively constrained the volume of inflows to limit currency speculation in 2009 and 2011, respectively, to prevent large outflows.[39] The latter two examples are connected to the GFC, which displayed the negative and multifaceted effects of unrestricted capital flows when subprime difficulties in the US led to banks collapsing in America and Europe while subsequently creating a sovereign debt crises, most notably in Greece. Gallagher provides an easily understandable summary of the root cause of such crises:

> Economic booms will significantly attract capital inflows from foreign investors looking for new investment opportunities [while] the initial economic euphoria, reflected in rising asset prices [will] produce an appreciation of the domestic currency and thus encourage[] the taking of short term positions in foreign currency. The euphoria also causes economic units to become more reckless in the risks they undertake and to resort to greater speculative financing.[40]

While some describe international economic and financial stability in terms of 'International Public Goods' (benefits that once provided to some must be provided to all and at all times),[41] others point towards the danger of not controlling financial flows – especially inflows.[42] Among other commentators, Alfaro notes that 'with completely open capital markets, the relevant source of systematic risk becomes the world market'.[43] Hence, in a system in which

---

[38] Benedict Clements and Herman Kamil, 'Are Capital Controls Effective in the 21st Century? The Recent Experience of Colombia' (International Monetary Fund 2009) IMF Working Paper No.09/30 3, 6 https://papers.ssrn.com/abstract=1356459.

[39] Gochoco-Bautista and Rhee (n 26) 1. See also Jeanne, Subramanian and Williamson (n 27) 13.

[40] Gallagher (n 36) 61 (referring to Christian E Weller, 'Financial Crises after Financial Liberalisation: Exceptional Circumstances or Structural Weakness?' (2001) 38 *The Journal of Development Studies* 98; Philip Arestis and Murray Glickman, 'Financial Crisis in Southeast Asia: Dispelling Illusion the Minskyan Way' (2002) 26 *Cambridge Journal of Economics* 237; Hyman P Minsky, 'The Financial Instability Hypothesis' (1992) The Jerome Levy Economics Institute Working Paper.

[41] Joyce (n 17) 4 [referring to Inge Kaul, Isabelle Grunberg and Marc A Stern, 'Defining Global Public Goods', *Global Public Goods: International Cooperation in the 21st Century* (Oxford University Press 1999)].

[42] See for instance Robert Wade and Frank Veneroso, 'The Gathering World Slump and the Battle over Capital Controls' (1998) 231 *New Left Review*. See also James Crotty and Gerald Epstein, 'In Defence of Capital Controls' (1996) 32 *Socialist Register* 118–49.

[43] Alfaro (n 24) 12.

'global investors care only about the expected return and volatility of their portfolio' the idea of imposing – or at least allowing for – a stability preservation mechanism 'segmenting the country's stock market from the rest of the world' is now favoured by many governments.[44] To some, this has proven to be successful, with Gallagher arguing that the countries 'with capital controls on inflows before the crisis were amongst the least hard hit by the sudden stop that occurred when the crisis went global in 2008'.[45]

2.2.3 Lack of Consensus

In reality, and despite the increasing revival of CFMs as a legitimate policy tool, even proponents admit that CFMs can unfairly distort competitive conditions.[46] This is especially the case in regard to currency manipulation which can artificially promote exports and discourage imports.[47] Gochoco-Bautista and Rhee have noted the occurrence of such conditions and highlighted the potential problems with flow from such strategies. In their words, while there are 'allegations that some countries with large and persistent current account surpluses may be using capital controls to deliberately prevent their currencies from appreciating … Intuitively, using capital controls to deliberately prevent currency appreciation is a clear example of beggar-thy-neighbor policies'.[48] Equally concerning is when governments use CFMs as a means to build up large reserves to act as currency security cushions, a practice largely relied upon in Asian economies where restrictions are seen as a form of 'precautionary insurance given the possibility of sudden capital flow reversals … to absorb the deflationary effects and exchange market pressures which followed'.[49] The protectionist dimension of CFMs has also been emphasised elsewhere, with Alfaro and others similarly describing policies 'aimed at maintaining persistent currency undervaluation' in Asia as well as in emerging South American economies.[50]

---

[44] Ibid. Gallagher (n 36) 67.
[45] Gallagher (n 36) 74.
[46] For a commentary on whether capital controls could be used as 'dynamic terms-of-trade manipulation' or as 'a form of intertemporal trade policy', see Arnaud Costinot, Guido Lorenzoni and Iván Werning, 'A Theory of Capital Controls as Dynamic Terms-of-Trade Manipulation' (2014) 122 *Journal of Political Economy* 77.
[47] 'Treasury Designates China as a Currency Manipulator' (*U.S. Department of the Treasury*, 5 August 2019) https://home.treasury.gov/news/press-releases/sm751.
[48] Gochoco-Bautista and Rhee (n 26) 2, 8–9.
[49] Ibid. 4.
[50] Alfaro (n 24) 4.

Overall, the two schools of thought therefore keep opposing one another. From a theoretical perspective, a well-known economic model promotes the 'theory of the six fears' according to which governments adopt CFMs for six main reasons. These include (i) fear of disrupting large and unforeseen inflows; (ii) a related fear of currency appreciation detrimental to export competitiveness; (iii) a fear of 'hot money' capable of generating short-term destabilizing distortions and flow reversals; (iv) a fear of low of monetary autonomy; (v) a fear of asset bubbles generated by volatile foreign inflows; and (vi) a fear of capital flights in case of capital flow reversals.[51] As the above indicates, the historical evidence indeed suggests that CFMs are often relied upon to address specific needs while targeting specific problems. Controls placed over short-term capital aim to counter the negative effects of volatility generated by speculation while, by contrast, controls over long-term (equity) capital rather reflect a country's sensitivity on foreign ownership issues rather than narrowly target issues of financial or monetary stability.[52]

Yet, for a long time the prevailing discourse has been largely CFM-averse and it has been argued that CFMs have overall been unable to impact flows in terms of volumes. On the contrary, CFMs could change the composition of flows only by progressively transforming shorter-term speculative flows into longer-term and more mature investment flows. Hence, to increase policy independence would tend to verify in practice, as other measures have proven fairly ineffective.[53]

---

[51] See for instance Isabella Massa ODI. For additional comments, see also Clements and Kamil (n 38). See also MacFarlane (n 1) 175; Neely (n 9) 21.

[52] Neely (n 9) 22.

[53] Kokeyne and others (n 20). For instance, Clements and Kamil found in 2013 that capital controls had mixed effects in emerging markets and 'no statistically significant impact' on non-FDI capital flows or on exchange rates but concluded that their capacity to alter the nature of cash flows and to increase domestic policymaking independence were more convincing. See Clements and Kamil (n 38) 17, 20. Further, Gabor notes that in Eastern Europe in 2008 some measures aimed at limiting currency appreciation actually had the opposite effect and 'perversely encouraged foreign currency borrowing'. See Daniela Gabor, '(De) Financialization and Crisis in Eastern Europe' (2010) 14 *Competition & Change* 248. Taking the example of Brazil and South Korea, others find that 'a mix of permanent and temporary macro prudential and [CFM] measures have been effective'. See Gallagher and Ocampo (n 11) 11; MacFarlane (n 1) 198–202. Qureshi similarly notes that 'evidence that capital controls may affect the composition of capital flows is stronger' than limited effectiveness in altering the overall volume of capital inflows. Qureshi and others (n 14) 2. See also Gochoco-Bautista and Rhee (n 26) 4.

2.2.4 Complementarity as a Convergence Point

All in all, it is therefore difficult to determine whether CFMs are more harmful than beneficial, but there is an agreement that restrictions have rarely 'been imposed in a well-thought-out way to correct clearly defined pre-existing distortions',[54] and that CFMs 'most often have been used as a tool to postpone difficult decisions on monetary and fiscal policies'.[55] The IMF has concurred with this idea, and while admitting that there is 'some evidence for the effectiveness of outflow controls in countries with favourable macroeconomic conditions', it also tempered its statement by suggesting that 'for controls on outflows to have a chance at being effective, they need to be supported by coherent macroeconomic policies'[56] – presumably to stop the 'herd' from rushing to withdraw capital from the country.

Stated differently, CFMs do not bring much as standalone measures but gain in relevance when used complementarily to adequate economic policy measures aimed at treating the diseases more than the symptoms. There is, in particular, one area in which most critics soften and (perhaps reluctantly) agree to the use of CFMs; that is, when the controls are implemented for 'prudential reasons' and in complement with other 'prudential' measures. Some commentators have written that 'capital controls and prudential measures can indeed reduce financial fragilities',[57] while others have emphasised that 'there is a good case to be made for using certain types of controls, notably prudential and countercyclical capital controls that can be effective in smoothing booms and busts in capital flows to developing and emerging-market economies'.[58] Jeanne et al., in particular, note the following:

> We find that capital controls can be part of the menu of options to be deployed in the last resort against incipient asset price bubbles ... However, our findings go further. Properly designed capital controls may even be effective as a regular instrument of economic policy and may be warranted in other situations that are not strictly related to capital booms and busts. One such situation would be when a country runs a structural current account deficit; maintaining capital controls can be a precautionary measure to prevent overvaluation of a currency (and thus penalize the tradable goods sector). India may be an example of this type of situation. Another situation in which capital controls may be warranted is when a country seeks to protect a fragile home banking sector from the destabilizing entry of foreign banks (or from other forms of capital inflows).[59]

[54] Neely (n 9) 19.
[55] Ibid.
[56] IMF, 'Liberalizing Capital Flows and Managing Outflows' (n 5) 56–57.
[57] Qureshi and others (n 14) 2.
[58] Jeanne, Subramanian and Williamson (n 27) 109.
[59] Ibid. 109–10.

Beyond complementarity, and as we shall discuss in subsequent chapters, the issue of whether there are suitable alternatives to CFMs – that is, tightening or expanding fiscal policies – therefore needs to be considered when assessing their desirability. Here, however, the possibilities are limited. For Gallagher and Ocampo, tightening fiscal policy to reduce capital inflows 'may also be suboptimal [because] [f]iscal policy adjustments take time, and therefore are not agile enough to respond to short-term shocks associated with the capital account'. Gallagher and Ocampo further add that '[s]uch response has also strong distributive effects, as it may imply cutting social public sector spending to give space to capital inflows that benefit richer sectors of society'.[60]

2.3 The Remaining Issue of CFMs

Whilst restrictions on free cross-border capital flows were once perceived as inefficient policy tools encouraging corruption,[61] they have progressively become a hybrid tool used to guard against the detrimental effects of liberalisation. CFMs are therefore no longer viewed as entirely problematic, but they are not considered as a fully desirable feature of international financial integration policy either. Their use should be considered in terms of complementarity and ought to be limited to safeguarding against abuse, namely 'for purposes of financial stability, and not for maintaining or acquiring international competitiveness'.[62] At the moment, however, this proposition remains in the realm of postulation because no formal framework exists, thus creating significant policy dilemmas for many policymakers.

2.3.1 Lack of a Guideline or Framework

Unsurprisingly, this poses the question of the framework applicable to managing CFMs. While CFMs are clearly part of the financial and monetary system, there is at this stage no international guideline or framework which directly regulates them – that is, allowing, restricting or simply coordinating[63] – and various discussions have therefore emerged. In particular, while the vast majority of scholarly and governmental literature

---

[60] Gallagher and Ocampo (n 11) 11.
[61] On corruption, see MacFarlane (n 1) 186–87.
[62] Gochoco-Bautista and Rhee (n 26) 8–9.
[63] This point is the subject of Chapter 3.

on CFMs has been authored by economists and political scientists who have largely focused on whether controls have delivered,[64] CFMs have only rarely been considered from a legal perspective. Beyond suggesting that the current debates on CFMs are mainly 'paternalistic' and judgmental,[65] this conclusion has various implications.

First, despite uncertainties, the reality is that CFMs have become a *de facto* instrument in the international financial regulation toolbox on which many countries rely to preserve domestic interests. The problem is that in the absence of a consensus as to when and how they ought to be used, those controls have become an unregulated instrument of monetary and economic competitiveness. Think, for instance, of China repeatedly being criticized for artificially maintaining the RMB at a low level to support exports and suppress imports. While this example is easy to conceptualize and express, it fails to provide the full picture. In the main, China is not alone in seeking to maintain a weak currency. Traditional financial advocates such as the US Federal Reserve, European Central Bank and Japan Central Bank all routinely engaged in quantitative easing (QE), and other 'non-standard' or 'unconventional' monetary policies which have raised liquidity but also by design had the effect of devaluating currencies while fostering trade and investment.[66] In fact, policymakers in surplus countries such as China have accused deficit countries (and in particular those that host global reserve currencies) of deliberately devaluing and weakening their currencies.[67] In this regard, the debates over CFMs are not limited to 'weighing trade-offs and effectiveness of capital controls in managing the risks to financial stability associated with large and volatile capital flows' but rather they encompass larger 'hot button political issues of 'currency wars' and 'currency manipulation''.[68]

Second, and as will be explained in Chapter 3, in practice global and cross-border capital movements have become so significant that they have

---

[64] See for instance Alfaro, Chari and Kanczuk (n 36); Vittorio Grilli and Gian Maria Milesi-Ferretti, 'Economic Effects and Structural Determinants of Capital Controls' (1995) 42 *IMF Economic Review* 517; Chikako Baba and Annamaria Kokenyne, 'Effectiveness of Capital Controls in Selected Emerging Markets in the 2000s' (International Monetary Fund 2011).

[65] Gochoco-Bautista and Rhee (n 26) 2 ('previous debates on capital controls have been paternalistic. The debates focused on whether capital controls are beneficial and effective in securing financial stability against volatile capital flows without raising funding costs for recipient countries').

[66] For an explanation of how QE policies operate, see for instance www.ecb.europa.eu/explainers/show-me/html/app_infographic.en.html

[67] Gochoco-Bautista and Rhee (n 26) 2.

[68] Ibid.

progressively fallen within the purview of the IMF, which has now come to embrace the view that transnational financial movements – and therefore CFMs – should now fall within the scope of its international financial and monetary stability mandate. Yet, in the absence of rules, should the Fund be entitled to take a lead on the matter, and how should members behave in relation to cross-border capital flows?

2.3.2 The Policymaking Dilemma

The above suggests that CFMs constitute a significant dilemma for policymakers. On the one hand, capital flows are acknowledged as having a potentially negative impact on economies due to volatility and shock propagation risks among increasingly connected economies. This is why the international community (via the IMF) now seeks to regulate their use through explicit if cautious legitimisation. On the other hand, the investors responsible for capital flows value the notion of liberalisation and free movement of capital. Hence, these actors tend to view the imposition of CFMs as a political message suggesting that (i) a country's economy is heading in the wrong direction and/or (ii) that the host authorities are not capable of managing the situation.

In either circumstance, CFMs thus send the message that investments are no longer safe and create a major policy issue. According to proven economic science theories, in practice the ability of states to operate financial markets in a sound manner is limited, *de facto*, by an 'impossible trinity', also known as the Mundell–Fleming model – developed by Nobel Prize Robert Mundell in the 1960s and based on Keynes' economic work dating from the 1930s.[69] The Mundell–Fleming model is key here because it introduces the idea that while financial governance usually focuses on three important goals – free capital flows, fixed exchange rates and independent monetary policy – in reality only two of those can be attained in any given period of time.[70] As Mo succinctly summarizes:

> In recent decades, the validity of the Impossible Trinity has been repeatedly verified. The forces of globalization have made capital controls among

---

[69] The Mundell–Fleming model is widely relied upon today, and has been described by economists as 'the workhorse for analyzing fundamental problems in international finance and the foundation for making related public decisions'. See Robert A Mundell, *International Economics* (Macmillan 1968). See also Neely (n 9) 18 (on the 'incompatible trinity'); Gallagher (n 36) 48–53; Joyce (n 17) 22.

[70] Mundell (n 69). See also Neely (n 9) 18. (on the 'incompatible trinity'); Gallagher (n 36) 48–53.

countries increasingly porous due to the enormous increase of trade in goods and services. Some countries intentionally open up their capital account in order to tap the potentially benefits brought to their economies. In many cases, they also desire to maintain exchange rate stability by adopting a fixed exchange rate regime. The phenomenon is common in developing and emerging economies. When the economies are small and open with immature and thin financial sector, exchange rate stability is particularly valuable to their international transactions. However, in the long-run, the choice is incompatible as predicted in the Mundell-Fleming model. The economies making such choice experience periodical booms and busts in their asset and financial markets. They result in the extensively documented financial and currency crises as in the Latin American and Asian countries that cause widespread pains and destructions. The experiences have made many developing economies extremely cautious in opening their currency and asset markets that becomes a formidable obstacle for further global integration and advancements. The global nature of the phenomenon suggests that the hazard is systemic and requires institutional solution. Achieving compatibility between financial/economic stability and capital mobility can remove the deadlock towards global integration that will be beneficial to both capital abundant and capital scarce economies.[71]

In other words, a country may wish to guarantee free capital flows and preserve its monetary autonomy, but in such a case it would not be able to avoid risks related to exchange rate volatility. This is the case with many of the world's leading economies. Alternatively, if a country wants to guarantee free capital flows and a stable exchange rate pegged to another currency or basket of currencies (e.g. the Hong Kong dollar is pegged within a narrow band to the US dollar) then by necessity it would lose independence over its monetary policy. Simply stated, and to follow the Hong Kong example, the US Federal Reserve's interests and policy orientations not only significantly impact but direct those of the Hong Kong Monetary Authority and the Hong Kong dollar. The third possibility is the situation in China, where exchange rates are maintained (some would say manipulated) through reserve efforts and the financial authorities fully control monetary policy, but there the imposition of CFMs has severely limited capital flows.

Stated differently, regulators must make a choice. They can impose CFMs, abandon monetary policy independence by linking their currency to another currency or conduct autonomous exchange policy and either raise interest rates in an attempt to stabilize the value of the currency or

---

[71] Mo Pak-Hung, 'Impossible Trinity, Capital Flow Market and Financial Stability' (2009) 62 *Kyklos* 611.

devalue their own currency as a means to stimulate growth.[72] However, in all cases they must take responsibility for creating one risk or another. As a result, while policymakers have long understood the importance of financial stability, they also increasingly recognise the need to manage the flows and effects of capital to restrict possible snowball effects, but they have no common framework to use. The lack of an adapted international legal framework, and the absence of a supranational authority holding a thoughtful and consistent position on the matter, further contribute to the difficulties.[73] Hence, the debate over CFMs is international, strategic, political, controversial and difficult to manage. In essence, the issue is therefore not whether countries should refrain from applying CFMs but rather it is about controlling capital flows in a sound and sustainable manner by ensuring that the financial markets evolve from debt-fueled speculation and bubbles into long-term and secure financing. This point will be further explored further in the remainder of the book.

---

[72] European Central Bank and others, 'Monetary Policy Spillovers, Capital Controls and Exchange Rate Flexibility, and the Financial Channel of Exchange Rates' (2019) 2019 Federal Reserve Bank of Dallas, Globalization Institute Working Papers www.dallasfed.org/~/media/documents/institute/wpapers/2019/0363.pdf.
[73] Korinek (n 13).

PART II

The IMF, Capital Flows and Controls

Having established that CFMs are an important element of financial and monetary policy, we now turn to whether and to what extent the IMF should monitor CFMs. The importance of coordinating monetary and financial policies is well documented, with authors recognising that 'global coordination is the key to effective capital flow management'.[1] Yet, in practice there are numerous obstacles to such coordination because, as Gallagher correctly notes, 'the losers of a capital control regime are highly concentrated and very powerful politically [while] the winners, in terms of the general public, are diffuse across the entire system [and] cannot connect the dots [...] to the extent that they will mobilize politically'.[2]

As the prevailing international financial authority and as the body tasked with securing the stability of the international monetary system, the IMF would appear to be the legitimate institution when it comes to promoting the coordination of international capital flow management. This suggestion is not without controversy, however, as over the past two decades, the Fund has been heavily criticised and its reputation harmed due to its performance in successive crises. In particular, influential commentators

---

[1] Kevin P Gallagher, *Ruling Capital: Emerging Markets and the Reregulation of Cross-Border Finance* (Cornell University Press 2015) 96–97. See also John Williamson, Olivier Jeanne and Arvind Subramanian, 'International Rules for Capital Controls' (VoxEU.org, 11 June 2012), https://voxeu.org/article/international-rules-capital-controls (discussing the view of some authors that 'currently, the international regime is permissive about the use of capital controls [and] countries can use them or not as they wish'). See also IMF, 'The Fund's Role Regarding Cross-Border Capital Flows' (International Monetary Fund 2010) 22, www.imf.org/en/Publications/Policy-Papers/Issues/2016/12/31/The-Fund-s-Role-Regarding-Cross-Border-Capital-Flows-PP4516; Olivier Jeanne, Arvind Subramanian and John Williamson, *Who Needs to Open the Capital Account* (Peterson Institute 2012); Annamaria Viterbo, *International Economic Law and Monetary Measures: Limitations to States' Sovereignty and Dispute Settlement* (Edward Elgar Publishing 2012) 115; Maria Socorro Gochoco-Bautista and Changyong Rhee, 'Capital Controls: A Pragmatic Proposal' (2013) No. 337, ADB Economics Working Paper Series 2.

[2] Gallagher (n 1) 96–97.

such as Stiglitz have suggested that the Fund was ill equipped and unable to prevent financial instability – with some going so far as to claim that the Fund even contributed to the creation of instability.³ Despite the battered reputation and lingering doubts regarding its capabilities, nonetheless, the Fund has *de facto* become the leading institution dealing with issues of capital movements and controls. Maybe this is because there is no other choice, but as the 'effective lender of last resort during an international panic',⁴ the Fund has long played (and still plays) a prominent role in matters relating to financial stability.

From a legal perspective, however, the Fund's role in capital account (de)regulation and financial stability matters comes despite the lack of a specifically designed framework or clear mandate to do so. This lack of mandate is one reason for the long history of ad hoc and inconsistent advice, and while in theory financial liberalisation has long been the mantra at the IMF, in reality the Fund has tolerated and even promoted capital restrictions. In fact, while the 'Institutional View' published in 2012 to legitimise the use of CFMs has been seen by some as a major move,⁵ this book analyses the Fund's legal and policy documents to suggest that the 'View' was less a tectonic shift and more so the result of a slow and steady evolution in thinking by fund staffers. Moreover, while some commentators have interpreted the Institutional View as implying that emerging economies 'now have official blessing' from the IMF to undertake autonomous monetary policies that will no longer be considered 'fundamentally distortionary',⁶ such a view does not correspond with the Fund continuing to set out the perimeters for their use and maintenance.

---

³ See for instance Joseph Stiglitz, 'The East Asian Crisis: How IMF Policies Brought the World to the Verge of a Global Meltdown', *Globalization and Its Discontents* (WW Norton & Company 2003). Krugman also described the Fund's work during the Asian Financial Crisis as a failure and asked whether 'the IMF made the best of a bad situation or it simply pour[ed] fuel on the fire', while Wade wrote that the Asian crisis was 'one of global crisis management'. See Paul Krugman, 'Saving Asia: It's Time To Get Radical: The IMF plan not only has failed to revive Asia's troubled economies but has worsened the situation. It's now time for some painful medicine.' (7 September 1998), *Fortune Magazine*, https://archive.fortune.com/magazines/fortune/fortune_archive/1998/09/07/247884/index.htm; Robert Wade and Frank Veneroso, 'The Gathering World Slump and the Battle over Capital Controls' (1998) 231 *New Left Review*.
⁴ Joseph P Joyce, *The IMF and Global Financial Crises: Phoenix Rising?* (Cambridge University Press 2012) 134.
⁵ IMF, 'The Liberalization and Management of Capital Flows: An Institutional View' (International Monetary Fund 2012), www.imf.org/external/np/pp/eng/2012/111412.pdf
⁶ Gallagher (n 1) 12, 135.

The 'View' should not be discounted, as it did formally shift away from the IMF's historical antagonism towards capital controls to an acceptance of temporary or longer-term 'measures that are specifically designed to limit capital flows'.[7] Nonetheless, more than a revolution, the 'View' simply codifies the Fund's 'integrated approach',[8] which overall favours liberalised markets while affirming that '[i]n certain circumstances, [CFMs] can be useful'. Stated differently, the move by the IMF does not create new powers; it usurps even greater control over CFMs than had previously existed. This usurpation of power raises a variety of questions that go to the core of the legality of the shift from an international law perspective. Chapters 3 and 4 explore the Institutional View and legal points which arise from the shifting mandate.

---

[7] IMF, 'The Liberalization and Management of Capital Flows: An Institutional View' (n 5).
[8] Ibid.

3

Shifting the IMF Mandate

In the absence of an international framework applicable to cross-border capital flows, there is little doubt that the Fund *had* to assert its authority over capital movements. Without the Fund, a legal lacuna would exist and financial movements would go largely unregulated. Yet, it is less certain whether the Fund ever had the formal legal authority to empower itself to act as a *de facto* financial authority.

As this chapter explains, a strict reading of the Articles of Agreement – which define the Fund's operational mandate – suggests that the Fund historically had no mandate over capital movements. Yet, by using a 'byroad' several decades ago the Fund has slowly but steadily begun appropriating and assuming authority over capital movements. Beginning with the materialisation of a mandate to oversee the development of stable exchange rate policies in the late 1990s, and the development in the late 2000s of a multilateral surveillance and coordination role which monitors the 'needs of the international monetary and financial system as they develop',[1] the Fund has placed itself in an increasingly important role in following and assisting governments which experience wildly fluctuating inward and outward capital flows – thus exercising what some have described as a post-crisis mandate.[2]

This grey area can be easily explained by the fact that the Fund's constitutive instrument never anticipated the growing importance of modern capital flows and therefore remained largely silent on the matter. What is surprising is the lack of available legal analysis of this mandate shift. The issue has been touched upon in research conducted by IMF staffers, academic economists and political scientists,[3] but the legal aspects have

---

[1] See *infra* Section 2.
[2] See for instance Adam Feibelman, 'The IMF and Regulation of Cross-Border Capital Flows' (2015) 15 *Chicago Journal of International Law* 409.
[3] See for instance Maria Socorro Gochoco-Bautista and Changyong Rhee, 'Capital Controls: A Pragmatic Proposal' (2013) No. 337 ADB Economics Working Paper Series 4; Manuela Moschella, 'The Institutional Roots of Incremental Ideational Change: The IMF and Capital Controls after the Global Financial Crisis' (2015) 17 *The British Journal of Politics and International Relations* 442.

hardly been considered in academic or other literature. Thus, the legal debate over capital movements has been limited, 'paternalistic' and focused simply on the question of 'whether capital controls are beneficial and effective'.[4] The legal analysts that have written on the issue generally (and oddly) skirt around the legal issues. For instance, Feibelman states that 'the scope of [the Fund's] jurisdiction to engage with its members regarding their treatment of capital flows is somewhat unclear'.[5] Former IMF senior legal counsel Deborah Siegel likewise does not fully address the issue but notes that the word 'framework' has only been used for 'convenience' without giving any legal authority to the Fund.[6]

To analyse the issue, this chapter explores the legal instruments used by the Fund to organise the shift and expansion of its mandate. The chapter makes two major points. First, while the Fund grounded its mandate expansion on the text and wording of the Articles of Agreement, further analysis of the Fund's approach reveals an 'Article IV byroad' which allowed the Fund to interpret its constitutive instrument to escape the historical distinction between 'capital movements' and 'current international transactions'.[7] Second, as eluded to in the introduction to Part II, the Fund's Institutional View of 2012 was not a radical break from tradition but merely a formalisation and crystallisation of the ideas and direction it has pursued since 2008. In other words, despite what has been commonly written, the Institutional View of 2012 itself did not create any new rights, nor did it change the Fund's legal mandate.

3.1 The Mandate under the Articles of Agreement

As a starting point, it should be noted that the Articles of Agreement do not highlight or even mention capital flow management. Instead, the mandate of the IMF is shaped by a historical distinction between 'current international transactions' and 'capital movements' which seems outdated and largely irrelevant to modern practice.[8] The Fund's authority over

---

[4] Gochoco-Bautista and Rhee (n 3) 2.
[5] Feibelman (n 2) 414.
[6] Deborah Siegel, 'Capital Account Restrictions, Trade Agreements, and the IMF', in *Capital Account Regulations and the Trading System: A Compatibility Review* (Boston University 2013) 72.
[7] This point was first made in Antoine P Martin and Bryan Mercurio, 'The IMF Mandate on Capital Controls: Legal Analysis of the Article IV Byroad and the Institutional View of 2012' (2017) 34(3) *Arizona Journal of International and Comparative Law* 529–56.
[8] For a similar argument, see for instance Deborah E Siegel, 'Using Free Trade Agreements to Control Capital Account Restrictions: Summary of Remarks on the Relationship to the Mandate of the IMF' (2003) 10 *ILSA Journal of International and Comparative Law* 297, 299.

issues of capital flow management is simply left unstated, which to some commentators implies that the Fund has no authority over CFMs. Such a view is myopic and out of touch with the Fund's *raison d'être*, however.

3.1.1 The (Official) Mandate of the Fund

The difficulty in establishing the Fund's authority to oversee capital policymaking pertaining to CFMs and capital controls stem from the fact that the Articles of Agreement have historically split capital movement policy supervision between the IMF and its member states. As a general rule, the Fund has always had a wide role in relation to stability coordination and facilitation. According to Article I, the purposes of the IMF are *inter alia*, to (i) promote international monetary cooperation, (ii) facilitate the expansion and balanced growth of international trade and (iii) promote exchange stability, to maintain orderly exchange arrangements among members and to avoid competitive exchange depreciation.

Article I Purposes

The purposes of the International Monetary Fund are:

(i) *To promote international monetary cooperation through a permanent institution which provides the machinery for consultation and collaboration on international monetary problems.*

(ii) *To facilitate the expansion and balanced growth of international trade, and to contribute thereby to the promotion and maintenance of high levels of employment and real income and to the development of the productive resources of all members as primary objectives of economic policy.*

(iii) *To promote exchange stability, to maintain orderly exchange arrangements among members, and to avoid competitive exchange depreciation.*

(iv) *To assist in the establishment of a multilateral system of payments in respect of current transactions between members and in the elimination of foreign exchange restrictions which hamper the growth of world trade.*

(v) *To give confidence to members by making the general resources of the Fund temporarily available to them under adequate safeguards, thus providing them with opportunity to correct maladjustments in their balance of payments without resorting to measures destructive of national or international prosperity.*

(vi) *In accordance with the above, to shorten the duration and lessen the degree of disequilibrium in the international balances of payments of members.*

At the same time, the Articles are opaque when it comes to assessing the Fund's competence to coordinate policy and monitor cross-border capital flows. On the one hand, Section 3 of Article VI ensures that the regulation of cross-border capital movements remains a state prerogative and makes it clear that the 'Members may exercise such controls as are necessary to regulate international *capital movements*'.[9]

Article VI Capital Transfers

Section 3. Controls of capital transfers

> Members may exercise such controls as are necessary to regulate international capital movements, but no member may exercise these controls in a manner which will restrict payments for current transactions or which will unduly delay transfers of funds in settlement of commitments, except as provided in Article VII, Section 3(b) and in Article XIV, Section 2.

On the other hand, Section 2(a) of Article VIII limits the ability of the states to *fully* control capital movements by providing that 'no member shall, *without the approval of the Fund*, impose restrictions on the making of payments and transfers for *current international transactions*'[10] or unduly delay transfers of funds in settlement of commitments (which also fall under the scope of current transactions).[11]

Article VIII General Obligations of Members

Section 2. Avoidance of restrictions on current payments

> (a) Subject to the provisions of Article VII, Section 3(b) and Article XIV, Section 2, no member shall, without the approval of the Fund, impose restrictions on the making of payments and transfers for current international transactions.

Furthermore, Section 1 of Article IV imposes an obligation on members 'to collaborate with the Fund and other members to assure orderly exchange arrangements and to promote a stable system of exchange rates'.

---

[9] Ibid. (emphasis added).
[10] Ibid. (emphasis added).
[11] Ibid. See Articles of Agreement of the IMF, Article VI.

3.1 THE MANDATE UNDER THE ARTICLES OF AGREEMENT

Article IV Obligations Regarding Exchange Arrangements

Section 2. *Avoidance of restrictions on current payments*

Recognizing that the essential purpose of the international monetary system is to provide a framework that facilitates the exchange of goods, services, and capital among countries, and that sustains sound economic growth, and that a principal objective is the continuing development of the orderly underlying conditions that are necessary for financial and economic stability, each member undertakes to collaborate with the Fund and other members to assure orderly exchange arrangements and to promote a stable system of exchange rates. In particular, each member shall:

(i) *endeavor to direct its economic and financial policies toward the objective of fostering orderly economic growth with reasonable price stability, with due regard to its circumstances;*
(ii) *seek to promote stability by fostering orderly underlying economic and financial conditions and a monetary system that does not tend to produce erratic disruptions;*
(iii) *avoid manipulating exchange rates or the international monetary system in order to prevent effective balance of payments adjustment or to gain an unfair competitive advantage over other members; and*
(iv) *(iv) follow exchange policies compatible with the undertakings under this Section.*

3.1.2 Explaining the Asymmetry

Such an asymmetry can be explained by historical factors. At the time of drafting, 'current transactions' most likely referred to payments and transfers, whereas the term 'capital movements' rather referred to currency exchange movements. The Articles of Agreement therefore created a 'capital movement vs current transactions' asymmetry[12] which allowed Members to manage 'capital movements' (exchange) – under IMF guidance – only as long as they did not interfere with 'current transactions' (payments and transfers) since these had to remain free. *A contrario*, this means that the Fund had full authority over monetary and exchange arrangement policies while Members had an obligation to cooperate with the Fund. Capital movements and current transactions were then considered as distinct elements because the Bretton Woods negotiations which led to the creation of the Fund did not emphasise trade or financial liberalisation – which is not as surprising as it seems since such issues were not a major concern to the

---

[12] For a similar argument, see Feibelman (n 2) 430 (defining the term 'asymmetry').

international community at that time. As a reminder, negotiating countries at Bretton Woods were largely focusing on and preparing for recovery and self-preservation following the end of hostilities in the Second World War.[13] Moreover, governments in the era from the Great Depression through to the end of the Second World War viewed high levels of tariff and other trade barriers as being necessary to build and protect nascent domestic industries,[14] and the prevailing sentiment at the time was that unrestricted capital movements favoured speculative trading which could negatively impact exchange rate stability. The views of the influential British economist John Maynard Keynes were gaining favour, and many influential thinkers believed that government interventionism was essential to economic stability and growth because it could best curb market failures.[15] Hence, the regulation of 'capital movements' was left under state control so that nations could ensure the preservation and support of domestic development efforts.[16] As a result, the drafters provided the IMF with the authority to ensure that cross-border 'current transactions' – that is, the financial transactions allowing for the realisation of international trade exchanges – would remain stable and under control. However, the idea of improving the countries' *current account* through capital movements facilitation (i.e. establishing a balance between the goods exchanged across borders) and the suggestion that free trade formed a key pathway to development did not emerge until much later.[17]

---

[13] IMF, 'The Fund's Role Regarding Cross-Border Capital Flows' (International Monetary Fund 2010) 23–24, www.imf.org/en/Publications/Policy-Papers/Issues/2016/12/31/The-Fund-s-Role-Regarding-Cross-Border-Capital-Flows-PP4516. See also Antoine Martin and Bryan Mercurio, 'The IMF and Its Shifting Mandate towards Capital Movements and Capital Controls: A Legal Perspective' (2017) 44 *Legal Issues of Economic Integration* 211, 215.

[14] See for instance Jeffrey A Hart and Joan Edelman Spero, *The Politics of International Economic Relations* (6th ed., Routledge 2013) 2–3, 15; IEO IMF, 'IMF's Approach to Capital Account Liberalization 2005' (International Monetary Fund) 17, www.imf.org/en/Publications/Independent-Evaluation-Office-Reports/Issues/2016/12/31/IEO-Evaluation-Report-on-the-IMF-s-Approach-to-Capital-Account-Liberalization-2005-18289

[15] Joseph E Stiglitz, 'The World Bank at the Millennium' (1999) 109 *The Economic Journal* 577, 578. See also Gochoco-Bautista and Rhee (n 3) 6.

[16] See Chapter 1. See also IMF, 'IMF's Approach to Capital Account Liberalization 2005' (n 14) 17.

[17] Ibid. Interpretations diverge as to what 'current transactions' actually encompassed at the time. Some IMF documents for instance conclude that the term then comprised international payments and transfers. See for instance IMF, 'The Fund's Role Regarding Cross-Border Capital Flows' (n 13) 18; Stiglitz (n 15) 577. Alternative sources, in contrast, clearly reject the idea that payment and transfers were ever included in the Fund's mandate. See for instance IMF, 'IMF's Approach to Capital Account Liberalization 2005' (n 16) 17; Philip J MacFarlane, 'The IMF's Reassessment of Capital Controls after the 2008 Financial Crisis: Heresy or Orthodoxy?' (2015) 19 *UCLA Journal of International Law and Foreign Affairs* 167, 176–79. See also Feibelman (n 2) 440–41(discussing the existence of an agreed repartition of roles between international organisations acting in the various trade and financial fields).

3.1.3 Consequences of a Restrictive Mandate in a Changing World

Nowadays, however, the concepts of current transactions and capital movements are blurred and almost indistinguishable. With the exponential growth of the financial sector over the past decades, the historical delineation between the current and capital accounts is both outdated and unrealistic. The liberalisation of international trade which occurred as a result of the GATT/WTO has led to a tremendous rise in the level of goods traded, which in turn has increased the need for cross-border financial transactions. More efficient cross-border financial services have also emerged together with the development of financial markets, while the expansion of commodity trading has transformed international finance into a self-standing activity capable of propping up or destroying the global economy irrespective of tangible trade in goods. Thus, we are now at a point where capital has become a tradable commodity much in the same way as goods and services.[18]

In such an environment, the concept of 'current transactions' has gained a very different meaning than at the Bretton Woods Conference or the drafting of the Articles of Agreement: the current transaction has at least in *de facto* terms been merged with the once very distinct concept of 'capital movements'.[19] It is also important to note, in fact, that while financial services and capital flows have grown exponentially over the decades, they have not been regulated or controlled by an international mechanism or institution in the same way as trade in goods has been overseen by the GATT/WTO.[20] Financial liberalisation coordination efforts only materialised as part of WTO negotiations through the GATS Annex on Financial Services during the Uruguay Round between 1995 and 1997,[21] as well as through bilateral and regional free trade agreements (FTAs) negotiated around the same time. Accordingly, the idea that such flows had to be managed began to gain serious traction in governmental and academic communities only from the 1990s.[22] Meanwhile, the Fund was

---

[18] See Ludger Schuknecht, 'A Simple Trade Policy Perspective on Capital Controls' (WTO 1998) WTO Staff Working Paper No. ERAD-98-11.
[19] See MacFarlane (n 17) 179. (showing the difference between both concepts).
[20] Antoine P Martin, 'Coordinating Modern Cross-Border Financial Services: No Global Policy, No Global Legal Framework, but Some Regional Opportunities' (2016) 50 *Int'l Law* 467.
[21] Ibid. See also WTO, 'Overview of the 1995 and 1997 Negotiations on Financial Services', www.wto.org/english/tratop_e/serv_e/finance_e/finance_fiback_e.htm
[22] See Feibelman (n 2) 431; Daniela Gabor, 'Paradigm Shift? A Critique of the IMF's New Approach to Capital Controls' (2011) Working Paper No. 1109 from The Bristol Business School, Department of Accounting, Economics and Finance, 5–6. Moschella (n 3) 451.

expected to oversee monetary and exchange rate stability factors as well as international financial stability at large, but it had no legal authority to establish a framework for the liberalisation or regulation of financial flows and services. While economists never demonstrated a robust correlation between capital account liberalisation and growth,[23] liberalisation became an embedded obligation in trade and investment agreements, and the need for supervision over the sector emerged.

3.2 Act Now, Apologize Later

Despite the lack of a solid mandate to do so, the IMF has played an important role in terms of capital-related policymaking. For starters, it has encouraged and implemented the 'Washington Consensus' doctrine of capital account liberalisation in its dealings with members. At the same time, the IMF has also sought to legitimise its actions, not so much in explicitly expanding its mission but more so in using the tools and text available to assert its authority over capital management. The Fund did so in several ways. First, the Fund shifted its focus from a purely monetary institution into a global financial institution. Second, the Fund interpreted its constituent documents in such a way to *ex post* legitimise the expansion of its mandate. Third, the Fund used the Institutional View in 2012 to further embed its legitimate mandate over issues relating to capital flows and management.

3.2.1 *From Monetary to Financial Institution*

Following its performance in the late 1990s and early 2000s, the Fund's reputation was damaged, and its lending activities were far below the levels it had seen in the previous decades. The global financial crisis marked a comeback for the Fund, as it again emerged 'as a leading player' in promoting, maintaining and ensuring global financial stability.[24] Since this time, the Fund's activities have progressively taken on an increasingly

---

[23] IEO IMF, 'The IMF's Approach to Capital Account Liberalization: Revisiting the 2005 IEO Evaluation' (International Monetary Fund 2015) 10, https://ieo.imf.org/en/our-work/Evaluations/Updates/The-IMFs-Approach-to-Capital-Account-Liberalization. See also Kevin P Gallagher and Jose Antonio Ocampo, 'IMF's New View on Capital Controls' (2013) 48 *Economic and Political Weekly* 10, 11 (referring to IMF economists concluding in 2012 that 'the international community should not seek to promote totally free trade in assets – even over the long run – because (…) free capital mobility seems to have little benefit in terms of long-run growth').

[24] Joseph P Joyce, *The IMF and Global Financial Crises: Phoenix Rising?* (Cambridge University Press 2012) 1.

financial dimension, which as should now be clear is beyond the scope of its original focus on monetary stability.

As just explained, the Fund's original mandate gave it the authority to promote international monetary cooperation, to facilitate the expansion and balanced growth of international trade and to promote exchange stability to maintain orderly exchange arrangements among members. The Articles of Agreement, however, have over time been amended to a significant extent. For greater clarity, let us take the original draft of the Articles of Agreements, as signed in 1944. At the time, the only mention of a financial competence could be found in Article VIII, which gave the Fund a mandate to collect and exchange information on monetary and financial problems:

> The Fund may arrange to obtain further information by agreement with members. It shall act as a centre for the collection and exchange of information on monetary and financial problems, thus facilitating the preparation of studies designed to assist members in developing policies which further the purposes of the Fund.[25]

An amendment to Article IV on the Obligations Regarding Exchange Arrangements was later added to supplement Article VIII:

> Recognizing that the essential purpose of the international monetary system is to provide a framework that facilitates the exchange of goods, services, and capital among countries, and that sustains sound economic growth, and that a principal objective is the continuing development of the orderly underlying conditions that are necessary for financial and economic stability.[26]

Moreover, while the very notion of 'Surveillance over exchange arrangements' did not exist in 1944, today Article IV reads:

> In order to fulfill its functions under (a) above, the Fund shall exercise firm surveillance over the exchange rate policies of members, and shall adopt specific principles for the guidance of all members with respect to those policies. Each member shall provide the Fund with the information necessary for such surveillance, and, when requested by the Fund, shall consult with it on the member's exchange rate policies.[27]

In parallel to these amendments, the Fund has developed financial activities on its own. For instance, the Financial Sector Assessment Programmes

---

[25] Article VIII, Section 5(c).
[26] Article IV, Section 1.
[27] Article IV, Section 3(b).

(FSAPs) were introduced in 1999 as part of Article IV consultations as 'a comprehensive and in-depth assessment of a country's financial sector' with a view to 'analyze the resilience of the financial sector, the quality of the regulatory and supervisory framework, and the capacity to manage and resolve financial crises'.[28] Described by the Fund as 'a key instrument of the Fund's surveillance', these programmes have over time become mandatory for twenty-nine countries designated by the Fund as 'Jurisdictions with Systemically Important Financial Sectors'.[29] In other words, while the Fund had no definitive financial prerogative at the time of its creation, over time and through amendments it has eventually gained a *de facto* authority to oversee financial sector stability programmes.

Owing to the significant evolution in financial practices, the Fund's operational scope also expanded towards capital controls over the years. As previously stated, the current international transactions at the core of the IMF mandate are no longer restricted to payments and transfers, while the distinction between the current and capital accounts has become an illusion. This point is made clear in the Fund's annual reports, where the 'Regulatory Framework for Foreign Exchange Transactions' now includes five major categories of foreign exchange transactions, including trade-related measures, current invisible transactions, accounts transactions and capital controls.[30] The term 'accounts transactions' itself refers to the regulatory measures imposed on resident and non-resident accounts, while 'capital controls' refers to 'adjustments in capital controls in response to changes in the global environment, especially in capital flows to emerging market economies'.[31] In other words, the distinction between current transactions and capital movements has become irrelevant as both account transactions and capital controls are now viewed as within the scope of a 'foreign exchange transaction', which is unquestionably included in its mandate. More recently, the Fund further relaxed its previous dogmatic position on

---

[28] See IMF, 'Financial Sector Assessment Program (FSSA)' (7 October 2019), www.imf.org/external/np/fsap/fssa.aspx

[29] These jurisdictions include the US, United Kingdom, China, France, Switzerland, Luxembourg, Hong Kong and others. See www.imf.org/external/np/fsap/mandatoryfsap.htm

[30] See for instance IMF, 'Annual Report on Exchange Arrangements and Exchange Restrictions' (International Monetary Fund 2012) 41. In practice, when looking at 'exchange arrangements', the IMF notes that a significant number of capital control measures were initiated between 2011 and 2012 as compared to the previous years, including a significant number of measures affecting capital and money market instruments, adjustments to controls on credit operations and measures aimed at easing capital inflows so as to compensate the reduced access to foreign funds. See ibid. 46–48.

[31] See IMF, 'Annual Report on Exchange Arrangements and Exchange Restrictions' (n 30) 45.

financial openness and even recommended against liberalisation in certain instances, mainly after a steady stream of staff research papers admitted that capital flows might have unwanted bubble and burst effects on economies. In the words of one IMF paper, free capital flows may actually '*lead to excessive exchange rate depreciation, credit busts, and asset price deflation, and thus may destabilize the domestic economy*'.[32]

Hence, since the aforementioned crises, and certainly following the GFC in 2008, the emerging consensus seems to favour two ideas. One is that the application of CFMs could prove useful to ensure the stability of the domestic and global economies against uncontrollable capital movements. The other is that, owing to its supervisory role on monetary matters, the Fund should also have a role to play in guaranteeing the stability of the international financial system.

3.2.2 Expansion through the 'Article IV Byroad'

In reality, the Fund has followed what can be described as an 'Act now, apologize later' approach. By creatively interpreting its constitutive instrument, the Fund developed an 'Article IV byroad' which progressively allowed it to address the 'asymmetry' and take an active role in overlooking capital movement matters as part of its exchange arrangement authority.

The byroad began with the 1977 Decision on Surveillance over Exchange Rate Policies (also known as the 'Hong Kong Declaration') which, as part of the second amendments of the IMF Articles of Agreement, was the first step towards shifting the Fund's mandate.[33] By the end of the 1970s, the international community had already made significant efforts to remove restrictions on current transactions – such as payments and transfers – while cross-border capital flows had increased in parallel to the growth of international trade. The Hong Kong Declaration completed the shift from the *par value* system to floating exchange rates,[34] but it also increased

---

[32] IMF, 'Annual Report on Exchange Arrangements and Exchange Restrictions 2014' (International Monetary Fund) 60 www.imf.org/external/pubs/nft/2014/areaers/ar2014 .pdf2 (emphasis added); Christopher J Neely, 'An Introduction to Capital Controls' (1999) 81 *Federal Reserve Bank of St. Louis Review* 20 (on the idea that the necessity to permit the rapid closure of positions in response to changing conditions creates an inherent 'destabilizing potential' because it increases exposure to global liquidity shocks). See Gabor (n 22) 6. See also MacFarlane (n 17) 172; Feibelman (n 2).

[33] IMF, 'IMF Executive Board Adopts New Decision on Bilateral Surveillance over Members' Policies' (International Monetary Fund) Public Information Notice No. 07/69, www.imf .org/en/News/Articles/2015/09/28/04/53/pn0769.

[34] See for instance MacFarlane (n 17) 182, 189.

the Fund's scope of action towards financial flows. In the main, the 1977 Declaration introduced the idea that the Fund's exchange stability prerogatives had to be considered more broadly because the isolated and unilateral controls operated by states over cross-border capital flows could impact global exchange stability. In other words, while Article VI had merely prevented members from manipulating exchange rates to prevent unfair adjustments, the revised Article IV broadened the Fund's role, transforming its competence from a stable exchange rate into a general authority to oversee the stability of the exchange system itself.[35] With the 1977 Decision, the Fund has become involved in assisting members to conduct currency policy adjustments in response to capital movement surges,[36] and the Fund's movement to gain competence over capital movements eventually continued into the 1990s, until it was stopped dead in its tracks when members rejected another amendment. Building on the general recognition of the systemic benefits flowing from trade and capital account liberalisation at the time, the Fund sought to further embed Washington Consensus thinking by proposing the elimination of the remaining difference in treatment between capital movements and current account transactions and instead creating a broad legal obligation for members to progressively liberalise policies and regulations on both trade and capital movements.[37]

This move towards a simplification of the system has been described in the economic literature as fulfilling three main functions: i) the view that 'an adequate and assured supply of foreign capital' was then seen as 'necessary' by the Fund; ii) a 'desire for symmetry' in the way current

---

[35] See *supra* Section 1.2.

[36] IMF, 'Public Information Notice' (n 33). Commenting on the integration, Siegel similarly notes that 'the revised Article IV recognized that the overall functioning of the international monetary system was impacted by a growth in international capital movements and liberalization of controls by some members'. See Siegel (n 8) 70. In contrast, Hieronymi argues that the second amendment was 'the one that basically made the IMF Irrelevant for the International Monetary System' and considers that 'the IMF has played no role at the global level and ... has had no influence whatsoever on the policies of the leading OECD countries' because it only served as a lending instrument but made 'feeble attempts at multilateral surveillance'. See Otto Hieronymi, 'From "Global Finance" to the Crisis of Globalization', in *Globalization and the Reform of the International Banking and Monetary System* (Palgrave Macmillan 2009) 91–92.

[37] See IMF, 'The Fund's Role Regarding Cross-Border Capital Flows' (n 13) 4. ('This could take the form of an obligation to ultimately liberalize capital movements, subject to safeguards and routine exclusion of prudential measures. Alternatively, and more neutrally, one might consider an amendment calling on members to collaborate with the Fund and others to ensure that capital movements are consistent with international monetary stability'.); Feibelman (n 2) 431; MacFarlane (n 17) 188. These sources provide further detail on the surrounding conditions.

account and capital account were treated – or in other words, an equality of treatment between trade transactions and capital flows; and iii) a necessity 'to establish an institutional and legal basis for its involvement in the expanding capital markets'.[38] With much controversy, Members however considered and ultimately refused to concede that capital account liberalisation should be an objective. By the same token, they also refused to surrender sovereignty over capital policymaking because of the fear that a complete prohibition of capital controls would eventually lead to financial instability.[39]

Despite the rejection of the proposed amendment, Members at all levels of development nonetheless continued to liberalise capital markets on a unilateral basis and through bilateral and regional trade and investment agreements.[40] The Fund, meanwhile, successfully continued to increase its influence on CFM policymaking – ironically, as a result of the negative effects created by liberalisation. In particular, the 1997 Asian Financial Crisis which in part was fuelled by rapid inflows and outflows of capital, helped persuade Members that capital account liberalisation should be organised, sequenced and integrated progressively as part of parallel economic reform programmes, integrated with suitable macroeconomic policies (exchange rate included), and occur only after ensuring that measures were taken to strengthen financial institutions and markets – the IMF's so-called integrated approach to capital account liberalisation.[41]

Though rarely mentioned by economic and political commentators, in 2006 the Fund's Legal Department in consultation with the Fund's Policy Development and Review Department released an important document that provided critical insights into the Fund's legal adaptation strategy.[42] The document rather cleverly relied on the 1977 Declaration as precedent to expound a carefully crafted argument advocating for the expansion of the Fund's mandate.

First, while the 2006 document admitted that an essential purpose of the international monetary system is to provide a framework that facilitates

---

[38] Joyce (n 24) 84. Jacques J Polak, 'The Changing Nature of IMF Conditionality', in *Essay in International Finance* (Princeton University Press 1991) 58.
[39] MacFarlane (n 17) 189–90.
[40] These agreements are discussed in Chapters 6 and 7.
[41] IMF, 'The IMF's Approach to Capital Account Liberalization' (n 23) 10.
[42] IMF, 'Article IV of the Fund's Articles of Agreement: An Overview of the Legal Framework' (International Monetary Fund 2006) Policy Paper 10, www.imf.org/en/Publications/Policy-Papers/Issues/2016/12/31/Article-IV-of-the-Fund-s-Articles-of-Agreement-An-Overview-of-the-Legal-Framework-PP3883

the exchange of goods, services *and* capital, the latter was never part of the Fund's purposes *per se*[43] – it placed a strong emphasis on the obligation of members to collaborate with the Fund on exchange arrangement matters. The document then relied on this obligation as the logical means to expand the IMF's scope of action.[44] In fact, the Legal and Policy Departments used the members' obligation to collaborate on exchange stability as the cornerstone of the Fund's constitutional re-interpretation over time. The document emphasised that in practice the Fund had *always* 'made considerable use' of the cooperation obligation to limit exchange rates' instability and competitive depreciation policies – even though the strict exchange policymaking fell out of its scope of application until the Amendment in 1977 to ensure the stability of the economic and financial system itself.[45] Highlighting the crucial importance of the cooperative approach in ensuring exchange stability at large, the document went on to state that it had always been intended that the Fund's overall mission would change over time to adapt to new circumstances in the political economy:

> 22. … Following a similar approach, the Fund could rely on the collaboration undertaking set forth in the present Article IV, Section 1 as a basis for either requiring or recommending that members take— or refrain from taking those actions that, while not included in any of the specific obligations listed in Article IV, Section 1, are considered by the Fund to be necessary in light of changing circumstances to assure orderly exchange arrangements and to promote a stable system of exchange rates.
>
> 27. … Although the legislative history is silent on the question, it must be assumed that, notwithstanding the continuity of language, *it was intended that the underlying meaning of this objective would change in a manner that takes into account the change made to the other objective of the obligation to collaborate* (i.e. the change from 'exchange stability' to a 'stable system of exchange rates', and the broad freedom given to members to put in place exchange arrangements of their choice). As noted above, even where the exchange arrangement actually includes a specified exchange rate, the right of the member to select this component would be constrained by its obligations regarding a stable system of exchange rates.[46]

Second, the Legal and Policy Development Departments relied on the vagueness of the Articles of Agreement to further support the idea that a

---

[43] Ibid. 18.
[44] Ibid. 16–28. See also Articles of Agreement of the IMF, Article 4 § 1.
[45] IMF, 'Article IV of the Fund's Articles of Agreement: An Overview of the Legal Framework' (n 42) 20–22, 25.
[46] Ibid. (emphasis added).

broader approach to exchange matters was needed. In the main, Article IV Section1(ii) requires each member to 'seek to promote stability by fostering orderly underlying economic and financial conditions and a monetary system that does not tend to produce erratic disruptions'. However, the document notes that while 'efforts in the Executive Board to insert the word "exchange" before "stability" were rejected [it was still] not clear whether the phrase "erratic disruptions" only refer[ed] to disruptions in exchange rates or whether it has a broader meaning'.[47] Said differently, the departments authoring the document offered a creative *ex post* interpretation of the Articles which clearly allowed explaining, justifying and grounding a mandate expansion.

Third, the document explained why a broader mandate was required, that is, 'there are different ways in which a member could potentially "manipulate" exchange rates within the meaning of Article IV [such as] excessive intervention in the exchange markets or through the imposition of capital controls'.[48] IMF lawyers and policy strategists, in other words, established a practical relationship between capital controls and exchange stability by emphasising that:

> most importantly, the Articles specifically confer upon members the right to exercise controls on capital movements. However, it has been understood that a member may not impose capital controls if such controls are used to manipulate the member's exchange rate in order to prevent balance of payments adjustment or to gain an unfair competitive advantage over other members.[49]

A contrario, therefore, the Fund's increasing authority towards the stability of the exchange system logically conferred competence to oversee members' capital policies. In a footnote, furthermore, the departments recalled that the Executive Board discussions relating to the 1977 Decision 'clarified that the imposition of capital controls or the capital flows that could occur in the absence of such controls could be legally used as an indicator justifying a need for discussion between the Fund and the member of the appropriateness of the member's exchange policies'.[50] Overall, the Legal and Policy Development Departments thus concluded that the Fund's competence to ensure the stability of the exchange system could evolve by using members' general obligation to

---

[47] Ibid. 31.
[48] Ibid. 34(a).
[49] Ibid. 15.
[50] Ibid. 7.

collaborate to promote a stable system of exchange rates. This, in fact, was clearly introduced as a means to reach grey areas of the system:

> 39. ... if the Fund wishes to provide further guidance to members as to those exchange rate obligations under Article IV, Section 1 that go beyond the obligation to avoid exchange rate manipulation, it may rely directly on the general obligation to collaborate to promote a stable system of exchange rates. As is discussed earlier, and consistent with the approach that was adopted prior to the adoption of the Second Amendment, the Fund could call on members to pursue such exchange rate policies that it views as being necessary to achieve the objective of achieving a stable system of exchange rates.

In retrospect, it is therefore interesting to note that although it established various connections between capital controls and exchange arrangements, the 2006 analysis drew conclusions as to the Fund's mandate evolution only in relation to exchange arrangements and merely invited the Fund to extend its competence – that is, provide further guidance – over exchange system stability at large because of the expanding nature of the concept, including towards capital controls. The document did not, however, elaborate on future shifts occurring in relation to capital movements. Thus, while the existing system under the 1977 Decision was lagging, the 2006 document increased the Fund's authority to pursue its legal coordination mandate only by taking a 'multilateral and medium-term perspective' towards exchange rates policymaking.

A year later, in 2007, a Decision of the Fund's Executive Board furthered the mandate shift by making clear that the Fund's future surveillance mandate 'shall be adapted to the needs of the international monetary and financial system as they develop' and shall focus on the members' policies that 'can significantly influence present or prospective external stability' whether in the context of exchange rate, monetary, fiscal or financial sector policies at large.[51] The instrument, it should be added, went even further by adding that the Fund would gain authority over Union policymaking[52] and by giving it the authority to authorise members to take on capital flow management policies under certain conditions:

> A member should intervene in the exchange market if necessary to counter disorderly conditions, which may be characterized *inter alia* by disruptive short-term movements in the exchange rate of its currency.[53]

---

[51] IMF, 'Public Information Notice' (n 33).
[52] Ibid.
[53] Ibid.

In essence, while most of the attention was focused on the 2012 View, the above thus suggests that these documents have been left unconsidered. Yet, they are extremely important to the jigsaw of the Fund's mandate because they show that the Fund's Legal and Policy Department were not afraid to suggest a *de facto* mandate expansion based on a progressive interpretation of the mandate in light of a changing global political economy. Somewhat surprisingly, nonetheless, the legal impact of the 2007 Decision is hardly ever mentioned in the literature despite being described by the Executive Board as an 'important starting point' or 'keystone' in the efforts to modernise the foundations of the IMF's surveillance function and, in so doing, crystalising thirty years of good practices in light of the current globalisation trend.[54]

3.2.3 The 2012 'Institutional View'

Leaving aside the direct and indirect attempts to amend the Articles of Agreement, the Fund eventually cemented its authority over CFMs through its so-called Institutional View of 2012, which is described by some commentators as a victory for emerging economies – even though they worked hard forming a 'unified voice' coalition and using the G20 as a forum to exercise pressure towards the acceptance of a 'new thinking' mindset.[55] Surprisingly, therefore, while the IMF's Executive Board has internally debated capital account liberalisation and controls since the 1980s,[56] the Executive Board's views and doctrinal position on cross-border capital controls have only recently attracted attention.[57]

Several documents outline the Fund's current view. For instance, an IMF report from 1997 insisted on the positive contribution of liberalisation but also noted that while 'controls on capital movements had proved largely ineffective … [they could] on occasion, provide temporary breathing room in dealing with balance of payments difficulties, although the controls'.[58] Controls, it was added, could also 'provide some protection against abrupt

---

[54] Ibid. (stating the Fund's surveillance function is 'the activity whereby the IMF monitors the economic and financial policies of its member countries in the interest of international monetary stability').

[55] Kevin P Gallagher, *Ruling Capital: Emerging Markets and the Reregulation of Cross-Border Finance* (Cornell University Press 2015) 12, 132.

[56] IMF, 'IMF's Approach to Capital Account Liberalization 2005' (n 16) 20.

[57] See IMF, 'Pursuing Equitable and Balanced Growth' (International Monetary Fund 2011) 26, www.imf.org/en/Publications/AREB/Issues/2016/12/31/Pursuing-Equitable-and-Balanced-Growth.

[58] IMF, 'Capital Account Convertibility and the Role of the Fund: Review of Experience and Consideration of a Possible Amendment of the Articles' (International Monetary Fund 1997) SM/97/32 13.

and sharp portfolio shifts by limiting capital mobility to the extent that it may be difficult to evade controls in the short run'.[59] This is, of course, provided that those are taken 'as part of a comprehensive package of stabilization and structural reform', that they are 'temporary and, to the extent possible, market based and transparent'.[60]

In line with this idea, a 2010 report prepared by the Strategy, Policy, and Review Department and the Legal Department also rather importantly stated:

> No presumption is made here that capital account liberalization is a goal in itself in all cases, but rather that a broader range of tools and advice, contemplating both the elimination and imposition of controls, may be more appropriate for domestic and systemic stability. It is recognized that international capital flows are only a type of financial flow – the type that crosses borders – and that the overall approach must fit in a broader vision of macro-prudential regulation and supervision.[61]

More recently, the IMF's official position on capital account issues resurfaced with the release of the 2012 Institutional View, which means that while the Fund's staff had in practice long shifted its views towards capital controls in its post-GFC advice, it could not rely on standardized guidelines to offer policymakers consistent advice.[62]

The lack of consistent advice did not go unnoticed.[63] In fact, as early as 2005, the Fund's IEO noted a lack of coherence in IMF advice and recommended that the Executive Board formally clarify the scope of IMF surveillance on capital account issues, provide clear guidance to staff on the official position and focus on the 'push factors behind international capital flows and how to minimize the volatility of capital movements'.[64] Similarly, while discussing the 2007 Decision on Bilateral Surveillance, the Fund's Annual Report for 2008 suggested that temporary capital controls could be used as financial and monetary

---

[59] Ibid. 15.
[60] Ibid. 10–11. It was added, furthermore, that 'the potential volatility and volume of [capital] flows can also occasionally undermine the "orderly underlying conditions" that are necessary for the stability of the international monetary system', and that 'The liberalization of capital flows underscores the importance of careful attention to the factors which could give rise to disruptive surges in capital flows'.
[61] IMF, 'The Fund's Role Regarding Cross-Border Capital Flows' (n 13) 5.
[62] See IMF, 'IMF's Approach to Capital Account Liberalization 2005' (n 16) 2.
[63] On the lack of consistency, see for instance Jean Tirole, *Financial Crises, Liquidity, and the International Monetary System* (Princeton University Press 2002) 47.
[64] IMF, 'IMF's Approach to Capital Account Liberalization 2005' (n 16).

stabilisation methods.[65] During the Global Financial Crisis (and in a clear reaction to the then-recent financial crisis in South America which showed similar trends as seen during the 1997–98 Asian Financial Crisis and 1998–99 Russian and Brazilian crises[66]), the Fund's International Monetary and Financial Committee (IMFC) called on the Fund to 'cover the full range of macroeconomic and financial policies that bear on global stability',[67] thus reiterating its authority to oversee capital movements at large.

While these reports sent strong signals on the evolving direction of the IMF, a major change occurred in 2010 in the wake of the GFC, when the Fund concluded that 'with liquidity being withdrawn as part of policy exits, new financial stability risks have surfaced'.[68] Until this time, traditional thought on the issues was that the significant capital flows to Asia and Latin America stemming from improving governance and outlook, abundant liquidities and low interest rates in advanced economies were a boon to the emerging world.[69] The Fund, however, expressed concerns that – despite limited evidence at the time – excessive flows could generate speculative bubbles and currency bubbles while the global financial sector linkages could spread financial vulnerabilities created by 'push and pull factors' (such as sudden stops in inflows followed by sudden outflows generated by future monetary and liquidity tightening policies) across economies.[70] In another cautionary note, the second Global Financial Stability Report published in October 2010 not only supported the use of macroeconomic policies and prudential regulations to deal with surges in temporary inflows, but also directly referenced the changing position of the Fund when it added that '[w]hen these [other] measures are not sufficient … capital controls may have a role in complementing the policy toolkit'.[71]

---

[65] IMF, 'Making the Global Economy Work for All' (International Monetary Fund 2008) Annual Report of the Executive Board 22–23, www.imf.org/en/Publications/AREB/Issues/2016/12/31/Annual-Report-of-the-Executive-Board-for-the-Financial-Year-Ended-April-30-2008

[66] See Olivier Jeanne, Arvind Subramanian and John Williamson, *Who Needs to Open the Capital Account* (Peterson Institute 2012) 9.

[67] IMF, 'Communiqué of the International Monetary and Financial Committee of the Board of Governors of the International Monetary Fund', (4 October 2009) Press Release No. 09/347, www.imf.org/en/News/Articles/2015/09/14/01/49/pr09347

[68] IMF, 'Meeting New Challenges to Stability and Building a Safer System' (International Monetary Fund 2010) IMF Global Financial Stability Report 3, www.imf.org/en/Publications/GFSR/Issues/2016/12/31/Meeting-New-Challenges-to-Stability-and-Building-a-Safer-System

[69] Ibid.

[70] Ibid. 29.

[71] Ibid. 135.

In November 2010, the aforementioned report prepared by the Strategy, Policy, and Review Department and the Legal Department comprehensively addressed the issues by providing background on the Fund's historical and prospective roles, emphasising staff difficulties in advising members due to a general lack of regulatory good practices guide in relation to cross-border capital movements, and calling for an official position on the matter. The document, furthermore, suggested that consideration be given to amending the Articles of Agreement,[72] and vigorously called on the Fund to take a strong leadership position in contrast to its status quo of doing things which, in the drafters' words, were 'not tenable' anymore.[73] In response, the Fund's Executive Board responded in early 2011 by admitting that while capital liberalisation efforts had generated 'substantial benefits by facilitating efficient resource allocation across countries', liberalisation had also generated growing volatility in worldwide cash flows which had played a 'key role' in the recent worldwide crisis.[74]

Around the same time, the IMFC of the Fund's Board of Governors sent its strongest signal of a pending change in official direction when it called for a 'comprehensive and balanced approach for the management of capital flows'.[75] The Fund's ideological evolution came in response to calls emanating from various actors in the international sphere, who increasingly demanded the flexibility to use capital controls and similar measures to manage the capital flows and markets. At the same time, these actors sought clarity from the Fund in light of its recent inconsistent practice. On a political level, the shift responded to a plea formulated into a G20 communiqué dated October 2010, which requested that the IMF

---

[72] See IMF, 'The Fund's Role Regarding Cross-Border Capital Flows' (n 13) 4 § V ('In the longer term, to provide a more complete framework to address the complex issues related to international capital flows, consideration could be given to amending the Articles of Agreement. This could take the form of an obligation to ultimately liberalize capital movements ... Alternatively, and more neutrally, one might consider an amendment calling on collaborate with the Fund and others to ensure that capital movements are consistent with international monetary stability'.).

[73] Ibid. 3 ('In the aftermath of the global crisis, and especially now with resurgent capital flows requiring a considered policy response, it is not tenable for the Fund to remain on the sidelines of a debate so central to global economic stability'.).

[74] IMF, 'Executive Board Discusses the Fund's Role Regarding Cross-Border Capital Flows' (IMF 2011) Public Information Notice (PIN) No. 11/1, www.imf.org/en/News/Articles/2015/09/28/04/53/pn1101

[75] IMF, 'Communiqué of the Twenty-Fourth Meeting of the IMFC: Collective Action for Global Recovery, Chaired by Mr. Tharman Shanmugaratnam, Deputy Prime Minister of Singapore and Minister for Finance' (IMF 2011) IMF Press Release No. 11/348, www.imf.org/en/News/Articles/2015/09/28/04/51/cm092411

'further work on macro-prudential policy frameworks, including tools to help mitigate the impact of excessive capital flows', and also committed 'advanced economies, including those with reserve currencies, [to now] be vigilant against excess volatility and disorderly movements in exchange rates'.[76] Having described the G20 declaration as a 'hard-won consensus on broad principles'[77] and admitting that currency management and capital controls could constitute 'legitimate policy choices',[78] the Executive Board lamented the lack of 'universal rules of the road' governing cross-border financial flows and reconsidered the Fund's mandate to oversee international monetary stability in relation to capital movements.

This reconsideration directly led to three main ideas. First, the Board found it necessary to formulate a coherent institutional view and guidelines for reducing vulnerabilities and reinforcing the Fund's surveillance role in relation to the capital account and capital flows: 'a more pro-active and systematic role for the Fund with respect to global capital flows seems desirable'.[79] Second, the Board called for expanded bilateral and multilateral efforts towards policy surveillance so as to avoid potential spill-overs. Third, the Board considered whether the IMF's Articles could be amended so as to provide for a 'more complete and consistent legal framework for addressing issues related to capital flows' and insisted on the necessity to improve policy advice while leaving sufficient room for 'country-specific circumstances' (i.e. to take into account the various liberalisation levels from one country to another).[80]

From an institutional perspective, the key element to the Fund's shift and expansion of mandate was therefore its surveillance function. Simply stated, the GFC (if not those before it) highlighted that national capital flow management policies could have large multilateral effects. Since 'a breakdown in the domestic stability of a large country [could] spill over into stress in other countries and even to the global system as a whole', the IMF, however, believed all economies could equally bear risks flowing from volatile cross-border capital flows. Hence, the conclusion of a 2011 IMF note commented that because domestic policymakers could

---

[76] G20, 'Communiqué of the Meeting of Finance Ministers and Central Bank Governors' (2010), www.g20.utoronto.ca/2010/g20finance101023.html
[77] IMF, 'The Liberalization and Management of Capital Flows: An Institutional View' (International Monetary Fund 2012), www.imf.org/external/np/pp/eng/2012/111412.pdf.
[78] Gabor (n 22) 4.
[79] IMF, 'Public Information Notice' (n 74) 4 § IV.
[80] Ibid. Referring to IMF, 'The Fund's Role Regarding Cross-Border Capital Flows' (n 13) 4, 47.

'not fully appreciate the multilateral transmission of their policies', the Fund now had an important bilateral and multilateral surveillance and supervision role to play.[81] This role includes cross-border flow and global liquidity monitoring, stability and spill-over controlling, policy coordination and dialogue promotion and efficient advising, among other duties.[82] Eventually, this led to the majority of the IMF Board of Directors welcoming in April 2011 a framework proposition which then appeared as a 'first-round articulation of the Fund's institutional views on responses to manage capital inflows' with a view to assimilating the framework into the Fund's surveillance mandate in the future.[83] A year later, in March 2012, the IMF released a final key document aimed at providing the Fund with an 'up-to-date and operational framework for policy advice on liberalising capital flows and on the management of capital outflows' which proposed an 'integrated approach' to capital flow liberalisation.[84] According to this 'integrated approach':

> (i) Capital flows must be considered 'within the broader context of macroeconomic and financial system stability', (ii) while respecting that 'the appropriate degree of liberalization can differ across countries, based on country specific conditions including the level of financial sector and institutional development', (iii) so that the 'economy and financial sector can handle the resulting flows without undue risk', (iv) especially when keeping in mind the 'broad linkage between domestic and cross-border financial liberalization'.[85]

This document, in particular, crystalized discussion held within the IMF's Executive Board in July 2001 in relation to conditionality in IMF funding

---

[81] On this point, Feibelman for instance notes that the 'distinct aim of multilateral surveillance' is to address threats to global financial stability that do not arise from the members' domestic instability but from the external or systemic effects of the members' domestic policies. Feibelman (n 2) [referring to IMF, 'Modernizing the Legal Framework for Surveillance: An Integrated Surveillance Decision' (International Monetary Fund 2012) Policy Paper 7–8, www.imf.org/en/Publications/Policy-Papers/Issues/2016/12/31/Modernizing-the-Legal-Framework-for-Surveillance-An-Integrated-Surveillance-Decision-PP4673]. See also Claus D Zimmermann, *A Contemporary Concept of Monetary Sovereignty* (Oxford University Press 2014), Chapter 5.

[82] IMF, 'IMF Executive Board Discusses the Multilateral Aspects of Policies Affecting Capital Flows' (International Monetary Fund 2011) Public Information Notice: No. 11/143 www.imf.org/en/News/Articles/2015/09/28/04/53/pn11143

[83] Ibid. IMF, 'IMF Executive Board Discusses Recent Experiences in Managing Capital Inflows' (2011) Public Information Notice No. 11/42 www.imf.org/en/News/Articles/2015/09/28/04/53/pn1142

[84] IMF, 'Liberalizing Capital Flows and Managing Outflows' (International Monetary Fund 2012) 3, www.imf.org/external/np/pp/eng/2012/031312.pdf

[85] Ibid. 21–22.

and called for a more 'integrated' and cautious approach to liberalisation.[86] It also acknowledged that CFMs may 'need to be temporarily reimposed under certain conditions without compromising the overall process of liberalization', while also noting that the 'reimposition of CFM on outflows' could be 'useful mainly in crisis or near crisis conditions, but only as a supplement to more fundamental policy adjustment'.[87]

In November 2012, seven years after the IEO first discussed the necessity of an official position on capital controls,[88] the IMF's shift in policymaking and incursion into the financial sector thus became complete with the publication of the Fund's 'Institutional View' on the liberalisation and management of capital flows. However, while the Institutional View is normally described as a revolutionary document, as explained in the previous subsection, the reality is that it merely synthesises the conclusions of the previous IMF policy and position papers and thus reiterates the various points stated previously. Of note is the call for greater liberalisation (as opposed to an objective of full capital account liberalisation). The Institutional View recognises that increasing capital flows represents a global policy challenge, even though they may be beneficial when certain conditions are met. Such conditions are low inflation; large foreign reserves; composition of external flows, including a relatively large share of FDI and equity flows; financial development reflected in growing financial market depth and enhanced regulation and supervision; enhanced institutional quality and governance and increased trade openness.[89] Increasing capital flows can also have disruptive and unexpected effects on economies. In other words, the Institutional View makes it clear that one size does not fit all, suggests that CFMs ought to be part of the 'toolkit' depending on specific circumstances and policy objectives (i.e. 'if capital flows pose risks to a member state's macroeconomic or financial system's stability')[90] and observes that while designed to be temporary and part of larger efforts, CFMs maintained on a long-term basis ought not to be precluded.[91]

---

[86] Ibid. 21. See also IMF, 'Seminar on IMF Conditionality' (10 July 2001) www.imf.org/en/News/Seminars/Conferences/2016/12/31/Seminar-on-IMF-Conditionality. IMF, 'IMF's Approach to Capital Account Liberalization 2005' (n 16) 55.
[87] IMF, 'Liberalizing Capital Flows and Managing Outflows' (n 84) 4.
[88] IMF, 'The IMF's Approach to Capital Account Liberalization' (n 23) 35.
[89] IMF, 'The Liberalization and Management of Capital Flows: An Institutional View' (n 77) 20.
[90] Ibid. 18. IMF, 'Annual Report on Exchange Arrangements and Exchange Restrictions 2014' (n 32) 63.
[91] IMF, 'The Liberalization and Management of Capital Flows: An Institutional View' (n 77).

Overall, the IMF's 2012 position on capital account issues should therefore be treated with caution. While it has overall been characterised as a radical departure from its own orthodoxy, and while some commentators have talked about a ground-breaking instrument described as the 'first and only systematic effort to manage global capital flows' characteristic of a new 'post-crisis mandate',[92] this view is somewhat exaggerative. As just explained, IMF staff papers had for some years paved the way for such a shift. In fact, the IMF approach to its dealings with countries suffering during the Global Financial Crisis reflected the changing stance on the use of capital controls. Hence, while the Institutional View crystallised the shifting view on the use of capital controls,[93] it is nothing but the culmination of a slow and steady movement within the Fund, marked essentially by the 'integrated approach' and the elaboration of the 'Article IV byroad'.

In line with this conclusion, some described the document as bringing about a slow, incremental ideological change in policymaking,[94] and being about a 'consolidated' and 'final cumulative paper ... based on a series of interim papers'[95] or a 'formalization of communiqués'.[96] The IMF itself introduced the publication of the Institutional View from March 2012 with a document described as the 'fourth in a series of Board papers developing a comprehensive Fund view on capital flows and the policies that affect them'. It also predicted that the 'next step' would be in the form of a 'subsequent paper, responding to the call by the [IMFC], integrat(ing) all of the elements covered in the series of papers thus far into a comprehensive, flexible, and balanced, approach for the management of capital flows, drawing on country experiences'.[97] As a clarifying document, it had no impact on the Fund's mandate to oversee capital movement issues: the strategic move described in the Institutional View, in fact, was formalized as part of the 1977 and 2007 Decisions, through the 2006 note by the IMF's Legal and Policy Development Departments.

Simply stated, therefore, the 'Institutional View' had no legal influence or effect on the Fund's expanding mandate, but the most relevant instrument in terms of mandate and legal evolution, however, is largely forgotten in the literature. The Fund's new mandate, indeed, was formalised through the Fund's Integrated Surveillance Decision of July 2012

[92] See Feibelman (n 2) 415, 438, 449. See also Gallagher and Ocampo (n 23) 10–11.
[93] Siegel (n 8) 72.
[94] Moschella (n 3) 443–44, 451.
[95] Siegel (n 8) 72.
[96] Gochoco-Bautista and Rhee (n 3) 8.
[97] IMF, 'Liberalizing Capital Flows and Managing Outflows' (n 84) at Executive Summary.

in which the Board, considering 'the need to promote global economic and financial stability to ensure the effective operation of the International Monetary System', took the decision that the Fund's assessments and policy advice would now have to 'incorporate relevant aspects of the global and regional economic and financial environment' while ensuring that the institution's legal mandate would evolve accordingly.[98] In legal terms, accordingly, the Integrated Surveillance Decision is far more important than the Institutional View in regards to the Fund's policymaking shift because it is the main and only tool capable of transforming the Fund's legal mandate. In contrast with the Institutional View, the Integrated Surveillance Decision has been adopted by a majority of the Executive Board. Under Article XII Section 3 of the Articles, the Executive Board is responsible for conducting the business of the Fund and, as such, is the authoritative body equipped with the decision-making power required to undertake and formalise such a mandate evolution. Thus, while the Institutional View reflects a policy evolution, the Integrated Decision is one of the instruments which decided, officialised and authorised a mandate evolution in affirmative and authoritative terms.

Interestingly, the Integrated Surveillance Decision relies on the 'Article IV byroad' approach described earlier. Clearly, the Decision does not relate to Article VI and does not grant the Fund a clear Article VI competence to deal with capital movements. The Decision, instead, relies on the increasing interconnectedness between exchange policymaking, current transactions and capital movements to extend the Fund's mandate covering Article IV monetary matters over capital movements. As a reminder, Article IV creates an obligation on members to foster 'economic and financial conditions and a monetary system that does not tend to produce erratic disruptions' and to refrain from manipulating exchange rates. The Decision expressly extends the Fund's surveillance role 'beyond' Article IV and 'encourages members to consider the effects of their policies on the effective operation of the international monetary system',[99] but it does so through the Fund's indirect role in relation to capital flows. The relevant paragraphs read:

6. ... Accordingly, exchange rate policies will always be the subject of the Fund's bilateral surveillance with respect to each member, *as will monetary, fiscal, and financial sector policies* (both their macroeconomic aspects and macroeconomically relevant structural aspects) ...

---

[98] IMF, 'Modernizing the Legal Framework for Surveillance: An Integrated Surveillance Decision' (n 81).
[99] Ibid. 2.

10. The international monetary system includes, in particular: (a) the rules governing exchange arrangements between countries and the rates at which foreign exchange is purchased and sold; (b) the rules governing the making of payments and transfers for current international transactions between countries; (c) *the arrangements respecting the regulation of international capital movements*; and (d) the arrangements under which international reserves are held, including official arrangements through which countries have access to liquidity through purchases from the Fund or under official currency swap arrangements.
11. The international monetary system is considered to be operating effectively when the areas it governs do not exhibit symptoms of malfunction such as, for example, persistent significant current account imbalances, an unstable system of exchange rates including foreign exchange rate misalignment, *volatile capital flows*, the excessive build up or depletion of reserves, or imbalances arising from excessive or insufficient global liquidity.
12. Therefore, in its multilateral surveillance, the Fund will focus on issues that may affect the effective operation of the international monetary system, including (a) global economic and financial developments and the outlook for the global economy, including risks to global economic and financial stability, and (b) the spillovers arising from policies of individual members that may significantly influence the effective operation of the international monetary system, for example by undermining global economic and financial stability. The policies of members that may be relevant for this purpose include exchange rate, monetary, fiscal, and financial sector policies and policies respecting capital flows.[100]

Hence, although the 2012 Decision did not create new obligations for the members,[101] it confirmed the 2007 Decision by reaffirming that 'Fund surveillance over members' policies and over the international monetary system shall be adapted to the needs of the international monetary and financial system as they develop'.[102] The Fund's mandate, in other words, did not change as a result of the 2012 Institutional View, but rather shifted because the Directors took the decision to further 'elucidate the place of

---

[100] Ibid. (emphasis added).
[101] Ibid. Preamble.
[102] Ibid. 3.

capital account issues in bilateral and multilateral surveillance'[103] and used their decision-making authority to make official and legitimise the evolution in clear legal terms through the 1977, 2007 and 2012 Decisions. These Decisions are the real ground-breaking instruments in the Fund's shifting mandate.[104] In contrast, the Institutional View provides no legal authority, competence or jurisdiction to the Fund but merely provides an informative status update on the IMF position on the issue of capital controls.

---

[103] IMF, 'The IMF's Approach to Capital Account Liberalization' (n 23) at Executive Summary.
[104] IMF, 'Article IV of the Fund's Articles of Agreement: An Overview of the Legal Framework' (n 42) (emphasising that this also deserves a mention, as it provided the views of the Fund's lawyers and strategists on the matter).

4

The Legality of the IMF's Mandate Expansion

Chapter 3 concludes that while the Fund may have usurped authority over capital movements through a variety of mechanisms, it remains the most relevant international financial body and is accordingly the most legitimate body to manage and deal with capital controls. Chapter 3 further demonstrates that the Fund's Institutional View of 2012 was not a revolutionary shift in policy regarding capital controls but rather a crystallisation of years of progressive evolution into an official guideline. What remains to be answered, therefore, is whether the Fund's self-initiated mandate expansion is legally valid.

This chapter explores the legality of the IMF's shift in mandate, and considers the overarching question of whether the institution was legally entitled to expand its mandate over time through *de facto* legal doctrines rather than express or implied consent of the members.[1] The analysis begins with a consideration of the legal basis to the Fund's initiative by examining the international legal theory on the legal personality of international organisations. The question asked is whether the mandate granted to an international organisation is strictly dependant on the wording of its constitutive instrument(s), or whether an organization's mandate could alternatively evolve in time so as to accommodate new *de facto* attributions and competences. The Fund's mandate shift is then tested by taking into account the power of soft law. As explained in more detail below, a key aspect in the legal literature is whether the constituent doctrine of 'separate will' or 'volonté distincte', which allows an organization to act independently – that is, without the express or implied consent of members – would apply to the IMF's mandate, as the move ensured the Fund maintained relevancy in an ever-changing world. Finally, the chapter concludes that, overall, the Fund's mandate expansion was in line with the

---

[1] The analysis in this chapter builds from Antoine P Martin and Bryan Mercurio, 'The IMF and Its Shifting Mandate towards Capital Movements and Capital Controls: A Legal Perspective' (2017) 44(3) *Legal Issues in Economic Integration* 211–35.

standards of international law applicable to international organisations. Thus, the Fund can legally monitor and discipline capital movements.

4.1 A Legally Valid Shift?

As noted above, the fact that the IMF assumed authority over capital movements does not necessarily mean that it was legally entitled to do so. In order to ascertain whether the Fund's expansion of mandate to include capital movements was legally valid, the following two factors must be analysed. First, we must establish the extent to which the Fund's unilateral and autonomous decision to expand its scope of operations is compatible with its constitutive instrument – the Articles of Agreement. Second, we must clarify whether the Fund's actions are in line with the international legal doctrine applicable to international organisations. Each factor is addressed in turn.

4.1.1 Legal Perspective on Mandate Evolutions

While considering the legal basis of the Fund's self-proclaimed mandate evolution, a first question relates to whether the mandate granted to an international organization is strictly dependant on the wording of its constitutive instrument(s) or whether the IMF's mandate could alternatively evolve in time to allow new *de facto* functions.

4.1.1.1 Legal Personality, Basic Principles

Under the international legal theory on the legal personality of international organisations, an international organisation is commonly described as 'an entity established by agreement ... which has states as its principal members'[2] and which has the capacity as a legal person to perform acts related to its purposes.[3] In this regard, the International Court of Justice noted that 'international organizations are subjects of international law which do not, unlike states, possess a general competence. International organizations are governed by the "principle of speciality", that is to say, they are invested by the States which create them with powers, the limits of which are a function of the common interests whose promotion those States entrust to them.'[4] Accordingly, determination

---

[2] Rebecca MM Wallace and others, *International Law* (8th ed., Sweet & Maxwell 2016) 89.
[3] On personality in general see Nigel White, *The Law of International Organisations: Second Edition* (2nd ed., Manchester University Press 2005) 32.
[4] 'Legality of the Use by a State of Nuclear Weapons in Armed Conflict', (1996) Advisory Opinion, ICJ Reports 78.

of personality (and mandate) under international law would normally require examining the organisation's constituent instruments, which traditionally have the objective of creating 'new subjects of law endowed with a certain autonomy, to which the parties entrust the task of realizing common goals'.[5]

Having said this, when an evolution or shift in roles, functions or mandates occurs in the international organisation, the issue is no longer the determination of legal personality but the identification of opportunities for development of the mandate. In such a case, merely examining the constituent instruments may prove limited, unless the said instruments clearly allow for such a development. Hence, public international law recognises several doctrines – most notably the attributed powers doctrine and the implied powers doctrine – with the purpose of clarifying such situations.

Developed in the 1920s, the doctrine of attributed or express powers came about in a time when state attitudes and approaches to international organisations were extremely guarded and cautious. Such an approach was confirmed in a series of cases involving the International Labour Organization (ILO) before the Permanent Court of International Justice (PCIJ), which held that only those powers expressly attributed by the founding members could establish an international organisation's legal personality and powers.[6] The Lotus Case in 1927 confirmed this interpretation when holding that an international organisation's powers could only emanate from the member state's attributions;[7] however, in practice, interpreting the principle of expressly attributed powers proved complex because both the organisations and judges had difficulty determining the reach of express empowerments, particularly in circumstances where the constituent instruments could not foresee future developments requiring an evolution or shift in mandate. As a result, the doctrine of attributed powers

---

[5] Ibid. 75.
[6] See 'Competence of the ILO to Regulate the Conditions of Labour of Persons Employed in Agriculture', (1922) Advisory Opinion, PCIJ (Series B), No. 2. 'Competence of the ILO to Examine Proposals for the Organization and Development of Methods of Agricultural Production', (1922) Advisory Opinion, PCIJ (Series B), No. 2 For comments on those cases, see in particular Jan Klabbers, *An Introduction to International Institutional Law* (Cambridge University Press 2002) 62, /core/books/an-introduction-to-international-institutional-law/1FE1D3FD31E46A7C0E0E26975E2A14ED
[7] 'Case of the SS Lotus', (1927) PCIJ (Series A), No. 10, 18.

became interpreted by commentators as restrictive in practice[8] and justified a new approach, that is, the doctrine of implied powers.

The doctrine of implied powers appeared in 1928 when the PCIJ found that an organisation's power could be implied from the existence of an explicit power.[9] The doctrine was commonly discussed in light of the Reparation for Injuries case which enshrined a functionalist approach to international legal personality. Discussing circumstances involving the United Nations (UN), the Court acknowledged that an international organisation's nature, as a subject of international law, 'depends on the needs of the community'.[10] Hence, more than a mere forum, the court recognised the United Nations (UN) as an autonomous actor equipped with functional organs and capable of acting 'in detachment from its members'.[11] In this case, the organisation's international legal personality was clearly associated with its very ability to 'carry out the intentions of its founders'[12] so that, in contrast with the previous doctrinal approach, the intentions behind the constitutive instruments became at least as relevant as the instruments themselves:

> [The United Nations] was intended to exercise and enjoy ... functions and rights which can only be explained on the basis of the possession of a large measure of international personality and the capacity to operate on the international plane ... its members, by entrusting certain functions to it, with the attendant duties and responsibilities, have clothed it with the competence required to enable those functions to be effectively discharged ... under international law, the Organization must be deemed to have those powers which, though not expressly provided in the Charter, are conferred upon it by necessary implication as being essential to the performance of its duties.[13]

The point is very significant because, as explained by White, the Reparation case tribunal 'recognised a right that cannot readily be implied from any of the express provisions of the charter [and] in so doing it recognised that the UN had rights of protection over individuals overlapping or in

---

[8] See White (n 3) 80.
[9] 'Interpretation of the Greco-Turkish Agreement of December 1st, 1926', (1928) PCIJ (Series B), No. 16. For an analysis, see Klabbers (n 6) 67.
[10] 'Reparation for Injuries Suffered in the Service of the United Nations', (1949) Advisory Opinion, ICJ Reports 178.
[11] Ibid. 178–79.
[12] Ibid. 179.
[13] Ibid. 179, 182–83.

competition with those customarily belonging to states'.[14] Subsequently, the International Court of Justice (ICJ) consistently applied this doctrine and admitted that international bodies such as the General Assembly were legitimate in implementing new mechanisms unforeseen at the time of the drafting of the constitutive instruments. For example, in the Effects of Awards case, a General Assembly's initiative was described as 'exercising a power which it had under the Charter' on an implied basis.[15] Similarly, in the Expenses case of 1962, the Court concluded that new peacekeeping attributions had been created in implied conformity with the constituent instruments to ensure the efficiency of the organisation. Likewise, in the Namibia Advisory Opinion of 1971, the ICJ recognised the authority of 'unexpressed' powers.[16] More recently, the ICJ re-confirmed this interpretation in the Nuclear Weapons case of 1996 when it reiterated that:

> The powers conferred on international organizations are normally the subject of an express statement in their constituent instruments. Nevertheless, the necessities of international life may point to the need for organizations, in order to achieve their objectives, to possess subsidiary powers which are not expressly provided for in the basic instruments which govern their activities. It is generally accepted that international organizations can exercise such powers, known as 'implied' powers.[17]

Overall, while an assessment of an organisation's constitutive provisions would appear to provide 'an objective test', in reality '[o]nce the treaty is concluded, it leads its own life'.[18] Hence, the constitutive instrument can be considered as having a 'declaratory effect', provided the international organisation it created has a mandate to evolve,[19] because

---

[14] See White (n 3) 84. A similar argument is also formulated by Klabbers (n 6) 68.
[15] 'Effects of Awards of Compensation Made by the UN Administrative Tribunal', (1956) ICJ Report 61.
[16] 'Legal Consequences for States of the Continued Presence of South Africa in Namibia (South West Africa) Notwithstanding Security Council Resolution 276' (1970), Advisory Opinion (1971) ICJ Reports 16,) para 98.
[17] ICJ Report (n 4) 79.
[18] Philippe Gautier, 'The Reparation for Injuries Case Revisited: The Personality of the European Union', in *Max Planck Yearbook of United Nations Law*, vol 4 (Kluwer Law International 2000) 335–36. See also White (n 3) 71.
[19] White (n 3) 71.

the member states, acting collectively, have conferred it substantive powers to act in line with its primary responsibilities.[20]

4.1.1.2 Applying International Law Requirements to the IMF Mandate Discussion

Let us now apply this theory to the discussion which surrounds the Fund's mandate. When applying those principles to the IMF situation, the starting point is to determine whether the IMF has legal personality and therefore is able to make decisions on its own. In theory, whether an international organisation has international personality usually depends on whether the organisation maintains a separate existence from its members, on whether majority votes are required to make things happen, on whether the entity is given treaty-making powers which would allow it

---

[20] On collective attributions, see Dan Sarooshi, 'Some Preliminary Remarks on the Conferral by States of Powers to International Organizations' (NYU School of Law 2003) Jean Monnet Working Paper 4/03 7. The doctrine behind conferred powers can then be analysed and implemented at several sub-levels, depending on whether the conferred powers have been delegated temporarily or transferred permanently to the international organisation. The point will, however, not be explored any further at this stage. See in particular Dan Sarooshi, *International Organizations and Their Exercise of Sovereign Powers* (Oxford University Press 2005) 55 (arguing that 'The first is that delegations of powers are revocable by a State; whereas in the case of transfers the conferrals will generally be irrevocable ... in the case of delegations the State retains for itself the right to implement the powers concurrent with, and independent of, the organization's exercise of powers; whereas in the case of transfers the organization has an exclusive competence to implement the conferred powers'.). Questions have also been raised as to the ability of international organisations to delegate their own powers. The issue is not applicable here but worth mentioning because it extends the analysis of the doctrine of delegated powers in light of the '*delegatus non potest delegare*' (non-delegation) doctrine. See Dan Sarooshi, 'The Essentially Contested Nature of the Concept of Sovereignty: Implications for the Exercise by International Organizations of Delegated Powers of Government' (2003) 25 *Michigan Journal of International Law* 1107, 1127–34. It should be added that a third approach, known as the inherent powers doctrine, has also been developed in an attempt at finding a happy medium between the two established approaches. According to this doctrine, organisational powers do not depend on the founders' intent but are granted by international law itself. In other words, if an international organisation has been equipped with legal personality, then international law also equips it with the powers necessary to fulfil its functions as long as they are not prohibited by the constitutive document. While this approach provides a practical way to give primacy to functionalism and needs-based thinking, it has remained theoretical and has not been followed in Court largely because it creates additional difficulties, such as the issue of implied prohibitions, that is, powers that were not expressly granted because the founding parties rejected the perspectives at the time. See Sarooshi, *International Organizations and Their Exercise of Sovereign Powers* 87. See also Klabbers (n 6) 75.

to negotiate with members in its own name and/or whether operational organs such as an executive board exist.[21] In practice, the Fund's Articles of Agreement suggest that the IMF maintains a separate existence from its members. In particular, its coordination and surveillance role (as provided under Article XII) clearly indicates that it has authority to deal with members in its own name, via the Managing Director, Board of Governors and Executive Board.[22] Hence, the Fund's constitutive instrument leaves no doubt as to the fact that it is an international institution equipped with specific decision-making organs and which thus benefits from a distinct international legal personality.[23] In this regard, the IMF should therefore be treated as any other organisation – such as the WTO, the OECD or OPEC – which all are considered as autonomous international organisations enjoying international legal personality and equipped to influence international affairs.[24]

The next step would be to determine the scope of action enjoyed by the Fund. As explained above, however, the Fund's mandate as provided within the Articles of Agreement arguably limits its scope of action. As a reminder, Article I provides that the Fund's purposes consist (i) in promoting international monetary cooperation, (ii) in facilitating the expansion and balanced growth of international trade and (iii) in promoting exchange stability to maintain orderly exchange arrangements among members, and to avoid competitive exchange depreciation.[25] Section 1 of Article IV, in addition, tasks the Fund with overseeing the monetary system and facilitating monetary cooperation to ensure

---

[21] White (n 3) 31–33, 41–42, 57–58.

[22] See Article XII, Organization and Management. However, the Executive Board has been criticised for being controlled by the rich funding countries and for being *de facto* under their control. In this regard, recipient countries often do not feel that they have much input into governance or the agenda of the institution, which has thus been described as 'inconclusive'. On the 'supplier country domination', see for instance Daniel D Bradlow, 'Rapidly Changing Functions and Slowly Evolving Structures: The Troubling Case of the IMF', *Proceedings of the ASIL Annual Meeting* (Cambridge University Press 2000). See also White (n 3) 126.

[23] In contrast, the G7 would rather constitute an example of an institution that lacks international legal personality. As constituted, the G7 merely serves as a forum where several of the largest countries (in economic terms) meet to discuss contemporary issues. On its own, the G7 does not possess supranational competence because it is simply not the objective of the institution to take decisions. For an extensive discussion on the international personality of international organisations, see White (n 3).

[24] See ibid. 55–57.

[25] Articles of Agreement of the IMF, Article I.

monetary stability. Section 3 of Article VI, however, insists that the ability to oversee cross-border capital movements remains a state prerogative,[26] except where capital movements relate to 'restrictions on the making of payments and transfers for *current international transactions*' or unduly delayed transfers.[27]

These constraints are not only certainly significant, they also give tremendous weight to the doctrines discussed previously. Should the attributed powers doctrine prevail, then an evolution in mandate aimed at giving the Fund some extra authority over capital flows would clearly go against the powers expressly granted to the Fund by the drafters of the Articles of Agreement. With the recognition and consistent application of the implied powers doctrine by international tribunals, however, the analysis would differ as the Fund would gain the ability to rely on the intent of its founders to justify mandate evolutions in line with the original purposes of the Fund.

In other words, under the currently applicable implied powers doctrine, the main purpose of the Fund prevails and the wording of the Articles of Agreement would actually tend to reinforce this analysis. In particular, the Articles' Purposes provision states clearly that 'The Fund shall be guided in all its policies and decisions by the purposes set forth in this Article'.[28] Hence, since its primary goal is to ensure monetary stability and in modern times it is well established and uncontroverted that monetary stability can be impacted by unpredictable capital flows, an evolution of the Fund's mandate to encompass capital movements into its monetary supervision mandate would be legally rational.

The main counter-argument here would be found in the inherent powers doctrine. While not relied upon in practice, such an approach would raise the issue of expanding the Fund's mandate in opposition to the intention of the founders, for whom capital controls historically were to remain a state prerogative. It is our opinion that the answer to this question can in reality be found within the implied powers doctrine, which clearly aims at bridging the gaps between original intent and necessary developments. Should the doctrine be tested, a potential solution could, for instance, be found in the Nuclear Weapons case where the Court considered whether the World Health Organization was legitimate in dealing

---

[26] Stating that '[m]embers may exercise such controls as are necessary to regulate international capital movements'.
[27] Section 2(a) of Article VIII (emphasis added).
[28] Articles of Agreement of the IMF, Article 1.

with the legality of nuclear weapons. While the Court admitted that an international organisation's mandate could evolve as provided under the implied powers doctrine, it did apply certain limitations to prevent abuses in mandate expansion. It is worth quoting the Court at length:

> The Court is of the opinion, however, that to ascribe to the WHO the competence to address the legality of the use of nuclear weapons even in view of their health and environmental effects would be tantamount to disregarding the principle of speciality; for such competence could not be deemed a necessary implication of the Constitution of the Organization in the light of the purposes assigned to it by its member States. The WHO is, moreover, an international organization of a particular kind. As indicated in the Preamble and confirmed by Article 69 of its Constitution ... the Charter laid the basis of a 'system' designed to organize international co-operation in a coherent fashion by bringing the United Nations, invested with powers of general scope, into relationship with various autonomous and complementary organizations, invested with sectorial powers. If, according to the rules on which that system is based, the WHO has, by virtue of Article 57 of the Charter, 'wide international responsibilities', those responsibilities are necessarily restricted to the sphere of public 'health' and cannot encroach on the responsibilities of other parts of the United Nations system. And there is no doubt that questions concerning the use of force, the regulation of armaments and disarmament are within the competence of the United Nations and lie outside that of the specialized agencies. For all these reasons, the Court considers that the question raised in the request for an advisory opinion submitted to it by the WHO does not arise 'within the scope of [the] activities' of that Organization as defined by its Constitution.[29]

In light of the case law, the IMF's *de facto* mandate evolution would remain within the scope of the implied powers doctrine as long as the mandate is expanded within the boundaries of its monetary stability attributions.

4.1.2 Additional Soft Law Testing

While testing the IMF's situation in light of the applicable legal doctrines suggests that the mandate evolutions put into place by the Fund would be lawful as a matter of public international law, it is also necessary to consider additional soft law arguments.

In particular, a key aspect in the legal literature is whether the constituent doctrine of 'separate will' or 'volonté distincte' allowing an organization to act independently of the will of its members would

---

[29] ICJ Report (n 4) 79–81.

apply in these circumstances to ensure it maintains relevancy in an ever-changing world, thus allowing the IMF to operate a mandate shift without the express or implied authority of the member states.[30] The separate will doctrine complements the previously considered doctrines, but while the implied powers doctrine focuses on controlling the ability of an international organisation to develop its mandate from an international legal perspective, separate wills are concerned with practice. To White, indeed, 'the driving force [of autonomous international organisations is] the practice of the organisation, which creates customary constitutional law that gradually fills in the legal framework created by the constitutive document' notwithstanding the intentions of the founding states. Hence, '[t]he stronger the constitution, the greater the separate will of the organisation'.[31] Against this basic principle, the remainder of this section will consider (i) the *de facto* evolutions in time and (ii) whether these are in line with the spirit of the Articles of Agreement, and it will clarify what would occur should an organisation fail to move forward with necessary adaptations.

4.1.2.1 Customary *de Facto* Evolution

In the IMF's case, the mandate shift has been formalised over the course of over thirty years through a series of Decisions adopted by a majority of the institution's decision-making body. The opportunity to provide a *de facto* evolution was emphasized in a 2006 report of the IMF's Legal and Policy Development Departments, which then argued that 'although the legislative history is silent on the question, it must be assumed that, notwithstanding the continuity of language, it was intended that the underlying meaning of this objective would change in a manner that takes into account the change made to the other objective of the obligation to collaborate'.[32] In reality, the shift occurred over time and through a number of legal instruments.

When opposition did arise, it was not in relation to the Fund's competence over capital movements *per se*, but rather over the Fund's attempt to enshrine full capital liberalisation through an amendment to the Articles

---

[30] See White (n 3) 30.
[31] Ibid. 71.
[32] IMF, 'Article IV of the Fund's Articles of Agreement: An Overview of the Legal Framework' (International Monetary Fund 2006) Policy Paper 27, www.imf.org/en/Publications/Policy-Papers/Issues/2016/12/31/Article-IV-of-the-Fund-s-Articles-of-Agreement-An-Overview-of-the-Legal-Framework-PP3883.

of Agreement. At some point the Member states objected to a provision which would expressly deprive them of the right to apply controls, even in case of emergency or necessity,[33] but otherwise the Fund's recent shift in policy prescription – that is, that CFMs can be a useful part of the policy toolbox – came at least partially as a response to calls emanating from various actors in the international community. In particular, the IMF's client states which rely on IMF staff advice when managing capital flows requested clarity and consistency. For example, in a communiqué dated October 2010 the G20 requested that the IMF 'further work on macroprudential policy frameworks, including tools to help mitigate the impact of excessive capital flows (including shadow banking)' and called on 'advanced economies, including those with reserve currencies, [to now] be vigilant against excess volatility and disorderly movements in exchange rates'.[34] In fact, the G20 Communiqué concluded with a request for the IMF to become even more involved in issues involving capital movements.[35] Thus, far from objecting to the IMF's expansion in mandate, the client states have indeed called upon the institution to do more to regulate capital flows to meet the objective of providing stability and predictability to the international financial system.

4.1.2.2 Soft Law Analysis: Interpreting the 'Spirit' of the Articles of Agreement

In our soft law approach, it is also relevant to consider whether the *de facto* evolution is in line with the spirit of the Fund's constitutive instrument. Interestingly, although the Fund's constitutive instrument provides no explicit jurisdiction to oversee or regulate issues involving capital movements, the Articles leave scope for the IMF to have a coordinating role beyond simply the regulation of monetary issues. In particular, the imposition of certain binding obligations on members could, in theory,

---

[33] Philip J MacFarlane, 'The IMF's Reassessment of Capital Controls after the 2008 Financial Crisis: Heresy or Orthodoxy?' (2015) 19 *UCLA Journal of International Law and Foreign Affairs* 167, 189.
[34] G20, 'Communiqué of the Meeting of Finance Ministers and Central Bank Governors' (2010), www.g20.utoronto.ca/2010/g20finance101023.html
[35] Ibid. '[T]hese actions will help mitigate the risk of excessive volatility in capital flows facing some emerging countries. Together, we will reinvigorate our efforts to promote a stable and well-functioning international monetary system and call on the IMF to deepen its work in these areas. We welcome the IMF's work to conduct spillover assessments of the wider impact of systemic economies' policies [and] call on the IMF to provide an assessment as part of the MAP on the progress toward external sustainability and the consistency of fiscal, monetary, financial sector, structural, exchange rate and other policies'.

be interpreted – and in practice has actually been interpreted by the IMF legal and policy development experts[36] – as giving the Fund a broad and long-lasting supervisory role which lends itself to a progressive expansion in scope. This is the case for a number of reasons.

First, the Fund has been provided with a legal means to expand its mandate to include capital movements. Remember that Article I of the Agreement makes it clear that the IMF aims to assist member states in the establishment of a multilateral system of payments in respect of current transactions between members *and* in the elimination of foreign exchange restrictions which may hamper the growth of world trade.[37] Article I also requires members to cooperate with the Fund in relation to exchange policymaking. Considering the close relationship between the growth of cross-border trade, the establishment of a multilateral system of payments closely linked with modern frontierless international finance and the important influence of international finance on foreign exchange stability, it is difficult to argue that the IMF's 1977 extension of mandate to oversee the stability of the exchange system does not encompass capital movements which are capable of having a substantial negative influence on the entire system. In other words, the IMF having a role in maintaining international financial stability seems to fit rather nicely with the general stability-oriented objective of the Fund's Articles of Agreement. Thus, although not exactly direct or straightforward, the Fund's 'Article IV byroad' strategy constitutes a valid way of dealing with capital movements through a mechanism designed for exchange rates. The IMF approach is also in line with the spirit of Article I of the Fund's constitutive instrument – cooperation for the greater good and stability of the global financial system.

Second, the Fund's 'Article IV byroad' strategy would be in line with the spirit of Section 3 of Article VI, which gives the IMF a 'firm' surveillance role to oversee the international monetary system. The surveillance role includes verifying that members respect specific obligations[38] to (i) ensure that their economic and financial policies foster 'orderly economic growth with reasonable price stability' and (ii) that member states 'seek to promote stability by fostering orderly underlying economic and financial conditions and a monetary system that does not tend to produce erratic disruptions'. In other words, the IMF has been granted an express and

---

[36] IMF Overview of the Legal Framework (n 32).
[37] Articles of Agreement of the IMF (emphasis added).
[38] 'The Fund shall oversee the international monetary system in order to ensure its effective operation, and shall oversee the compliance of each member with its obligations'.

specific mandate to liberalise foreign exchanges while limiting unwanted market disruptions. The need to provide a stable system and limit negative market disruptions is exactly the reason for the move by the IMF to include capital movements in its mandate. In fact, it can even be argued that the 'spirit' behind the Articles of Agreement – in granting the Fund a firm surveillance role and in identifying orderly economic growth, stability and the fostering of orderly financial conditions as policy goals for the state members – considered the possibility that a certain degree of coordination would at some point be necessary outside of purely monetary considerations.

4.1.2.3 Necessary Adaptation

The above interpretation recognises the reality of the situation on the ground. Conditioning modern prerogatives to a strict legal mandate dating from the 1940s would ignore the reality of modern international finance – with both financial flows at the macro level and a host of individual entities acting separately to preserve their own interest against the individual actions of their counterparts having global consequences. Said differently, the IMF needed to adapt in order to remain credible and relevant.

On a more basic level, the IMF was perhaps forced to reform in a *de facto* manner following the abandonment of the gold standard in 1971 by the US, which triggered several subsequent important events. Highlighting the 'undefined nature' of the Fund's role, Bradlow commented on the Fund's loss of purpose:

> After the collapse of the Bretton Woods system in 1973 and the adoption of the Second Amendment to the IMF's Articles of Agreement in 1978, when each member state regained the right to choose its own exchange-rate policy, the IMF lost its well-defined monetary mission. This created a problem for the IMF. If a member state had no specific exchange-rate obligation and was basically free to choose its own exchange-rate policy, then what was the IMF supposed to be monitoring in its annual consultations with that country?[39]

Over time, the IMF become not only the lender of last resort[40] but also the international financial 'know-it-all' for member states – the latter more so

---

[39] Bradlow (n 22) 153.
[40] There have been some disagreement among economists as to whether the IMF should act as a lender of last resort at all, especially considering the presence of short-maturity loans and with senior debt status being secured by governments bonds. Instead, it has been argued that the fund should act as a 'delegated monitor' and that the international community ought to 'refocus[] the IMF as an official (as opposed to a de facto) advocate for rigor'. See Jean Tirole, *Financial Crises, Liquidity, and the International Monetary System* (Princeton University Press 2002) 110–15.

due to member states' increasing reliance on the Fund for advice on 'out of mandate' issues. In regards to the former, the IMF began frequently including capital movement issues when conditioning lending on the ability and willingness of the client state to adopt certain macroeconomic and reform measures – this seemed like a natural extension of the mandate as it is almost unfathomable that the Fund could operate in a holistic manner without having the authority to discuss or intervene in matters pertaining to international capital flows.

Interestingly, many of the criticisms levelled at the IMF and World Bank suggest that their effectiveness had been compromised over time by the inability to adapt to the increasing complexity of the 'intertwined' problems they faced, leaving them unable to respond to the international community's changing reaction and coordination need.[41] Recalling that 'trade flows dominated capital flows at the time when the Fund began', Wade wrote during the Asian Crisis about the necessity of giving 'Power to the Fund' and argued for 'a necessary modernization of the Articles of Agreement 'to reflect the new realities of capital flows'.[42] Similarly, Bradlow argued that the 'unsatisfactory performance' of international organisations such as the IMF over the years was rooted in their 'failure to adapt their structure and operating practices to their changing functions [so that] unless they correct[ed] these problems, they [would] never be able to fulfil their responsibilities effectively'.[43] Discussing the IMF's new role towards stabilising 'both of the monetary system and of the world economy in general',[44] Stiglitz similarly noted that in practice the World Bank similarly had no choice but to (i) shift from a post-war reconstruction financing organization into a development funding institution while (ii) broadening its objectives and instruments to adapt to the idea that development is not only about GDP but also about raising living standards, democratic leadership and sustainability.[45] He concludes that 'what the Bank does and how it does it will undoubtedly evolve with the continuing changes in the global environment and [with] our understanding of

---

[41] Bradlow (n 22) 412–13. See also Daniel D Bradlow and Claudio Grossman, 'Limited Mandates and Intertwined Problems: A New Challenge for the World Bank and the IMF' (1995) 17 *Human Rights Quarterly* 411, 412–13.

[42] Robert Wade and Frank Veneroso, 'The Gathering World Slump and the Battle over Capital Controls' (1998) 231 *New Left Review*.

[43] Bradlow (n 22) 157.

[44] Joseph E Stiglitz, 'The World Bank at the Millennium' (1999) 109 *The Economic Journal* 577, 581.

[45] Ibid. 587–88.

development that is, both our views of its objectives and our beliefs about how they can most effectively be accomplished'.[46]

Highlighting the difficulty for 'source' and 'recipient' countries to manage capital flows, Gallagher and Ocampo insist on the need to set up coordination towards sound financial policymaking,[47] while Korinek similarly notes that IMF supervision over capital flows has a role to play because sound financial management differs at the individual and macro (national and supranational) levels.[48] Providing a political analysis of the issue, Moschella concludes that 'the Fund's surveillance function (which entails giving advice on policies directed towards international capital flows) and the Fund's crisis assistance role, (which may lead the Fund to provide financing to address capital account crises) eventually figure among the institutional considerations that justif[ied] the adjustment of the Fund's thinking on controls'.[49] To the author, the Fund had to operate a 'punctuated shift', which was in practice facilitated by a combination of a 'dynamic of ideational change' and a 'permissive environment' – created by (i) the non-rejection of the trend by members and (ii) the fact that IMF staff – in the absence of an official position – eventually took the lead in formulating the Fund's approach when confronting countries facing large capital flow management issues:[50]

> Recent advances in historical institutionalist literature have convincingly shown that ... institutions also allow for an endogenous dynamic of change ... because even the most formal institutions exhibit some degree of ambiguity that opens up the way to new interpretations ... In short, institutions have a double nature: they serve both as structures that constrain thinking and acting, and as constructs that can be changed by actors. As a result, while they provide some space for the development of new ideas due to their need for continuous interpretation and application ... the development of new ideas is not contingent upon the disruption of old institutions, the process of ideational innovation does not require the development of a completely new approach to institutions but may take place through marginal adjustments ... For instance, the modalities

---

[46] Ibid. 595.
[47] See the arguments formulated in Kevin P Gallagher and Jose Antonio Ocampo, 'IMF's New View on Capital Controls' (2013) 48 *Economic and Political Weekly* 10, 12.
[48] Anton Korinek, 'The New Economics of Prudential Capital Controls: A Research Agenda' (2011) 59 *IMF Economic Review* 523, 526.
[49] Manuela Moschella, 'The Institutional Roots of Incremental Ideational Change: The IMF and Capital Controls after the Global Financial Crisis' (2015) 17 *The British Journal of Politics and International Relations* 442, 454.
[50] Ibid. 443–44, 448.

through which the IMF conducts its bilateral and multilateral surveillance, or those through which it provides financial assistance to crisis-hit countries, have been significantly adapted over time within the parameters of the Fund's original objectives.[51]

Putting aside the strict interpretation of the original mandate and looking at the role of the Fund from a common-sense approach, an IMF report concluded rather simply that 'in the aftermath of the global crisis, and especially now with resurgent capital flows requiring a considered policy response, it [was] not tenable for the Fund to remain on the side-lines of a debate so central to global economic stability'.[52]

---

[51] Ibid. 448, 454 [referring to James Mahoney and Kathleen Thelen, 'A Theory of Gradual Institutional Change', *Explaining Institutional Change: Ambiguity, Agency, and Power*, vol. 1 (Cambridge University Press 2010)]; Vivien A Schmidt, 'Discursive Institutionalism: The Explanatory Power of Ideas and Discourse' (2008) 11 *Annual Review of Political Science* 303.

[52] IMF, 'The Fund's Role Regarding Cross-Border Capital Flows' (International Monetary Fund 2010) 3, www.imf.org/en/Publications/Policy-Papers/Issues/2016/12/31/The-Fund-s-Role-Regarding-Cross-Border-Capital-Flows-PP4516. The paper went on to conclude that the Articles of Agreement would allow for a re-interpretation of the Fund's mandate due to the increasing significance of capital flows on international financial stability described as the fundamental mission of the organisation.

PART III

Legal Frameworks, Rules and Conflicts

Having determined in the previous chapters that CFMs are increasingly considered to be a legitimate policy tool, and that the IMF has re-aligned its approach to reflect this, this chapter now turns to examine the regulatory framework of international economic law. Part III thus addresses the question of the rules applicable to capital controls under international economic law, namely the multilateral WTO, bilateral and regional FTAs and BITs.

The question of the applicable legal framework is important, but as usual when capital controls are discussed, somewhat controversial. Yet again, most of the 'legal' scholarship originates from economists and political scientists. Perhaps the most prominent scholarship encompassing the legal ecosystem surrounding capital controls is from the political economist Kevin P Gallagher, who sees a large gap between the policy dynamics – 'new thinking in economics' – and the existing regulatory framework. For Gallagher, the IMF and G20 have proclaimed that 'countries have the policy space to regulate capital flows … [yet] obstacles [make] the reregulation of cross-border finance difficult [as] many countries across the world lack the political space and the policy space to regulate them effectively'.[1] The obstacles to which Gallagher refers are the commitments these countries make when entering into the WTO, FTAs and IIAs. While the accuracy of this conclusion is debatable, the point here is simply that legal scholars have essentially not weighed in on the debate; instead, the legal analysis has been left to those without formal legal training and with perhaps an agenda which colours their interpretation of the legal documents.[2]

---

[1] Kevin P Gallagher, *Ruling Capital: Emerging Markets and the Reregulation of Cross-Border Finance* (Cornell University Press 2015) 6.

[2] One of the few legal articles on the issue is a student note authored by Duncan E. Williams, 'Policy Perspectives on the Use of Capital Controls in Emerging Market Nations: Lessons from the Asian Financial Crisis and a Look at the International Legal Regime' (2001–2002) 70 *Fordham Law Review* 561–623.

Part III has two objectives. First, to clarify the legal framework applicable to CFMs from both a trade and investment perspective. Second, to provide solid, unbiased legal analysis of the issues. The prevailing view among some commentators is that the global international economic law framework tends to prevent domestic regulators from taking capital controls and other capital movement–restricting measures. For example, a task force organised by Gallagher in 2013 and published by the Pardee Center at Boston University opined that broad obligations contained in FTAs and BITs could conflict with the 'right' to implement capital controls and other CFMs.[3] While Chapter 3 demonstrated there is no unfettered 'right' to take CFMs, as the IMF has claimed authority over capital accounts, Gallagher and his team are correct in stating that capital controls and CFMs can potentially run afoul of commitments taken in the various strains of various international economic law.

With IMF loan and assistance packages now regularly including CFMs, recipients of such assistance could be placed in a difficult position; on the one hand, an IMF-advised CFMs may breach the applicable international economic law framework in place (and in the case of an IIA an investor may hold the government liable for monetary damages). On the other hand, a Member refusing an IMF request to put CFMs in place as part of a support program might lose IMF support. Likewise, should the member impose CFMs but exclude trade or investment treaty partners from their application, it would likely conflict with IMF non-discrimination provisions. On the potential for conflict, Siegel asserts that trade and investment agreements 'are potentially on a collision course with the [IMF] because of how [they] deal with capital transactions'[4] while the IMF finds 'the limited flexibility afforded by some [trade and investment agreements] in respect to liberalization obligations may create challenges for the management of capital flows'.[5] The IMF, therefore, points at a problem but fails to consider potential solutions.

Another issue worth considering is the use of exception clauses and safeguards in trade and investment agreements. While the majority of

---

[3] Kevin Gallagher and Leonardo Stanley (eds), 'Capital Account Regulations and the Trading System: A "Compatibility Review"' (Pardee Center for the Study of Longer-Range Development, Boston University 2013).

[4] Deborah Siegel, 'Capital Account Restrictions, Trade Agreements, and the IMF', in Kevin Gallager and Leonardo Stanley (eds), 'Capital Account Regulations and the Trading System: A "Compatibility Review"' (Pardee Center for the Study of Longer-Range Development, Boston University 2013).

[5] IMF, 'Liberalizing Capital Flows and Managing Outflows' (13 March 2012).

FTAs and IIAs contain language exceptions similar to those in the GATS, others contain few to no safeguards. In this regard, a CFM that could be deemed to be consistent with a GATS exception could nevertheless be held to be inconsistent with a bilateral/regional FTA or IIA. Likewise, as the scope and depth of exceptions differ widely between and among bilateral/regional FTAs and IIAs, a CFM deemed to be consistent with one FTA or IIA could be inconsistent with another agreement due to differing textual language. Again, the IMF identified the problem of fragmentation and conflict but failed to consider potential solutions; instead, the IMF merely suggested that 'these agreements in many cases do not provide appropriate safeguards or proper sequencing of liberalization and thus could benefit from reform'.[6] This is unhelpful. What is worse is that most countries have failed to heed the IMF warning, and agreements continue to be negotiated which contribute to or do not attempt to resolve the potential conflict.

Chapter 5 focuses on the multilateral trade framework, that being the WTO and its GATS. Chapter 6 covers FTAs, while Chapter 7 analyses IIAs. Chapter 8 offers concluding analysis.

---

[6] Ibid.

5

The Multilateral Trade Framework

This chapter assesses the compatibility of capital controls and other CFMs with the multilateral trade framework; that is, the WTO's GATS. The GATS contains several provisions that relate to controls and restrictions on services in general, and to financial services in particular.[1] This chapter begins by setting out the framework for obligations in the GATS relevant to cross-border capital movements before explaining and evaluating the relevant exceptions. While the exceptions should in theory allow capital controls to be put in place in a manner that is consistent with the GATS, each of the exceptions contain uncertainties which, depending on how they are interpreted, could mean capital controls would fall outside of the scope of the exceptions.[2] Recent jurisprudence, however, should provide some comfort to governments seeking to make use of exceptions in the financial services sector, namely the so-called prudential exception. In this regard, the GATS should not be viewed as a major impediment to the implementation of CFMs implemented in good faith and for prudential reasons.

---

[1] The financial services industry pushed hard for the inclusion of services in the multilateral trading system and for the launch of the Uruguay Round of trade negotiations. See Juan A. Marchetti and Petros Mavroidis, 'The Genesis of the GATS (General Agreement on Trade in Services)' (2011) 22(3) *European Journal International Law* 689, 692–94.

[2] This issue has in the past been extensively discussed at the Committee on Trade in Financial Services, with consensus yet to emerge. See for instance the minutes of meetings of the Committee on Trade in Financial Services held on 26 April 2010 (S/FIN/M/63, 25 June 2010), 9 March 2011 (S/FIN/M/67, 12 April 2011), 31 October 2011 (S/FIN/M/71, 4 November 2011) and 27 June 2012 (S/FIN/M/73, 30 July 2012). See also 'Communication from Ecuador: Proposal for Fwork on Regulatory Measures in Financial Services, for Inclusion in the Ministerial Declaration' (S/FIN/W/80, 7 October 2011); 'Communication from Ecuador: Proposal to Discuss Progress on Macro Prudential Regulation and Its Relationship with GATS Rules' (S/FIN/W/84 26 June 2012).

5.1 Obligations under the GATS

The GATS contains certain obligations which apply to all measures 'affecting trade in services'.[3] The most crucial obligation in this respect is that of the most favoured nation (MFN) clause (which does contain an exception where Members have expressly indicated the nature of the deviation in a list of exemptions).[4] In regard to market access, Members must undertake specific liberalisation commitments pertaining to market access and national treatment for each sector and sub-sector and for each of the four modes of supply. This approach, referred to as a 'positive list', is used for all sectors of services, but in reality combines a positive aspect where Members select the sectors, sub-sectors and modes of supply which they are willing to liberalise combined with the negative listing of limitations to these commitments. The system, therefore, provides for a variable geometry of commitments between and among members.

The incorporation of services into the WTO framework remains somewhat incomplete. Not only have issues such as subsidies, procurement and emergency safeguards been left for future negotiations, but the agreement itself also envisaged the progressive liberalisation of initial market access and national treatment commitments. The 'positive list' model of the GATS also leaves gaps in coverage and a significant amount of protectionism. Thus, while the GATS provides a rich set of rules, the level of liberalisation commitments is weak. With no meaningful advances to the GATS since its inception, services operate 'with yesterday's rulebook [of] weak, incomplete, rules and the limited, regulatory precaution-laden, pre-Internet, commitments of 1994'.[5]

The GATS Annex on Financial Services provides additional context, including by defining the term 'financial service' through an illustrative list of examples and clarifying that Members remain able to regulate for prudential policy objectives. Finally, the GATS Understanding on Commitments in Financial Services is a plurilateral agreement (meaning Members can opt in or remain outside its scope) which obliges Members to adhere to a series of obligations in connection with their liberalisation commitments in related sectors and sub-sectors.

It is important to note at the outset that the GATS does not require Members to liberalise capital flows. The obligation contained in Article XI

---

[3] GATS, Article I:1.
[4] GATS, Article II.
[5] See Pierre Sauvé, 'Towards a Plurilateral Trade in Services Agreement (TISA): Challenges and Prospects' (2014) 5(1) *Journal of International Commerce, Economics and Policy* 1, 3.

(Payments and Transfers) is conditional upon a Member committing to liberalise – that is, to allow partial or complete market access and national treatment in a specific sector:

1. Except under the circumstances envisaged in Article XII, a Member shall not apply restrictions on international transfers and payments for current transactions relating to its specific commitments.
2. Nothing in this Agreement shall affect the rights and obligations of the members of the International Monetary Fund under the Articles of Agreement of the Fund, including the use of exchange actions which are in conformity with the Articles of Agreement, provided that a Member shall not impose restrictions on any capital transactions inconsistently with its specific commitments regarding such transactions.

Under the 'positive list' approach to scheduling commitments, WTO Members are not obliged to offer market access or national treatment to any sector, but any legal obligation taken – even conditional and limited – is binding on the Member. In other words, if a Member commits to market access (Article XVI) or national treatment (Article XVII) liberalisation of a services sector in its schedule of commitments, it will also liberalise current movements in connection to that service. The obligation is thus conditional upon a binding liberalisation commitment being made in the schedule. Correspondingly, there is no obligation to liberalise flows for sectors left uncommitted – controls can be maintained without being inconsistent with GATS rules. Thus, Members remain free to adopt CFMs aimed at restricting cross-border capital flows without breaching WTO obligations. To be clear, the prohibition of restrictions on capital transactions does not conflict with the IMF's limited and conditional right to apply controls to regulate capital movements under Article VI:3 of the IMF's Articles, but by making a specific market access commitment in the GATS the Member is voluntarily electing not to make use of all the scope provided by the Fund.

Footnote 8 to Article XVI further clarifies by stating that Members undertaking a market-access commitment relating to Mode 1 (cross-border supply of services) must commit to allowing cross-border movement of capital where such cross-border movement of capital is an 'essential part' of the service. This undertaking would appear to relate to both inflows as well as outflows. Footnote 8 reads:

> If a Member undertakes a market-access commitment in relation to the supply of a service through the mode of supply referred to in subparagraph 2(a) of Article I and if the cross-border movement of capital is an essential

part of the service itself, that Member is thereby committed to allow such movement of capital. If a Member undertakes a market-access commitment in relation to the supply of a service through the mode of supply referred to in subparagraph 2(c) of Article I, it is thereby committed to allow related transfers of capital into its territory.

Whereas capital movement is not an 'essential part' of all cross-border suppliers of services (i.e. architectural services), it could be argued that capital movements are an essential part of almost every financial services sector.[6] This obligation would therefore be an obvious limitation on Members' ability to implement capital controls – examples here would be that a minimum loan period for loans provided by non-residents would be inconsistent with a market access commitment on the supply of cross-border lending services or unremunerated reserve requirements for non-residents on certain investments for a period of time. However, an alternative reading of footnote 8 is that it is limited to covering only the capital movements inherently linked with the service itself, leaving payments and repatriation of capital outside the purview of the footnote. Under such a reading, while the taking of deposits or a loan made from a non-resident bank to a domestic customer would involve both a services transaction and an essential capital movement (in the form of the taking of the deposit or loan and movement of money, respectively) the provision of financial advisory services requires no capital movement and would not fall within the scope of footnote 8.[7]

Similarly, where the service is supplied through Mode 3 (commercial presence), Members are required to liberalise capital inflows in the establishment and post-establishment phases. This prohibits restrictions on capital inflows in all sectors where a Mode 3 market access commitment has been made.[8] There is a view among some scholars that this would

---

[6] The only possible exclusions would be services listed in Article 5 of the Annex on Financial Services under letter (i) advisory, intermediation and auxiliary services, and (ii) provision and transfer of financial information, and financial data processing.

[7] See Bryan Mercurio, Ross Buckley and Erin Fu Jiangyuan, 'The Legitimacy of Controlling Capital Flows under International Economic Law during a Retreat from Globalization' (2021) 70 *International and Comparative Law Quarterly* 59, 88 (citing Federico Lupo-Pasini, 'Movement of Capital and Trade in Services: Distinguishing Myth from Reality Regarding the GATS and the Liberalization of the Capital Account' (2012) 15(2) *Journal of International Economic Law* 581, 594. It could be argued, however, that capital movement is not an essential part of the service since the bank could raise capital in the host country. Bert De Meester, 'Liberalization of Financial Flows and Trade in Financial Services under the GATS' (2012) 46(3) *Journal of World Trade* 733, 774.

[8] It should be noted that the capital transfers provision is non-negotiable and thus not subject to limitation in a Member's Schedule of Commitments. WTO Secretariat Background Note 'Financial Services', S/FIN/W/73, (3 February 2010) para. 20.

prohibit not only restrictions on the inflow of capital when setting up and operating a business but also 'any restriction on the outward movements of capital necessary to provide the service would be prohibited since otherwise the commitment in question would be without value'.[9] This view is persuasive, and it must be remembered that foreign investment is only one part of a two-way transaction. A cross-border loan must be paid back by the recipient, and equity investment will likely receive dividends. Moreover, it is well settled in the jurisprudence that a commitment in Mode 3 includes not only the right to supply consumers in the territory of the host Member but also the right to export services from that Member.[10] In the financial services context this would, for example, allow a foreign bank operating in another Member's jurisdiction to offer loans to borrowers located outside of that jurisdiction.[11]

There is no clarification or statement pertaining to whether Mode 2 (consumption abroad) applies to outflows and inflows, which is understandable given the time period when the GATS was drafted but somewhat regrettable as it is often unclear in electronic transactions if it is the service or the consumer which is crossing the border.[12]

The national treatment provision of the GATS can also serve as a limitation on the use of controls on capital inflows where specific commitments have been made in Modes 1 and 3 to restrict Members' discretion to adopt controls on capital flows. More specifically, Article XVII:1 of the GATS provides that where a Member has made a liberalisation commitment in its Schedule, and subject to any conditions and qualifications set out therein, 'each Member shall accord to services and service suppliers of any other Member, in respect of all measures affecting the supply of services, treatment no less favourable than that it accords to its own like services and service suppliers'. Thus, while the national treatment provision does not prohibit the use of capital controls, Members

---

[9] See for instance Annamaria Viterbo, 'How to Make the GATS a Code of Conduct for Capital Controls', in Kevin Gallagher and Leonardo Stanley (eds), 'Capital Account Regulations and the Trading System: A "Compatibility Review"' (Pardee Center for the Study of Longer-Range Development, Boston University 2013) 14. See contra, Lupo-Pasini (n 7) 602.

[10] Panel Report, *Mexico: Measures Affecting Telecommunications Services*, WT/DS204/R, adopted 1 June 2004, para. 7.375, and Panel Report, *China: Certain Measures Affecting Electronic Payment Services*, adopted 16 July 2012, WT/DS413/R, paras 7.617–7.619.

[11] See Gabriel Gari, 'GATS Disciplines on Capital Transfers and Short-Term Capital Inflows: Time for Change?' (2014) 17 *Journal of International Economic Law* 399, 414–15.

[12] The issue remains contentious and divisive at the WTO. See WTO Secretariat Background Note (n 8) paras 47–51.

taking such measures must ensure they do not accord a less favourable treatment to services and service suppliers of other Members. Taxes on non-residents' portfolio investments in domestic securities or taxes on the outflow of foreign currency could potentially run afoul of the provision. It is also not hard to come up with measures which *de facto* restrict, limit or otherwise treat a foreign service or service provider less favourably. While this author is not aware of any Member that has sought to apply capital controls having made any relevant commitments in the GATS, the point here is merely that the provision has the potential to restrict the use of controls on Members that have made specific commitments in the relevant sectors.

Finally, it should be noted that the GATS does not cover 'services supplied in the exercise of governmental authority'.[13] Article I:3(c) defines that as 'any service which is supplied neither on a commercial basis, nor in competition with one or more service suppliers', and Article 1:b of the Annex on Financial Services provides a list of activities that are to be regarded as such, including in b(i) as 'activities conducted by a central bank or a monetary authority or by any other public entity in pursuit of monetary or exchange rate policies'.[14] The instrumental question is therefore whether capital controls are included within that definition, and thus exempted from the scope of the GATS. While some economists take a broad view that would carve out all macroeconomic measures,[15] the weight of legal interpretation is on a narrower approach that limits the carve-out to financial service–type activities such as exchange market interventions.[16] The latter view seems correct in that a capital control is a particular measure but it is not an 'activity'. The activities listed in Article 1:b are specific types of services. Finally, carving out any and all activities conducted by the Central Bank, monetary and finance authorities would lead to an absurd result that conflicts with the objective and purpose of the Agreement, and in particular conflict with Article XI:1 on transfers and payments.

---

[13] GATS, Article I:3(b).
[14] The other two activities named are (ii) activities forming part of a statutory system of social security or public retirement plans and (iii) other activities conducted by a public entity for the account or with the guarantee or using the financial resources of the government.
[15] See for instance Masamichi Kono and others, 'Opening Markets in the Financial Services and the Role of the GATS' (WTO Special Studies, 1997) 3.
[16] See for instance Bart De Meester, 'The Global Financial Crisis and Global Support for Banks: What Role for the GATS?' (2010) 13(1) *Journal of International Economic Law* 27, 29–30; Lupo-Pasini (n 7) 97; Gari (n 11) 426–27.

5.2 Exceptions under the GATS

The commitments outlined above does not mean that when a Member makes a market access or national treatment commitment capital controls can never be introduced for that sector. On the contrary, it simply means that the Member seeking to introduce the control would need to rely on an exception in order to remain compliant with the GATS. The most relevant exceptions would be Article XII (BoP difficulties), Article XI:2 (to satisfy a request by the IMF) or paragraph 2(a) of the Annex on Financial Services (prudential measure designed to ensure the integrity and stability of the financial service sector). The use of these provisions, however, is not without barriers and issues. Each will be addressed in turn.

5.2.1 Balance of Payment Difficulties

Recall that Article XI:1 begins with the phrase '[e]xcept under the circumstances envisaged in Article XII'. This caveat explicitly provides that the liberalisation commitment is subject to the restrictions to safeguard balance of payments set out in Article XII. Article XII is extensive, with paragraph 1 essentially providing that in times of balance of payments problems or external financial difficulties or threat thereof, Members are allowed to 'adopt or maintain restrictions on trade in services on which it has undertaken specific commitments, including on payments or transfers for transactions related to such commitments'. The article continues by recognising that balance of payment pressures for Members in the process of economic development or economic transition 'may necessitate the use of restrictions to ensure, *inter alia*, the maintenance of a level of financial reserves adequate for the implementation of its programme of economic development or economic transition'.

The BoP exception is not self-judging and is limited in several ways. For instance, the paragraph states that restrictions (a) shall not discriminate among Members; (b) shall be consistent with the IMF Articles of Agreement; (c) shall avoid unnecessary damage to the commercial, economic and financial interests of any other Member; (d) shall not exceed those necessary to deal with the circumstances described in paragraph 1; (e) shall be temporary and be phased out progressively as the situation specified in paragraph 1 improves. In addition, while Members can 'give priority to the supply of services which are more essential to their economic or development programmes', they cannot adopt or maintain such restrictions 'for the purpose of protecting a particular service sector'.[17] The text of Article XII reads:

1. In the event of serious balance-of-payments and external financial difficulties or threat thereof, a Member may adopt or maintain restrictions on trade in services on which it has undertaken specific commitments, including on payments or transfers for transactions related to such commitments. It is recognized that particular pressures on the balance of payments of a Member in the process of economic development or economic transition may necessitate the use of restrictions to ensure, inter alia, the maintenance of a level of financial reserves adequate for the implementation of its programme of economic development or economic transition.
2. The restrictions referred to in paragraph 1: (a) shall not discriminate among Members; (b) shall be consistent with the Articles of Agreement of the International Monetary Fund; (c) shall avoid unnecessary damage to the commercial, economic and financial interests of any other Member; (d) shall not exceed those necessary to deal with the circumstances described in paragraph 1; (e) shall be temporary and be phased out progressively as the situation specified in paragraph 1 improves.
3. In determining the incidence of such restrictions, Members may give priority to the supply of services which are more essential to their economic or development programmes. However, such restrictions shall not be adopted or maintained for the purpose of protecting a particular service sector.

While Article XII makes no specific mention of capital controls, such measures would fall within the scope of the provision. This is clear for two reasons – first, the article does not provide for an exhaustive list of situations where 'restrictions on trade in services' can take place. The article does list two possible restrictions (payments or transfers for transactions related to such commitments), but these appear to be mere examples and not a limitation of usage. This interpretation is based on the use of the word 'including' in the sentence, which again points to examples rather than a defined list. This interpretation is further strengthened by the reference to Article XII in Article XI:2: (Payments and Transfers): 'provided a Member shall not impose restrictions on any capital transactions inconsistently with its specific commitments regarding such transactions,

---

[17] GATS, Article XII:3.

except under Article XII or at the request of the Fund'. Simply stated, the reference would be nonsensical if capital controls did not fall within the scope of Article XII.

What is less clear is whether the balance of payments provision applies to restrictions on capital outflows or whether it applies to both inflows and outflows. This issue was raised and became contentious during the negotiations of the OECD's Multilateral Agreement on Investment (MAI). With some of the negotiating parties believing that the BOP clause should apply to inflows and outflows whereas other negotiating parties sided with the views of IMF staff that inflows were not usually harmful to BoP difficulties – quite the opposite, in fact – and that the provision should only apply in regards to outflows, which was believed to be the most significant cause for the depletion of monetary reserves and balance of payment problems difficulties.[18]

With Article XII yet to be invoked and interpreted by a dispute settlement panel, the issue remains unresolved and uncertain.[19] That being said, the view limiting Article XII to outflows is more persuasive. Article XI:1 justifies the BoP exception, in part, on the necessity of Members' in the process of economic development or economic transition to use of the restrictions 'to ensure, inter alia, the maintenance of a level of financial reserves adequate for the implementation of its programme of economic development or economic transition'. This sentence quite clearly refers to outflows, as inflows do not threaten financial reserves. Far from seeking to maintain reserves, controls on inflows serve to take pressure off an appreciating currency which can be caused by an oversupply of foreign currency.[20]

Other potential limitations or problems with using Article XII include the fact that a Member taking the measure would have to prove that the allowable safeguards are non-discriminatory, are limited, will be phased out and are necessary to deal with the crisis. This implies that capital control measures taken in accordance with the BoP provision are inherently constrained as they must be well defined and short term, and can only remain in effect for as long as the underlying circumstances necessitate. The larger problem may be whether capital controls can be formulated

---

[18] See Statement by the IMF, 'The Relationship between the Multilateral Agreement on Investment and the International Monetary Fund' [DAFFE/MAI/RD(96)35, 2 September 1996].

[19] For useful discission of the positions, see WTO Secretariat Background Note 'Exceptions and Balance of Payments Safeguards' (WT/WGTI/W/137, 2002).

[20] See Gari (n 11) 449.

in such a way as not to discriminate against other Members. In line with Article XII:2(a), the IMF has stated that measures should not discriminate on the basis of residency but on currency (i.e. currency-specific reserve requirements or limitations on foreign currency borrowings).[21] This, however, may not be possible because CFMs inherently discriminate in some respects between residents and non-residents.[22] Moreover, while it may be technically possible to draft currency-related measures in a manner that is consistent with the BoP, provision it is questionable whether such a narrowly tailored measure would actually serve the purpose of alleviating the underlying BoP difficulties.

5.2.2   To Satisfy a Request from the IMF

Article XI:2 is an exception to the general prohibition contained in paragraph 1 which prohibits Members from adopting or maintaining restrictions on payments and transfers as well as on capital transactions in a manner that is not consistent with their specific commitments. More specifically, Article XI:2 attempts to avoid conflict between the WTO and IMF by allowing restrictions to be placed on capital flows – even where such restrictions would be inconsistent with paragraph 1 of Article XI – so long as the restrictions are adopted 'at the request' of the IMF. Article XI:2 reads:

> Nothing in this Agreement shall affect the rights and obligations of the members of the International Monetary Fund under the Articles of Agreement of the Fund, including the use of exchange actions which are in conformity with the Articles of Agreement, provided that a Member shall not impose restrictions on any capital transactions inconsistently with its specific commitments regarding such transactions, except under Article XII *or at the request of the Fund*. (emphasis added)

The IMF would have the authority to make such a request under Article VI, Section 1(a) of the Articles of Agreement:

> A member may not use the Fund's general resources to meet a large or sustained *outflow* of capital except as provided in Section 2 of this Article, and *the Fund may request a member to exercise controls to prevent such use of the general resources of the Fund.* If, after receiving such a request, a member fails to exercise appropriate controls, the Fund may declare the member ineligible to use the general resources of the Fund. (emphasis added)

---

[21] IMF, 'The Liberalization and Management of Capital Flows: An Institutional View' (14 November 2012).
[22] See Viterbo (n 9) 16–17.

The rationale for the restraint is to ensure that IMF resources are spent in accordance with the Fund's mandate. The authority granted appears to be wide in scope, and would certainly include situations where a loan/stabilisation agreement or other lending programme with a borrowing member includes a CFM. But it is clear that the restraint is dealing with outflows. Thus, it only makes sense that the reference to a 'request of the Fund' in Article XI:2 of the GATS is likewise limited to GATS Members' right to impose restrictions on capital outflows. The provision would not apply to Members seeking to control inflows. The only possible exception would be if the Fund could use a mechanism other than Article VI to make a request; here, Gari speculates that since the Fund has recently shifted its position on capital controls, 'it is not unreasonable to expect circumstances where the Fund could recommend its Members to deploy controls on capital inflows as part of its surveillance, financial or technical assistance functions', but questions whether such an action could be construed as a 'request of the Fund' to impose restrictions on capital transactions within the meaning of GATS Article XI:2.[23]

The Appellate Body in *Argentina–Textiles* (1998) took a narrow view of the exception in holding that Members can deviate from the obligations set out in a WTO covered agreement only when the measure arises from a 'legally binding agreement' stemming from the IMF Articles which requires the member to take certain action.[24] In that case, Argentina could not prove that its 3 per cent statistical tax levied on imports was required or requested by any agreement the country had with the IMF. Even if Argentina did have a legally binding agreement in place with the IMF, the Appellate Body held that nothing in the Agreement between the IMF and the WTO, the Declaration on the Relationship of the WTO with the IMF or the Declaration on Coherence 'justifies a conclusion that a Member's commitments to the IMF shall prevail over its [GATT] obligations'.[25] In this regard, the Appellate Body continued:

> The Agreement Between the IMF and the WTO, however, does not modify, add to or diminish the rights and obligations of Members under the WTO Agreement, nor does it modify individual States' commitments to the IMF. It does not provide any substantive rules concerning the resolution

---

[23] Gari (n 11) 420.
[24] Appellate Body Report, *Argentina–Textiles*, WT/DS56/AB/R, adopted 22 April 1998, para. 69. See also Panel Report, *Dominican Republic–Cigarettes*, WT/DS302/R, adopted 26 November 2004, para. 7.154.
[25] Appellate Body Report, *Argentina–Textiles*, para. 70.

of possible conflicts between obligations of a Member under the WTO Agreement and obligations under the Articles of Agreement of the IMF or any agreement with the IMF. However, paragraph 10 of the Agreement Between the IMF and the WTO contains a direction to the staff of the IMF and the WTO Secretariat to consult on 'issues of possible inconsistency between measures under discussion'[...][26]

This decision has been interpreted as meaning that without a request from the IMF resulting in a binding agreement, a WTO member cannot make use of Article XI:2. Under such an interpretation, the entire exception may therefore be illusory as the IMF does not in practice request a Member to introduce a CFM; rather, a borrower 'voluntarily' reaches an agreement with the IMF. Thus, the IMF never technically 'requests' the country to initiate CFMs. In other words, since loan agreements are implemented on a voluntary basis, following consultations and a 'recommendation' by the Fund, they are not within the scope of the provision.

This decision is particularly damning to the use of Article XI:2 to excuse controls on inflows of capital because an IMF recommendation that a Member implement controls on inflows made in the context of Article IV consultations or as a lending condition cannot create a legally binding obligation. No country is obligated to follow the recommendation, and there is no breach of international law for failing to abide by a recommendation made by the IMF.

5.2.3 Prudential Measures

Perhaps the most important exception is contained in paragraph 2(a) of the GATS Annex on Financial Services, which allows Members to adopt prudential measures despite their specific sectoral commitments related to market access and national treatment. As the placement of the exception implies, this exception applies only to the financial service sector. The exception does not, therefore, apply to, and cannot be invoked to justify, other sectors; for example, the provision could not apply to justify a tax on inflows inconsistent with market access commitments undertaken in the telecommunications sector. When applicable, the exception takes precedence over obligations arising from GATS Article VI (Domestic Regulation). Paragraph 2(a) reads:

> Notwithstanding any other provisions of the Agreement, a Member shall not be prevented from taking measures for prudential reasons, including

[26] Ibid. para. 72.

for the protection of investors, depositors, policy holders or persons to whom a fiduciary duty is owed by a financial service supplier, or to ensure the integrity and stability of the financial system. Where such measures do not conform with the provisions of the Agreement, they shall not be used as a means of avoiding the Member's commitments or obligations under the Agreement.

The first part of the provision suggests that WTO Members retain a wide degree of autonomy to control financial services in case of financial instability or threat thereof. In fact, the provision does not even require prudential measures to be non-discriminatory, nor is there any need to prove the 'necessity' of taking the measures, as there is in the general exceptions clause of Article XIV. The only somewhat controversial aspect would be that the use of the wording 'taking measures' in the first sentence limits applicability to new measures. Such language could be interpreted as being narrower in scope than the 'adopting or maintaining' language used in some free trade agreements.[27]

Despite the apparent wide scope, some commentators have argued that the provision is limited and without value. For example, according to IMF working papers dating to 2011, prudential measures seek to limit systemic risk on financial institutions, as opposed to targeting capital account transactions, and do not discriminate between residency and currency.[28] Such an interpretation appears unduly narrow, as the text of the provision seems to encompass macro-prudential regulations such as capital controls. Other commentators assert that the prudential clause applies only to outflows (and therefore measures taken in regards to inflows do not fall within the scope of the clause) or that the clause only covers Basel-type measures such as bank capital requirements and buffers (and thus capital controls do not fall within the scope of the clause).[29] Again, such interpretations are without textual support.

One of the more interesting arguments is that the last sentence of paragraph 2(a) means that such prudential measures cannot contradict existing GATS obligations and that the prudential provision would

---

[27] See Chapter 6 for examples.
[28] See Karl F Habermeier, Annamaria Kokenyne and Chikako Baba, 'The Effectiveness of Capital Controls and Prudential Policies in Managing Large Inflows' (5 August 2011) IMF Staff Discussion Notes No. 11/14; Anton Korinek, 'The New Economics of Capital Controls Imposed for Prudential Reasons' (2011) 59 *IMF Economic Review* 523.
[29] See generally Korinek (n 28).

perhaps never permit governmental action in practice.³⁰ More specifically, commentators holding this position contend that the last sentence has a self-cancelling effect that prevents WTO Members from taking measures inconsistent with their WTO obligations.³¹ Thus, to those commentators, the prudential exception does not actually allow a WTO Member to address systemic risks, because attempting to do so would breach their WTO commitments.

Reading the provisions with state regulatory needs in mind and with a view to avoiding contradictions within the same treaty as required by Article 31 of the Vienna Convention on the Law of Treaties,³² a more reasonable reading yields a different result. The provision reads that where threats are identified, prudential measures may legitimately contradict WTO obligations, provided that they are not used as a pretext to initiate protectionist measures and escape general obligations under the Agreement. In other words, the last sentence of paragraph 2(a) is not self-cancelling, but rather constitutes a good faith clause or safeguard against abuse in a similar fashion to the chapeau of Article XIV of the GATS and Article XX of the General Agreement on Tariffs and Trade (GATT), but without the burden of proving the measures are 'necessary'

---

[30] See Kevin Gallagher and Leonardo Stanley (eds), 'Capital Account Regulations and the Trading System: A "Compatibility Review"' (Pardee Center for the Study of Longer-Range Development, Boston University 2013), 6–8, 18. In particular, see Viterbo, (n 9) 20 (stating that '[t]he last sentence of the clause should be deleted or at least thoroughly clarified'). See also Todd Tucker, 'The Looming GATS Conflict with Capital Controls', 31–32 (stating that '[o]ne way to craft a better defense against the range of grounds for attacking a CAR explored in this paper is to expand the [prudential measures defence] to ensure that it applies to CARs, and to remove its arguably self-canceling language'). But see also the Executive Summary, 6 ('It should be stressed that there has not been a case where this language has been tested with respect to CARs. Some Task Force members believe that existing language will be sufficient.'). See also for instance Lori Wallach and Todd Tucker, 'Answering Critical Questions about Conflicts between Financial Regulation and WTO Rules Hitherto Unaddressed by the WTO Secretariat and other Official Sources' (22 June 2010) Public Citizen 3, www.citizen.org/sites/default/files/memo_-_unanswered_questions_memo_for_geneva.pdf ('As the second sentence makes clear, prudential measures are only allowed under GATS if they don't violate any of the GATS rules, which are very expansive, or operate to reduce a member country's commitments or obligations.'); Todd Tucker and Lori Wallach, 'To Promote Economic Stability, Nations Must Free Themselves from WTO Financial Deregulation Dictates' (October 2009) Public Citizen 8, www.citizen.org/sites/default/files/introductiontowtoderegulation.pdf ('[T]he provision may only be used to defend regulatory policies if such policies do not undermine the commitments and obligations established through the other WTO rules. This effectively eviscerates the use of the provision … self-cancelling second sentence').

[31] See Ibid.

[32] Vienna Convention on the Law of Treaties, Article 31 (23 May 1969) 1155 U.N.T.S. 18232.

or not 'arbitrary or unjustifiable discrimination between countries where like conditions prevail, or a disguised restriction on trade in services'.[33]

Support for this interpretation is expressed in various doctrinal discussions and carries the weight of the commentaries. For instance, a 2010 note by the IMF concluded that '[t]he Annex on Financial Services includes a 'prudential carve out' clause that recognizes the right of WTO members to introduce and maintain prudential measures ... regardless of any other provisions of the GATS' and suggests that '[s]ince the Annex on Financial Services does not provide any definition or indicative list of prudential measures that would be covered by this provision, governments have considerable leeway in introducing prudential measures that fit their needs'.[34]

Other commentators have stated that the prudential provision allows financial regulatory authorities to 'take measures to ensure the integrity and stability of the financial system or to protect consumers of financial services even if these measures are inconsistent with other provisions of GATS'.[35] In this regard, Key notes that '[t]he only issues are whether the measure is, in fact, prudential, and whether it is being used to avoid a country's obligations or commitments under the GATS'.[36] Similarly, Cottier and Krajewski find that WTO Members may adopt prudential measures without interference from the WTO because the system 'preserves national regulatory autonomy and enables each country to adopt those rules which [it] deems appropriate'.[37] Finally, in an extensive analysis of prudential provisions, Barbee and Lester conclude the concerns over the phrasing of the clause are only 'speculative and have been overstated'[38] and that the prudential exception provides considerable policy space for regulators to safeguard the integrity and stability of the financial system, provided 'the non-protectionist purposes offered to justify the measure [is] authentic and real'.[39]

---

[33] GATS, Article XIV.
[34] IMF, 'Reference Note on Trade in Financial Services', Prepared by the Strategy, Policy, and Review and Legal Departments (9 July 2010) para. 14, www.elibrary.imf.org/view/journals/007/2010/056/article-A001-en.xml
[35] See Sydney J. Key, *The Doha Round and Financial Services Negotiations* (AEI Press 2003) 47.
[36] Ibid. 50.
[37] Thomas Cottier and Markus Krajewski, 'What Role for Non-Discrimination and Prudential Standards in International Law?' (2010) 13 *Journal of International Economic Law* 817, 827.
[38] Inu Barbee and Simon Lester, 'Financial Services in the TTIP: Making the Prudential Exception Work' (2014) 45 *Georgetown Journal of International Law* 953, 954.
[39] Ibid. 954, 961.

Perhaps more importantly, several governments have come to similar conclusions on the role and efficiency of prudential measures. This includes direct statements on the high degree of autonomy granted to the WTO Members, notwithstanding the inclusion of the last sentence in paragraph 2(a) of the Annex. For instance, former US Treasury Secretary Timothy Geithner stated that the controversial part of prudential provision was to be read as a guard against abuse and concluded that US investment treaties and FTAs provided 'very substantial and adequate flexibility for government policy makers to mitigate such risks, including through the so-called prudential exception and through the monetary and exchange rate policy exception'.[40] The effectiveness of the prudential exception provisions has also been confirmed by jurisdictions as diverse as Macao, Costa Rica and the EU.[41]

The issue has now been addressed in the WTO dispute of *Argentina–Financial Services*, where both parties to the dispute weighed in on the issue. The respondent, Argentina, viewed the second sentence of the prudential exception in a similar fashion to the chapeau of GATS Article XIV (General Exceptions):

> Argentina asserts that the second sentence of the prudential exception performs the same function as the preamble to Article XIV of the GATS, i.e. to prevent abuse in the use of the exception. Argentina explains that the second sentence of the prudential exception requires that WTO-inconsistent measures taken for prudential reasons not be, in actual fact, measures whose objective is to avoid the disciplines of the GATS. According to Argentina, this provision is aimed at determining whether the measure is genuinely being applied in a manner consistent with its prudential objective and not for the purpose of avoiding a Member's commitments or obligations under the GATS.[42]

The complainant, Panama, viewed the provision slightly differently, preferring a more objective test:

> 7.803 … Panama argues that the purpose of the second sentence of paragraph 2(a) of the Annex on Financial Services is to limit the possibility

---

[40] Ibid. 962 (quoting Letter from Timothy Geithner, Treasury Secretary, to Rep. Barney Frank, 'Inside U.S. Trade' (July 19, 2012), http://insidetrade.com/iwpfile.html?file=dec2012%2Fwto2012_2846a.pdf.

[41] See KH Lei, 'Financial Services in the Current WTO Framework, Monetary Authority of Macao' (2006), http://docplayer.net/5989501-Financial-services-in-the-current-wto-framework.html. See further, Antoine P Martin and Bryan Mercurio, 'Towards Convergence of Trade and Investment Law? A Right to Prudential Measures for the Preservation of Financial Stability' (2018) 51(3) *The International Lawyer* 553.

[42] Panel Report, 'Argentina: Measures Relating to Trade in Goods and Services', (30 September 2015) WT/DS453/R, para. 7.783.

of measures being freely taken for allegedly prudential reasons. For this condition to be satisfied, Panama considers that there must be a relationship of means and ends between the measure taken and the prudential objective pursued. Panama agrees with Argentina that the academic literature has described the second sentence of the prudential exception as equivalent to a good faith obligation that requires a rational relationship of means and ends between the measure taken and the prudential objective pursued.

7.804. Panama argues ... the prohibition on using prudential measures as a means of avoiding commitments and obligations is intended to prevent abuses. Moreover, it ensures that the right of Members to avail themselves of exceptions is exercised reasonably or prudently and in such a way as not to frustrate the rights accorded to other Members by the substantive rules of the GATS.

7.805. Panama considers that ... a panel should examine whether the design, structure and architecture of the measure (or its application in practice) correspond with the prudential reasons on which it is allegedly based. In other words, it should examine whether there is a genuine relationship of means and ends between the measure and its stated objectives. In this connection, Panama considers that if a measure is not suitable, fit or appropriate for achieving its presumed prudential objective, then it should be understood that its utilization is inconsistent (wholly or in part) with the objective pursued. In these circumstances, the use of a measure that does not match the purported prudential reason will not be underpinned by a prudential reason. In the absence of a supporting prudential reason, such use (or part thereof) should be treated as what it is: a means of avoiding commitments or obligations, and therefore prohibited under the second sentence of paragraph 2(a) of the Annex on Financial Services.

7.806. Panama considers that the analysis of this element should be based on an objective assessment ... and that the objective of a measure can most often 'be discerned from the design, the architecture, and the revealing structure' of the measure.

Panama concluded its submission with an example, stating that if a measure is not designed to protect financial services consumers and its application does not help to achieve that objective, the relationship between means and ends required by the second sentence of paragraph 2(a) of the Annex on Financial Services does not exist, and 'consequently, it will be understood that the measure is being used as a means of avoiding commitments or obligations under the GATS and it will not be justified by the prudential exception'.[43] The Panel in *Argentina–Financial Services* did not make any rulings on the second sentence of paragraph 2(a); therefore, we still do not have any jurisprudence on the issue.

---

[43] Ibid. para. 7.807.

The Panel and Appellate Body in the *Argentina–Financial Services* dispute did weigh in on several aspects of the prudential exception and with relevant jurisprudence supplementing doctrinal analysis, commentators and governments alike are no longer forced to base their conclusions on the effectiveness of prudential exception solely on a textual analysis of treaty language.[44] For this reason, it is worth exploring the dispute in some depth.

In *Argentina–Financial Services*, Panama challenged a set of Argentine measures designed crack down on tax evasion implemented following an economic crisis.[45] The necessity discussion focused on both regulatory exceptions and prudential measures for eight financial, taxation, foreign exchange and business registration measures.[46] According to Argentina, the measures constituted 'anti-abuse measures which [were] essential tools for enforcing national tax laws, guaranteeing taxation and tax collection, preventing fraudulent practices, tax evasion and tax avoidance, as well as the erosion of national tax bases'.[47] Panama claimed the measures infringed Argentina's market access commitments in the financial services sector.[48]

The Panel found that certain measures taken by Argentina were inconsistent with the MFN obligation in GATS Article II:1 and could not be justified as measures taken for 'prudential reasons' under paragraph 2(a) of the GATS Annex.[49] After reversing the Panel's finding of an MFN violation, the Appellate Body declared 'moot' the Panel's analysis regarding the prudential exception.[50] Nevertheless, and 'somewhat unusually',[51] the Appellate Body spent eight pages discussing and ruling on the Panel's

---

[44] See for instance Barbee and Lester (n 38) 954; U.N. Conference on Trade and Development, 'Policy Space to Prevent and Mitigate Financial Crises in Trade and Investment Agreements' (May 2010) UNCTAD/GDS/MDP/G24/2010/1, 8.

[45] See Panel Report, *Argentina–Financial Services*, paras 2.1–2.62.

[46] Ibid. para 2.9.

[47] Ibid. Annex B-31, WT/DS453/R/Add.1, para. 2.

[48] Ibid. paras. 3.1–3.3.

[49] Ibid. para. 7.949. The panel did not find the measures were inconsistent with Argentina's commitments under Article XVII (national treatment) or Article XVI (market access commitments). See Ibid. paras 7.525 and 7.431, respectively.

[50] See Appellate Body Report, 'Argentina: Measures Relating to Trade in Goods and Services', WT/DS453/AB/R, adopted 9 May 2016, para. 6.83 ['this … renders moot the Panel's analysis of … whether measures 5 and 6 may be justified pursuant to paragraph 2(a) of the GATS Annex on Financial Services.']. The Appellate Body also reversed but made no decision under Article XVII, with the result being that Argentina was not found to have breached any WTO obligation. See Ibid. para. 7.2.

[51] Andrew D Mitchell, Jennifer K Hawkins and Neha Mishra, 'Dear Prudence: Allowances under International Trade and Investment Law for Prudential Regulation in the Financial Services Sector' (2016) 9 *Journal of International Economic Law* 787, 790.

interpretation of the prudential clause, justifying its decision to do so by stating that 'several of the issues raised in Panama's appeal have implications for the interpretation of provisions of the GATS'.[52] While the findings and decisions of the Appellate Body in this case can only be regarded as *obiter dicta*,[53] and while capital controls were not at issue in the dispute, it is nevertheless worthwhile to review this case, as the Panel and Appellate Body reports are the only ones to consider whether certain Argentine measures – including requirements relating to re-insurance services and requirements for access to the Argentine capital market – could qualify under paragraph 2 of the GATS Annex on Financial Services as measures taken for prudential reasons, that is, to protect investors, financial service suppliers or, more generally, the integrity and stability of the financial system.[54]

The Panel began its analysis by stating:

> it can be inferred from the wording of paragraph 2(a) of the Annex on Financial Services that Argentina must demonstrate that two requirements have been met in order to avail itself of the exception, namely: (i) that the measure in question was taken for prudential reasons and (ii) that the measure is not being used as a means of avoiding its commitments or obligations under the GATS.[55]

The Panel next identified a third requirement in applying the prudential exception, that the party seeking to make use of the exception 'must also demonstrate that the measure in question is a measure "affecting the supply of financial services"' pursuant to paragraph 1(a) of the Annex on Financial Services.[56]

The Panel then proceeded to analyse the Argentina measures under the three prongs of the test.[57] In analysing whether the measures in question were taken for prudential reasons, the Panel drew a firm distinction between 'prudential measures' and 'measures taken for prudential reasons' and concluded that in order to fall within the provision 'it is the reason which must be "prudential" and not the measure *per se*'.[58] In other words,

---

[52] Appellate Body Report, *Argentina–Financial Services*, para. 6.84.
[53] See also Mitchell, Hawkins and Mishra (n 51) 790.
[54] Panel Report, 'Argentina–Financial Services', para. 7.821. Argentina argued that the two measures at issue 'are preventive measures that seek to protect the insured and the consumers of financial services from risks that could undermine public confidence and affect the functioning of Argentina's financial markets'. Ibid. 7.785.
[55] Ibid. para. 7.821.
[56] Ibid. para. 7.822.
[57] Ibid. paras. 7.822, 7.825.
[58] Ibid. para. 7.861.

the prudential factor does not relate to a certain type of measure but to the circumstances justifying the measure.[59]

The Panel also rejected Panama's assertion 'that the respondent must [further] demonstrate that the measure [at issue] constitutes a "domestic regulation".'[60] Instead, the Panel held that 'paragraph 2(a) of the Annex on Financial Services covers all types of measures affecting the supply of financial services within the meaning of paragraph 1(a) of the Annex and not only those measures that could be characterized as 'domestic regulations' within the meaning of Article VI of the GATS'.[61] The Appellate Body rejected Panama's appeal,[62] holding that 'the Panel's interpretation, that paragraph 2(a) of the Annex on Financial Services "covers all types of measures affecting the supply of financial services within the meaning of paragraph 1(a)" of the Annex, comports with our interpretation of paragraph 2(a)'.[63]

In explaining the concept of prudential reasons, the Panel then considered the circumstances characteristic of prudential decisions, that is, a prevention role, a prudential cause and a temporal aspect.[64] Each of these three characteristics will be addressed in turn.

5.2.3.1 Prevention Role

Starting from a dictionary definition, the Panel introduced the idea that prudential measures are 'preventive or precautionary' in nature[65] and could thus include an 'extremely broad' number of measures in quantitative terms.[66] Taking a more legal approach, it then expressed concerns as to the 'serious systemic implications of the narrow interpretation' of such provisions,[67] and found the prudential reasons listed in paragraph 2(a) to be indicative rather than exhaustive.[68] Following the jurisprudence of the GATT/GATS General Exception clause, it thus concluded that prudential measures under paragraph 2 should be read in a broad manner.

---

[59] Ibid. ('[T]he exception makes it possible to exempt or exonerate any measure affecting the supply of financial services that has been taken "for prudential reasons".').
[60] Ibid. para. 7.826.
[61] Ibid. para. 7.847.
[62] Ibid. paras. 6.252–6.262.
[63] Ibid. para. 6.262. See further Mitchell, Hawkins and Mishra (n 51) 804–5.
[64] See Ibid. paras. 7.864–7.945.
[65] Ibid. para. 7.868.
[66] Ibid. para. 7.869.
[67] Ibid. para. 7.848.
[68] Ibid.

The Panel overall found that Members 'are entitled to determine the level of protection they consider appropriate'[69] and that the 'nature and scope of financial regulation at different times reflect the knowledge, experience and scales of values of governments at the moment in question'.[70] In this regard, the Panel stated that Members: 'should have sufficient freedom to define the prudential reasons that underpin their measures, in accordance with their own scales of values' such as 'the protection of investors, depositors, policy holders or persons to whom a fiduciary duty is owed by a financial service supplier' or 'the integrity and stability of the financial system'.[71]

5.2.3.2 Prudential Cause

The Panel then set out an important distinction between a prudential measure and a measure taken for prudential reasons.[72] Analysing the text of paragraph 2(a) of the Annex on Financial Services on the basis of the ordinary meaning of its terms as provided under the Vienna Convention on the Law of Treaties, the Panel again resorted to the dictionary and found that a 'measure taken "for" prudential reasons would … be a measure with a prudential cause'.[73] In so doing, the Panel seemed to give 'deference to Members' autonomy determining their prudential reasons, and a preference for a broader understanding of this concept, which the Panel considered "evolutionary".'[74] The Panel stated:

> The nature and scope of financial regulation at different times reflect the knowledge, experience and scales of values of governments at the moment in question. We therefore consider that WTO Members should have sufficient freedom to define the prudential reasons that underpin their measures, in accordance with their own scales of values.[75]

---

[69] Ibid. para. 7.870 (citing Panel Report, 'United States: Measures Affecting the Cross-Border Supply of Gambling and Betting Services', WT/DS285/R, adopted 20 April 2005, as modified by Appellate Body Report WT/DS285/AB, para. 168); Appellate Body Report, 'Korea: Measures Affecting Imports of Fresh, Chilled and Frozen Beef', WT/DS161/AB/R, WT/DS169/AB/R, adopted 10 January 2001, para. 176.
[70] Ibid. para. 7.871.
[71] Ibid. para. 7.871. Such an interpretation, the Panel stated, is in accordance with the fourth recital of the preamble to the GATS, which recognizes 'the right of Members to regulate, and to introduce new regulations, on the supply of services within their territories in order to meet national policy objectives'. Ibid. para. 7.872 (quoting GATS, Preamble).
[72] Ibid. paras. 7.880–7.892.
[73] Ibid. para. 7.888. 'A measure taken "for" prudential reasons would therefore be a measure with a prudential cause'. Ibid.
[74] Ibid. para. 7.873; Mitchell, Hawkins and Mishra (n 51) 805.
[75] Ibid. para. 7.871.

The Panel rejected Panama's contention that 'an assessment of whether measures were taken "for" prudential reasons requires an examination of whether a delay in adopting the measures would result in a real prudential risk, while also rejecting the appropriateness of a "necessity" enquiry',[76] instead holding that a rational relationship must exist between 'the measure and its prudential objective' and that 'the measure must be fit for the purpose of preventing the event, or the effects resulting therefrom, which the measure is intended to avoid' is in line with the notion that in 'the measure's design, structure and architecture there must be a rational relationship of cause and effect between the measure and the prudential reason for it'.[77] The Panel stated:

> [T]he word 'for' in the phrase 'measures for prudential reasons' denotes a rational relationship of cause and effect between the measure and the prudential reason. Thus, the Member taking the measure in question must demonstrate that in its design, structure or architecture there is a rational relationship of cause and effect between the measure it seeks to justify under paragraph 2(a) and the prudential reason provided. A central aspect of this rational relationship of cause and effect is the adequacy of the measure to the prudential reason, that is, whether the measure, through its design, structure and architecture, contributes to achieving the desired effect.[78]

The Panel went on to state that whether a measure has been taken 'for prudential reasons' (i.e. whether there is a rational relationship of cause and effect between the measure and the reason), must be determined 'on a case-by-case basis, taking into account the particular characteristics of each situation and each dispute'.[79] The Panel ultimately found the measures to be of a prudential type under paragraph 2(a) but that they had not been taken 'for prudential reasons' and were thus inconsistent with the latter requirement.[80]

The Appellate Body did not contradict the Panel. Instead, it reiterated that a Member shall not be prevented from taking measures for prudential reasons,[81] confirmed the idea that measures deemed prudential in nature could fall under the scope of an Annex exception but insisted that no exception could be used to escape existing commitments.[82] In essence, therefore, the Appellate Body substantiated the Panel's conclusions as to a right of the Members to regulate and made it clear that the exception provisions of the GATS were designed with these considerations in mind.[83]

---

[76] Mitchell, Hawkins and Mishra (n 51) 805. See also Panel Report, *Argentina–Financial Services*, paras. 7.883–7.885.
[77] Panel Report, *Argentina–Financial Services*, para. 7.889.
[78] Ibid. para. 7.891.
[79] Ibid.
[80] Ibid. paras. 7.946–7.949. For the complete reasoning, see paras. 7.893–7.944.
[81] Appellate Body Report, 'Argentina–Financial Services', paras. 6.254–6.255, 6.272.
[82] Ibid. paras. 6.244–6.246.
[83] Ibid. para. 6.260.

5.2.3.3 Temporal Aspects

The Panel finally considered whether measures taken for prudential reasons must be temporary in nature and whether they may be taken as a result of an imminent threat. In so doing, it took a holistic approach and focused on two main points.

First, the Panel emphasised that anticipatory prudence was legitimate because – financial crises being varied, complex and susceptible to emerge suddenly – it is difficult for governments to anticipate their consequences. The Panel admitted that the risks stemming from financial instability evolve as crises unfold[84] and, in fine, concluded that paragraph 2(a) of the Annex on Financial Services authorized WTO Members to protect their financial systems from systemic risks in a forward-looking, precautionary and anticipatory '*ex ante*' prudential manner.[85] The Panel's finding that the risk, injury or danger twhat a government is seeking to guard against do 'not necessarily have to be imminent',[86] therefore, contrasts with the conclusions of investment tribunals on the matter (as discussed in Chapter 7).

Second, in holding that a measure taken for prudential reasons required a prudential cause, the Panel could easily reject Panama's assertion that 'prudential measures should be transitional, provisional or short-term in nature'.[87] Instead, the Panel found that the time factor was to be read in light of the causes justifying the measures and thus concluded that measures taken for prudential reasons 'can remain in place ... for as long as the factual circumstances that justified their adoption continue to exist'.[88] Furthermore, the panel insisted that 'nothing in the ordinary meaning of the words "prudential reasons"

---

[84] Panel Report, *Argentina–Financial Services*, para. 7.878 ('it is important to understand that "systemic" problems may be incubating or gestating over the course of time and erupt rapidly; hence the importance of being prepared for them in advance').

[85] Ibid. para. 7.790 (Financial crises 'are typically latent and extremely difficult to identify beforehand, making it practically impossible to deal with those risks by taking corrective measures. This is precisely why paragraph 2(a) of the Annex on Financial Services authorizes WTO Members to take measures for prudential reasons to deal with risks of a systemic nature ex ante'). In this regard, the Panel also cited the third-party submissions of the EU, US, and Brazil. See Ibid. para. 7.873.

[86] Ibid. para. 7.879.

[87] Ibid. para. 7.890.

[88] Ibid. para. 7.890 ('an "imminent" danger may give rise to long-lasting measures to avoid the recurrence of similar situations in the future ... they may be urgent measures to confront an imminent risk, temporary or provisional measures, or even permanent (or long-lasting) measures, which might be taken even in the absence of an imminent risk that would prevent fulfilment of one of the motives or reasons mentioned in that paragraph.' It is, therefore, 'the nature of the situation that threatens a particular prudential objective that will dictate the nature of the measure').

conveys the idea of a time-limit' and added that 'as a matter of principle' difficulties raising prudential concerns 'may give rise to long-lasting measures to avoid the recurrence of similar situations in the future'.[89] Such a position demonstrates an awareness of the trade regime as part of a larger, integrated world system as opposed to myopically focusing on trade-specific obligations.

***

In analysing the measures, the Panel deemed the paragraph 2(a) prudential provision to be an exception, referring not only to the fact that the word 'notwithstanding' implies a derogation from a commitment but also to the Guidelines for the Scheduling of Specific Commitments under the GATS and the Explanatory Note by the Secretariat entitled 'Scheduling of Initial Commitments in Trade in Services', both of which refer to paragraph 2(a) as an exception. The Appellate Body agreed paragraph 2(a) is an exception and referred to it as such throughout its report. Accordingly, after the complainant establishes its *prima facie* case of inconsistency, the burden of proof shifts, and it is for the respondent to justify its measures under the prudential exception.

Here, the Panel accorded considerable deference to Argentina's identification of prudential reasons for its measures. In so doing, the Panel rejected Panama's suggestion to assess those reasons based on international standards, finding 'the GATS does not seek to identify measures that could be characterized as *specifically* prudential, such as those usually cited in the context of the standards defined by the Basel Committee on Banking Supervision'.[90] This bodes well for those seeking regulatory sovereignty, as the Panel implicitly recognises the complexity of the financial sector and the vastly different opinions and views among governments on the most appropriate form of prudential regulation to establish and maintain financial stability and control risks. The decision is also in line with the desire of Members for the exception to be broad and provide sufficient policy space to governments and maintain regulatory flexibility in this sector, as evidenced by the negotiating history of the GATS.[91]

---

[89] Ibid. para. 7.890.
[90] Panel Report, *Argentina–Financial Services*, para. 7.861.
[91] See for instance GATT Group of Negotiations on Services, Working Group on Financial Services Including Insurance, 'Communication from the European Communities' (10 July 1990) MTN.GNS/FIN/W/1; GATT Group of Negotiations on Services, Working Group on

One technical question remains unresolved, however, that being how a panel is to conduct its analysis on paragraph 2(a). Given the Panel and Appellate Body reports in *Argentina–Financial Services* extensively referenced and agreed the paragraph broadly corresponds with Article XIV, the general exceptions provision of the GATS, one would have anticipated that an appropriate view of paragraph 2(a) would be that the first sentence corresponds to the sub-provisions of Article XIV of the GATS – that is, the policy measures covered – while the second sentence is akin to the chapeau and concerns the application of the measures. The Panel in *Argentina–Financial Services*, did not proceed in this manner; instead, the Panel examined the tax exchange information issue as part of its analysis of the first sentence. Finding the first sentence had not been satisfied, the Panel did not proceed to analyse the measure under the second sentence. While perhaps reasonable, the Panel's approach of evaluating the design and application of the measure under the first sentence as to whether a measure has been taken 'for prudential reasons' leaves it unclear whether i should be considered when evaluating if the measure was taken 'as a means of avoiding the Member's commitments or obligations' under the second sentence.

That being the case, and in line with the prevailing view of commentators and governments, it is now clear that the provisions contained in the GATS Agreement and relevant Annex provide ample scope for Members to utilise the prudential carve-out as a safeguard in times of financial instability and crisis.

Financial Services Including Insurance, 'Communication from the United States' (12 July 1990) MTN.GNS/FIN/W/2; GATT Group of Negotiations on Services, Working Group on Financial Services Including Insurance, 'Note on the Meeting of 12–13 July 1990' (10 August 1990) MTN.GNS/FIN/2; GATT Trade Negotiations Committee, 'Communication from Canada, Japan, Sweden and Switzerland' (3 December 1990) MTN.TNC/W/50; GATT Trade Negotiations Committee, 'Communication from Canada, Japan, Sweden and Switzerland: Addendum' (15 October 1991) MTN.TNC/W/50/Add.2.

6

Bilateral and Regional Trade Agreements

Having clarified the extent to which the WTO's GATS Agreement contributes to creating a CFM-friendly environment for the Member States, let us turn to the next layer of international law applicable to countries seeking to operate controls on cross-border capital flows – bilateral and regional free trade agreements (FTAs). Due in part to the inability of the WTO to foster and complete fruitful trade discussions over the past two decades, bilateral and regional FTAs have become a major conduit for developing and organising a legal framework for capital movements across borders. To some commentators, further liberalisation in the financial services sector is 'an important reason ... for the conclusion of [agreements] on services outside the WTO'.[1] As previously discussed, the contribution of FTAs towards building a stable financial environment is contentious, with some commentators arguing that FTAs represent a threat for those countries desiring or even requiring prudent financial regulation.

The situation is complex because while FTAs are typically instruments designed to open, and trade and financial market liberalisation is not the only objective. While FTAs do indeed contemplate the liberalisation of signatories' capital accounts and the facilitation of payments and transfers as a means to foster trade in goods and trade in financial services between countries, the agreements do more than simply require the free flow of capital. Indeed, and in line with the rules established in the multilateral framework discussed in the previous chapter, FTAs also provide a variety of exceptions and carve-outs aimed at providing signatories with regulatory policy space. The amount and degree of policy space provided differ between and among agreements, but the trend is for treaties to include more and stronger protections for signatories.

---

[1] Carlo M. Cantore, '"Parallel Convergences" in Free Trade Agreements on Financial Services: Select Issues', in Rhea Tamara Hoffmann and Markus Krajewski (eds), *Coherence and Divergence in Services Trade Law: European Yearbook of International Economic Law* (Springer 2020) 194.

This chapter begins with a short introduction on the legal status and review of FTAs in the WTO. The chapter then proceeds to look in more detail at the typical provisions relating to financial services found in FTAs before turning to common FTA exclusions and exceptions. In so doing, four modern agreements are extensively referred to as examples – CPTPP, USMCA, RCEP and CETA. While many substantive obligations and exceptions are based on and resemble the GATS, the provisions contained in FTAs can be deeper and more comprehensive than those of the multilateral trading system. Properly drafted, such FTAs should provide comfort to governments seeking to make use of targeted CFMs that they will be able to do so without violating their bilateral and regional trade agreements.

6.1 Free Trade Agreements and the GATS

Article V of the GATS, entitled 'Economic Integration', allows WTO Members to derogate from the most favoured nation principle and negotiate FTAs which are more trade liberalising than the GATS. Article V of the GATS imposes conditions on the negotiation of FTAs, requiring such agreements to have 'substantial sectoral coverage', with footnote 1 of Article V clarifying that this refers to the 'number of sectors, volume of trade affected and modes of supply' and that '[i]n order to meet this condition, agreements should not provide for the a priori exclusion of any mode of supply'. Article V also requires that FTAs eliminate 'substantially all discrimination' between the parties and that they refrain from introducing new discriminatory measures against non-parties. Article V has not been interpreted by any dispute settlement panel and therefore the exact parameters of the provision remain uncertain.

Since the entry into force of the WTO on 1 January 1995 there have been 188 FTAs notified to the WTO Secretariat under Article V of the GATS (as of December 2021), with the vast majority coming post-2000. The rapid increase in FTAs is the result both of the failure of the multilateral trading system to advance the agenda in the unsuccessful Doha Development Round and also to the 'incomplete' nature of the GATS, which left several issues unresolved (including subsidies, domestic regulation and safeguards) and suffered from weak market access commitments due to the highly regulated nature of the service sectors and trepidation at offering binding and virtually irreversible commitments at the WTO. Of the 188 agreements, the WTO Regional Trade Agreements Database reveals that 173 contain at least one provision relating to capital transfers. Upon closer inspection, approximately 70 per cent of the notified agreements contain specific disciplines on financial services, under 10 per cent make reference to the existing disciplines of the GATS and approximately 10 percent do not explicitly cover financial services. These figures should not be a surprise, given that financial services remain heavily regulated and thus Members are using FTAs to reduce barriers and access more markets.

6.2 Typical Provisions Included in Free Trade Agreements

This section reviews provisions typically appearing in modern FTAs aiming to facilitate capital movements in relation to trade in goods and/or trade in services. Many FTAs are modelled on the GATS but contain deeper and wider liberalization commitments. Other FTAs have opted for a 'negative list' approach, whereby market openings apply across the board except for scheduled reservations. In other words, in a 'negative list' approach to scheduling commitments, everything is liberalised except where reservations have been taken for existing or future non-conforming measures. These agreements also usually contain a 'standstill' clause binding the parties' restrictions on trade in services to the level existing at the time of entry into force of the trade agreement in relation to the substantive provisions such as most favoured nation, national treatment and market access.[2] Modern FTAs also commonly contain a 'ratchet' clause which serves to raise the level of commitment every time a party unilaterally (or as part of another trade agreement) amends its laws and regulations to provide fewer restrictions than those set out in the agreement.[3] In other words, if a party makes additional concessions relating to market access in a subsequent trade agreement (or unilaterally offers greater market access), the higher level of access is automatically brought into the original agreement and the concession cannot be reversed. The ratchet moves in only one direction. The trend is also towards multi-issue trade agreements providing for investment (commercial presence in services terminology) through separate disciplines on trade in services and investment, thus facilitating a greater level of linkage between trade and investment across signatory parties.

---

[2] Agreements containing investment chapters and standalone BITs also routinely include a standstill clause for other provisions, including limitations on the nationality of senior management and board of directors. See for instance CPTPP, Article 11.10.1(a); USMCA, Article 17.10.1(a); CETA, Article 13.10.1(a).

[3] See for instance CPTPP, Article 11.10.1(c); USMCA, Article 17.10.1(c); CETA, Article 13.10.1(c).

Two types of provisions commonly appear in modern FTAs which serve to facilitate capital flows in the form of capital account liberalization and payments and transfers. Such clauses have become standard but may differ to some extent between and among agreements. In addition to provisions enabling the freer flow of capital movements or facilitating the establishment of foreign financial institutions are a variety of exceptions, including investment-related, trade-related and financial stability-related exceptions.

6.2.1 Provisions on the Current and Capital Account

Provisions explicitly seeking to liberalize the capital account and ensure free movement across borders are the most direct way to facilitate free capital movements. Such provisions essentially aim to create visibly liberal macroeconomic and monetary policy frameworks and tend to reference the IMF, which has long favoured an open capital account. These provisions remain rare but are commonly utilised by some countries.

Such an approach has been adopted by the EU in the CETA as well as in agreements with Singapore, South Korea and Vietnam. The relevant provisions in those agreements are nearly identical regarding the current account but slightly different in relation to capital movements, with the agreements with South Korea and Vietnam being more comprehensive and liberalising. Article 30.4 of the CETA in relation to the current account reads as follows:

> The Parties shall authorise, in freely convertible currency and in accordance with Article VIII of the Articles of Agreement ... any payments and transfers on the current account of the balance of payments between the Parties.[4]

Article 30.5 of the CETA on the movement of capital simply requires the parties to consult 'with a view to facilitating the movement of capital ... by continuing to implement their policies regarding the liberalisation of the capital and financial account, and by supporting a stable and secure framework for long term investment'. Nearly identical language is used in Article 16.7 of the EU-Singapore FTA. In contrast, Article 8.2 of the EU–Korea FTA binds the parties 'to impose no restrictions on the free movement of capital relating to direct investments made in accordance with the laws of the host country, to investments and other transactions liberalised in accordance with Chapter 7 (Trade in Services, Establishment and Electronic Commerce) and to the liquidation and repatriation of such

---

[4] See also EU–Singapore, Article 16.7.1; EU–Vietnam, Article 17.9.1.

invested capital and of any profit generated therefrom'.[5] The provision goes on to state that neither party may 'introduce any new restrictions on the movement of capital between residents of the Parties and shall not make the existing arrangements more restrictive'.

6.2.2 Provisions on Payments and Transfers

Most FTAs contain provisions specifically drafted to facilitate the flow of payments and transfers across borders, again with slight differences between and among agreements to account for differing contexts. Where financial flows relate to foreign investments, the provisions are drafted so as to provide investors with a right to be paid and to operate money transfers freely under the investment provisions of the treaty. Payment and transfer provisions are also commonly included in the trade sections of FTAs, as commercial presence (Mode 3) is a form of a supply of service. For this reason, investment and trade provisions on payments and transfers increasingly converge to become a single provision.

In the investment context, FTAs tend to include provisions aimed at creating a framework of unencumbered payments and transfers in the chapter on investment promotion and protection. As such, these provisions essentially incorporate the capital account provisions mentioned previously, while adapting them to an investment promotion context. For instance, Article 9.9 of the CPTPP provides:

1. Each Party shall permit all transfers relating to a covered investment to be made freely and without delay into and out of its territory. Such transfers include:
   (a) contributions to capital;
   (b) profits, dividends, interest, capital gains, royalty payments, management fees, technical assistance and other fees;
   (c) proceeds from the sale of all or any part of the covered investment or from the partial or complete liquidation of the covered investment;
   (d) payments made under a contract, including a loan agreement;
   (e) payments made pursuant to Article 9.7 (Treatment in Case of Armed Conflict or Civil Strife) and Article 9.8 (Expropriation and Compensation); and
   (f) payments arising out of a dispute.

---

[5] See also EU–Vietnam, Article 17.9.2.

6.2 TYPICAL PROVISIONS INCLUDED IN FREE TRADE AGREEMENTS

2. Each Party shall permit transfers relating to a covered investment to be made in a freely usable currency at the market rate of exchange prevailing at the time of transfer.

These provisions are then made subject to exceptions, where a government 'may prevent or delay a transfer through the equitable, non-discriminatory and good faith application of its laws relating to' the following:

(a) bankruptcy, insolvency or the protection of the rights of creditors;
(b) issuing, trading or dealing in securities, futures, options or derivatives;
(c) criminal or penal offences;
(d) financial reporting or record keeping of transfers when necessary to assist law enforcement or financial regulatory authorities; or
(e) ensuring compliance with orders or judgments in judicial or administrative proceedings.

Thus, the provisions not only facilitate payments and transfers but also leave room for exceptions, provided that the said restrictions are equitable, non-discriminatory and applied in good faith. In doing so, the signatories therefore send an important signal to investors that the country is investment friendly, yet they also preserve a certain margin of manoeuvre.

Note that while these provisions are not present in all FTAs,[6] provisions with the exact or similar wording can be found in most contemporary FTAs, including the CETA,[7] RCEP,[8] USMCA[9] and agreements between the US and South Korea,[10] Chile[11] and Australia,[12] and Australian agreements with Chile[13] and South Korea.[14]

Payments and transfer facilitation may also be included in trade provisions, although such provisions may not be required when transfers and payments are already liberalised under the investment provisions discussed before.[15] When included, capital flow facilitation is usually structured around two aspects of trade: trade in goods and trade in financial services.

---

[6] There is, for example, no investment chapter in the Korea–EU agreement.
[7] CETA, Article 8.13.
[8] RCEP, Article 10.9.
[9] USMCA, Article 9.9.
[10] KORUS, Article 11.7.
[11] US–Chile FTA, Article 10.8.
[12] AUSFTA, Article 11.8.
[13] Australia–Chile FTA, Article 10.10.
[14] KAFTA, Article 11.8.
[15] For instance, the Chile–US FTA provides for payment and transfers under its investment chapter but not under its trade in services or financial services chapters.

Most provisions aimed at facilitating free payments and transfers in a trade context are governed by a variety of provisions relating to trade in financial services. The first type of provision facilitating capital movements is general and similar to the provisions mentioned previously in the investment context. Article 10.12 (Payments and Transfers) of the CPTPP is a typical provision in this regard, which provides:

1. Each Party shall permit all transfers and payments that relate to the cross-border supply of services to be made freely and without delay into and out of its territory.
2. Each Party shall permit such transfers and payments that relate to the cross-border supply of services to be made in a freely usable currency at the market rate of exchange that prevails at the time of transfer.

Article 10.12(3) then provides that a government 'may prevent or delay a transfer or payment through the equitable, non-discriminatory and good faith application of its laws that relate to' the following:

(a) bankruptcy, insolvency or the protection of the rights of creditors;
(b) issuing, trading or dealing in securities, futures, options or derivatives;
(c) financial reporting or record keeping of transfers when necessary to assist law enforcement or financial regulatory authorities;
(d) criminal or penal offences; or
(e) ensuring compliance with orders or judgments in judicial or administrative proceedings.

Article 10.12 is then 'incorporated into and made a part of' the chapter on financial services by virtue of Article 11.2.2(c) to the extent that cross-border trade in financial services is subject to obligations pursuant to the provisions on cross-border trade contained in Article 11.6.

Other agreements with identical wording or wording to the exact substance include the USMCA, AUSFTA, KAFTA and KORUS.[16] One notable departure is the slightly more restrictive language used in the RCEP, with Article 8.19 providing:

1. Except under the circumstances envisaged in Article 17.15 (Measures to Safeguard the Balance of Payments), a Party shall not apply restrictions on international transfers or payments for current transactions relating to its commitments.

---

[16] See USMCA, Article 15.2 and 17.2.2(b); AUSFTA, Article 10.10(1) and Article 13.1.2(b); KAFTA, Article 7.10 and 8.2(c); KORUS, Article 12.10 and 13.2(c).

2. Nothing in this Chapter shall affect the rights and obligations of a Party as a member of the IMF under the IMF Articles of Agreement, as may be amended, including the use of exchange actions which are in conformity with the IMF Articles of Agreement, as may be amended, provided that the Party shall not impose restrictions on any capital transaction inconsistently with its commitments under this Chapter regarding such transactions, except under Article 17.15 (Measures to Safeguard the Balance of Payments) or on request of the IMF.

The CETA is perhaps an outlier among modern agreements with no provision on payments and transfers included in the trade in services chapter, but with the similar provision in the investment chapter (Article 8.13) being explicitly incorporated into the chapter on financial services (Article 13.2.3).

The second type of provision facilitating capital movements from a trade perspective can be found in the commitments on market access. Such provisions do not permit payments and transfers per se, but rather in the context of financial services permit the cross-border development and establishment of financial institutions capable of operating these transfers and payments (subject to reservations taken as part of the annexes on non-conforming measures). Article 11.5 of the CPTPP provides a typical market access provision:

> No Party shall adopt or maintain with respect to financial institutions of another Party or investors of another Party seeking to establish those institutions, either on the basis of a regional subdivision or on the basis of its entire territory, measures that:
>
> (a) impose limitations on:
>   (i) the number of financial institutions whether in the form of numerical quotas, monopolies, exclusive service suppliers or the requirement of an economic needs test;
>   (ii) the total value of financial service transactions or assets in the form of numerical quotas or the requirement of an economic needs test;
>   (iii) the total number of financial service operations or the total quantity of financial services output expressed in terms of designated numerical units in the form of quotas or the requirement of an economic needs test; or
>   (iv) the total number of natural persons that may be employed in a particular financial service sector or that a financial institution may employ and who are necessary for, and directly related to, the supply of a specific financial service in the form of numerical quotas or the requirement of an economic needs test; or

(b) restrict or require specific types of legal entity or joint venture through which a financial institution may supply a service.[17]

To complement provisions aimed at facilitating the establishment of foreign financial institutions, FTAs regularly also ensure access to payment and clearing systems. Article 11.15 of the CETA provides:

> Under terms and conditions that accord national treatment, each Party shall grant financial institutions of the other Party established in its territory access to payment and clearing systems operated by public entities, and to official funding and refinancing facilities available in the normal course of ordinary business. This Article is not intended to confer access to the Party's lender of last resort facilities.

The third type of provision facilitating capital movements from a trade perspective can be found as part of the signatories' commitments on new financial services. This provision goes beyond permitting the establishment of financial institutions across borders and is aimed at facilitating the development of new financial services provided by non-bank actors. Article 11.7 of the CPTPP provides:

> Each Party shall permit a financial institution of another Party to supply a new financial service that the Party would permit its own financial institutions, in like circumstances, to supply without adopting a law or modifying an existing law. Notwithstanding Article 11.5(b) (Market Access for Financial Institutions), a Party may determine the institutional and juridical form through which the new financial service may be supplied and may require authorisation for the supply of the service. If a Party requires a financial institution to obtain authorisation to supply a new financial service, the Party shall decide within a reasonable period of time whether to issue the authorisation and may refuse the authorisation only for prudential reasons.[18]

Provisions on new financial services are not found in all FTAs, but where they feature are drafted in a general manner as per the above example.

6.2.3 Exclusions and Exceptions

Trade agreements do not only provide for liberalisation; they also allow signatories to make use of built-in exceptions. Such exceptions can be broad or narrowly tailored. This section reviews some of the more

---

[17] See also the provisions on access to clearing systems (11.15) and free establishment of new financial services (11.17). See also USMCA, Article 17.5, 17.15 and 17.7. Similar provisions exist in other modern agreements; see for instance CETA, Article 13.6; KAFTA, Article 8.4.

[18] See also KORUS, Article 13.6; USMCA, Article 17.7.

common and useful exceptions relating to capital flows. Most agreements tend to provide for broader limitations related to financial stability preservation as part of the financial services or exceptions chapters. Again, the exact wording and scope of the provisions take various forms and allow the signatories to take a variety of restrictions.

6.2.3.1 Services Supplied in the Exercise of Governmental Authority and Government Procurement

Similar to the GATS, modern FTAs also contain exclusion clauses for services supplied in the exercise of governmental authority and government procurement. Article 11.2.3 of the CPTPP provides a typical exclusion clause in that it states the financial services chapter shall not apply to measures adopted or maintained by a party relating to activities or services: (1) forming part of a public retirement plan or statutory system of social security or (2) conducted for the account or with the guarantee or using the financial resources of the party, including its public entities. The provision does not apply where a party allows services or activities to be conducted by financial institutions in competition with a public entity or a financial institution.[19] The CPTPP then adds an exception providing that the agreements do not apply to measures taken by any public entity in pursuit of monetary and related credit policies or exchange rate policies.[20] The caveat is that the exclusion does not affect a party's obligations pertaining to performance requirements in the investment chapter, specifically transfers and payments. Whereas some agreements have different eroding and placement – for instance, the EU–Japan EPA contains an exclusion for 'activities conducted by a central bank or a monetary authority or by any other public entity in pursuit of monetary or exchange rate policies'[21] – the effect is the same.

Modern trade agreements also follow the GATS in excluding measures governing the procurement by governmental agencies of services purchased for governmental purposes and not with a view to commercial resale or with a view to use in the supply of services for commercial sale. Some agreements, including the CETA, essentially reproduce Article XIII of the GATS model by excluding government procurement from the application of the provisions governing MFN, MA, NT, cross-border

---

[19] See also USMCA, Article 13.2.5; CETA, Article 13.2.5.
[20] CPTPP, Article 11.11.2. See also USMCA, Article 17.11.2; CETA, Article 13.17.1; Korea–EU FTA, Article 7.44(2).
[21] EU–Japan EPA, Article 8.58.2(a).

supply of financial services, senior management and board of directors and performance requirements, with the exclusion being services purchased for governmental purposes and not with a view to commercial resale.[22] Other agreements include a more direct exclusion that exempts 'government procurement of financial services' from the scope of application of the discipline on trade in financial services.[23]

6.2.3.2 Balance of Payments

One common exception is for balance of payment (BoP) difficulties. The USMCA provides a comprehensive BoP provision in the form of Article 32.4 (Temporary Safeguard Measures), which provides the following:

2. This Agreement does not prevent a Party from adopting or maintaining a restrictive measure with regard to payments or transfers for current account transactions in the event of serious balance of payments and external financial difficulties or threats thereof.
3. This Agreement does not prevent a Party from adopting or maintaining a restrictive measure with regard to payments or transfers relating to the movements of capital:
   (a) in the event of serious balance of payments and external financial difficulties or threats thereof; or
   (b) if, in exceptional circumstances, payments or transfers relating to capital movements cause or threaten to cause serious difficulties for macroeconomic management.

The provision goes on to provide that measures taken must not be inconsistent with the principles of most favoured nation and national treatment or with the expropriation provision of the investment chapter of the agreement, and must be consistent with the Articles of Agreement of the IMF; avoid unnecessary damage to the commercial, economic, and financial interests of another Party and not exceed those necessary to deal with the circumstances described in paragraph.[24] The BoP restrictions shall not be used to avoid necessary macroeconomic adjustment, must be 'temporary and be phased out progressively as the situations specified in paragraph 2 or 3 improve' and shall not exceed 12 months in duration, with the possibility of a further one-year

---

[22] CETA, Article 13.10.7(a)–(b).
[23] CPTPP, Article 11.2.4; USMCA, Article 17.2.4.
[24] USMCA, Article 32.4.4.

6.2 TYPICAL PROVISIONS INCLUDED IN FREE TRADE AGREEMENTS

extension in exceptional circumstances. Sub-paragraph (e) deals with restrictions on capital outflows, stating that such restrictions:

> [shall] not interfere with investors' ability to earn a market rate of return in the territory of the restricting Party on assets invested in the territory of the restricting Party by an investor of a Party that are restricted from being transferred out of the territory of the restricting Party.

Moreover, the BoP restrictions must be submitted to the IMF for review and approval under Article VIII of the Articles of Agreement of the IMF.

Article 29.3 of the CPTPP provides for an almost verbatim BoP provision, with the only difference being the length of the initial restriction is eighteen months as opposed to one year. The CETA also provides for a comprehensive exception for BoP difficulties, with Article 28.5.1 stating that where a party 'experiences serious balance-of-payments or external financial difficulties, or threat thereof, it may adopt or maintain restrictive measures with regard to capital movements or payments, including transfers'. The safeguard must be taken on an MFN basis; be consistent with the IMF's Articles of Agreement; avoid unnecessary damage to the commercial, economic and financial interests of a Party and be temporary and phased out progressively as the situation improves and shall not exceed 180 days (with the possibility of a further period of 180 days in exceptional circumstances).[25] Sub-paragraph 4 deals with trade in services and allows for the adoption of restrictive measures in order to safeguard its balance of payments or external financial position so long as the restriction is taken in accordance with the GATS. Sub-paragraph 7 establishes a link with the IMF, as it requires the parties to 'accept all findings of statistical and other facts presented by the [IMF] relating to foreign exchange, monetary reserves, balance-of-payments, and their conclusions shall be based on the assessment by the IMF of the balance-of-payments and the external financial situation of the Party concerned'.

The RCEP contains a similar but less detailed BoP exception, with Article 17.15 allowing parties to adopt or maintain restrictions on trade in services on which it has undertaken commitments (including on payments or transfers for transactions related to such commitments) and to adopt or maintain restrictions on payments or transfers related to covered investments 'where a party is in serious balance of payments and external financial difficulties or under threat thereof, or where, in exceptional circumstances, payments or transfers relating to capital movements cause

---

[25] CPTPP, Article 28.5.2.

or threaten to cause serious difficulties for macroeconomic management'. Such restrictions must be consistent with the IMF Articles of Agreement; avoid unnecessary damage to the commercial, economic and financial interests of any other party; not exceed those necessary to deal with the difficulties; be temporary and be phased out progressively as the situation improves (note there is no precise temporal limitation) and be applied on an MFN basis to parties to the RCEP.[26]

Note that while a BoP exception is now commonplace in FTAs, the inclusion of such a clause is not universal and is not included in many FTAs. In particular, numerous US FTAs, including the AUSFTA and KORUS, do not contain a BoP exception.

6.2.3.3 Prudential Exception

Almost all the FTAs covering financial services notified to the WTO contain a prudential exception.[27] Of particular interest to commentators is the scope for the signatories to take CFMs for prudential reasons, and how such clauses are drafted.

A large percentage of prudential exceptions are modelled on and closely resemble paragraph 2(a) of the GATS Annex on Financial Services. Such agreements list two groups of measures covered: those intended for 'the protection of investors, depositors, policy holders or persons to whom a fiduciary duty is owed by a financial service supplier' and those intended 'to ensure the integrity and the stability of the financial system as a whole'. As a reminder, the clause reads in full:

> Notwithstanding any other provisions of the Agreement, a Member shall not be prevented from taking measures for prudential reasons, including for the protection of investors, depositors, policy holders or persons to whom a fiduciary duty is owed by a financial service supplier, or to ensure the integrity and stability of the financial system. Where such measures do not conform with the provisions of the Agreement, they shall not be used as a means of avoiding the Member's commitments or obligations under the Agreement.

This is not really an exception but rather a clause that excludes the application of other provisions of the agreement.

Another grouping of FTAs (often including a party or parties from Central America) are modelled on or replicate the text of Article 1410(1)

---

[26] RCEP, Article 17.15.3.

[27] Those that do not contain a prudential exception are often special cases, such as the European Economic Area (between the EU and EFTA), Iceland–Faroe Islands, China–Hong Kong and China–Macau.

6.2 TYPICAL PROVISIONS INCLUDED IN FREE TRADE AGREEMENTS 135

of the NAFTA, which arguably broadens the application of the clause as it shifts the GATS language of 'a Member shall not be prevented from taking measures' to '[n]othing in this Part shall be construed to prevent a Party from adopting or maintaining reasonable measures for prudential reasons'. The provision then goes on to provide three types of measures:

(a) the protection of investors, depositors, financial market participants, policyholders, policy claimants, or persons to whom a fiduciary duty is owed by a financial institution or cross-border financial service provider;
(b) the maintenance of the safety, soundness, integrity or financial responsibility of financial institutions or cross-border financial service providers; and
(c) ensuring the integrity and stability of a Party's financial system.

More recent US FTAs are slightly broader in that they cover not only provisions on financial service but also telecommunications, e-commerce and investment. These agreements also move the essence of point (b) to a footnote. US FTAs are likewise clauses that exclude the application of other provisions of the agreement rather than an exception.

Interestingly, FTAs negotiated by EFTA tend to resemble the NAFTA-era clause but add a 'necessity test' in a second paragraph which states: 'These measures shall not be more burdensome than necessary to achieve their aim, and shall not discriminate against financial service suppliers of another Party in comparison to its own like financial service suppliers'.[28] EFTA agreements are also unique, as some replicate the chapeau of Article XIV of the GATS while others contain a clause similar to the second sentence of paragraph 2(a) of the Annex on Financial Services and still others contain a national treatment clause in the exception or a best endeavours clause to ensure compliance with international standards. All of these variations appear in EFTA agreements with Ukraine and Central America (Panama and Costa Rico), as well as in the FTA between Ukraine and Montenegro. In this regard, the EFTA FTAs are clearly exceptions and not simply articles that exclude the application of other provisions. This is also the case with some FTAs negotiated by the EU, which also include a necessity test and national treatment obligation,[29] as well as the East African Community which requires the party making use of the prudential clause to 'furnish proof that the action was appropriate, reasonable and justified'.[30]

---

[28] See EFTA FTAs with Mexico, Singapore, Korea, Colombia, Central America, Ukraine and Montenegro.
[29] See for instance EU FTAs with Georgia and Moldova (Article 91).
[30] East African Community, Article 25.

Other agreements blend elements of exception clauses and those that exclude the application of other provisions. An example of such a hybrid clause can be seen in Article 3(1) of the Annex on Financial Services of the ASEAN–Australia–New Zealand FTA:

> Notwithstanding any other provision of this Agreement, a Party shall not be prevented from taking measures for prudential reasons, including for the protection of investors, depositors, policy holders or persons to whom a fiduciary duty is owed by a financial service supplier, or to ensure the integrity and stability of the financial system or to ensure the stability of the exchange rate[7] subject to the following:
>
> (a) where such measures do not conform with the provisions of this Agreement, they shall not be used as a means of avoiding the Party's commitments or obligations under this Agreement;
> (b) for measures to ensure the stability of the exchange rate such measures shall be no more than necessary and phased out when conditions no longer justify their institution or maintenance; and
> (c) for measures to ensure the stability of the exchange rate such measures shall be applied on a most-favoured-nation basis.

> [7] The measures to ensure the stability of the exchange rate shall not be adopted or maintained for the purpose of protecting a particular sector.

While most of this article allows the parties to deviate from their commitments ('shall not be prevented'), invocation of the article for the purposes of stability of exchange rate contains a necessity test and MFN obligation, while footnote 7 prohibits measures taken to protect a particular sector.

The CPTPP adopts a slight variation of the typical US model, with Article 11.11 providing:

> a Party shall not be prevented from adopting or maintaining measures for prudential reasons, including for the protection of investors, depositors, policy holders, or persons to whom a fiduciary duty is owed by a financial institution or cross-border financial service supplier, or to ensure the integrity and stability of the financial system. Where such measures do not conform with the provisions of this Agreement referred to in this paragraph, they shall not be used as a means of avoiding the Party's commitments or obligations under such provisions.

The clause then goes on to state that nothing in the relevant chapters of the agreement 'shall apply to non-discriminatory measures of general application taken by any public entity in pursuit of monetary and related credit policies or exchange rate policies' and that:

> a party may prevent or limit transfers by a financial institution or cross-border financial service supplier to, or for the benefit of, an affiliate of or person related to such institution or supplier, through the equitable, non-discriminatory, and good faith application of measures relating to maintenance of the safety, soundness, integrity, or financial responsibility of financial institutions or cross-border financial service suppliers. This paragraph does not prejudice any other provision of this Agreement that permits a Party to restrict transfers.[31]

In a footnote, the CPTPP also expressly states that 'the term "prudential reasons" includes the maintenance of the safety, soundness, integrity or financial responsibility of individual financial service suppliers as well as the safety, and financial and operational integrity of payment and clearing systems'.[32]

An exact or substantially similar clause appears in the USMCA (Article 17.11), KORUS (Article 13.10), Korea–EU FTA (Article 8.3) and many others. In contrast, the RCEP contains a stand-alone provision on prudential measures [Annex 8A (Article 4)]. Meanwhile, the CETA agreement provides two stability-related exception clauses. One under the Exceptions chapter allows generally restrictive measures on capital movements 'Where, in exceptional circumstances, capital movements and payments, including transfers, cause or threaten to cause serious difficulties for the operation of the economic and monetary union of the European Union' for a period not exceeding 180 days,[33] with the other being a stand-alone provision in the Financial Services chapter allowing prudential measures be taken to preserve depositors, suppliers and the financial system as a whole.[34]

The CETA goes even further with Annex 13-C establishing a 'dialogue on the regulation of the financial services sector ... based on the principles and prudential standards agreed at multilateral level'. Perhaps more importantly, Annex 13-B provides further details and establishes that prudential measures are acceptable where the parties act in good faith and are in line with a list of non-exhaustive 'High-Level Principles', which include a right of each party to 'determine its own appropriate level of prudential regulation ... and enforce measures that provide a higher level

---

[31] See also KORUS, Article 13.10.
[32] KORUS, Article 7.38, footnote 40. See also Chile–US FTA, footnote 3 of Chapter 12.
[33] CETA, Article 28.4.
[34] CETA, Article 13.16.

of prudential protection than those set out in common international prudential commitments'.[35] The article goes on to provide that '[r]elevant considerations in determining whether a measure meets the requirements of Article 13.16.1 include the extent to which a measure may be required by the urgency of the situation and the information available to the party at the time when the measure was adopted',[36] and also states a measure is deemed to meet the requirements of Article 13.16.1 if it has a prudential objective and is not so severe in light of its purpose that it is manifestly disproportionate to the attainment of its objective so long as it is a disguised restriction on foreign investment or an arbitrary or unjustifiable discrimination between investors in like situations.[37] The last principle is that a non-manifestly disproportionate measure should be in line with international prudential commitments that are common to the parties and taken in pursuance of the resolution of a financial institution that is no longer viable or likely to be no longer viable, in pursuance of the recovery of a financial institution or the management of a financial institution under stress; or in pursuance of the preservation or the restoration of financial stability, in response to a system-wide financial crisis.[38]

There is limited jurisprudence on the prudential exception in FTAs, with the only case being a 2006 arbitral award under Chapter 11 of the NAFTA.[39] Even there, the tribunal's discussion of the prudential exception [Article 1410(1)] in *Fireman's Fund v Mexico* can be viewed as *obiter dictum*, as the measures at issue were not found to violate the treaty's expropriation clause. Nevertheless, they clarified that a measure that results in discrimination between a national and foreign service suppliers could still be considered reasonable under Article 1410(1):

> The Tribunal, noting that the exception applies to all provisions of Part Five ('Investments, Services and Related Matters') of the NAFTA applicable to Financial Services, including the National Treatment article (Article 1405), concludes that Article 1410(1) permits reasonable measures of a prudential character even if their effect (as contrasted with their motive or intent) is discriminatory. The Tribunal rejects the contention that a measure discriminatory in effect is *eo ipso* unreasonable.[40]

---

[35] CETA, Annex 13-B s8(a).
[36] Ibid. s8(b).
[37] Ibid. s8(d).
[38] Ibid. s8(e).
[39] *Fireman's Fund Insurance Company v Mexico* (17 July 2006) ICSID Case No. ARB(AF)/02/01, Award.
[40] Ibid. para. 162.

The tribunal then proceeded to confirm that the prudential exception contained two objectives: (1) it establishes a 'regulatory prerogative' to ensure the integrity of the financial system, and (2) it prevents abuses of such prerogative through arbitrary measures and the like.[41] In so doing, the tribunal found that the prudential exception provides the government with a substantial degree of regulatory autonomy but that 'backhanded avoidance' of obligations would not be permitted.[42] Despite the heading of the article calling it an 'exception', it is clear from the tribunal's analysis that in fact the prudential clause operates differently and that the only condition for its use is that the adopted prudential measure must be 'reasonable'. Therefore, according to the tribunal's analysis, 'only measures that are manifestly not linked with a prudential objective and lead to the backhanded avoidance of obligations or commitments can be targeted', meaning evaluations of cost and benefits and potential less restrictive measures are not to be undertaken.[43]

While the tribunal's interpretation and distinction between 'backhandedness' and 'discrimination' is not entirely clear, the issue was not further discussed and did not prove determinative, given that the measures were not found to be an expropriation. The case is nevertheless instructive as to the interpretation of prudential exception clauses. Cantore analyses the dispute at length and finds that despite the differences in structure and wording of Article 1410(1) of the NAFTA with paragraph 2(a) of the GATS Annex on Financial Services, 'the provision does not substantially differ'.[44] Cantore continues:

> The function performed by the provision is, substantially, that of giving regulators a wide margin of discretion in addressing micro and macroprudential concerns. In particular, the very idea of 'integrity and stability' of the financial system is, in and of itself, wide and leaves space for domestic sovereignty with regard to the policy choices regulators consider appropriate.[45]

This is the case with all the modern prudential exception clauses. While drafted differently, and even while the nature of the clauses differ, in many respects all modern clauses advance from and add clarity to paragraph 2(a) of the Annex on Financial Services contained in the GATS.

---

[41] Ibid. paras. 163–65.
[42] Carlo M. Cantore, *The Prudential Carve-Out for Financial Services: Rationale and Practice in the GATS and Preferential Trade Agreements* (Cambridge University Press 2018) 125–26.
[43] Ibid. 129.
[44] Ibid. 126.
[45] Ibid.

6.2.3.4 Monetary Policy Exclusions

In addition to the standard carve-out for monetary and related credit policies or exchange rate policies, a select number of agreements further elaborate upon or expand the scope of the exclusion. For instance, the Korea–EU FTA entitles the parties to restrict capital movements when these 'cause or threaten to cause serious difficulties for the operation of monetary policy or exchange rate policy' – which in a footnote is associated with, amongst others, BoP issues. Meanwhile, the KORUS notes that the agreement shall not prevent Korea from taking measures under its Foreign Exchange Transactions Act as long as various fairness requirements are respected – temporary, avoidance of unnecessary damage, national treatment, MFN standards and so on. In a more comprehensive manner, Annex 10-C of the Chile–Australia FTA highlights Chile's sovereignty on payments and transfers.

6.2.3.5 Limiting Investment Disputes in Financial Services

In certain agreements, regulatory space may be preserved by way of specific provisions aimed at limiting the possibility of investment disputes grounded on payments and transfer limitation measures. Indeed, an increasingly common provision often entitled 'Investment disputes in financial services' provides for the creation of a joint committee composed of the financial regulators of both signatories prior to any investor-state dispute involving financial stability concerns. The committees, once constituted, can make a joint determination acknowledging that the complex financial situation of the responding party constitutes 'a valid defence to the claim', a decision which shall be binding on the ISDS tribunal, and any decision or award issued by the tribunal must be consistent with that determination.[46]

In essence, while ISDS applies to investors in the financial services sector, not only for disputes arising from the investment chapter but also inconsistencies with the national treatment and MFN obligations of the chapter on financial services, these provisions serve as a filter mechanism for disputes relating to measures allegedly taken for prudential reasons. Article 13.21 of the CETA, read together with Annex 13-B, is a useful model of such a provision, and sets out that if the Financial Services Committee or the CETA Trade Committee decides that the measures at issue come within the scope of the prudential exception, the decision is not just

---

[46] See for instance CPTPP, Article 11.22; USMCA, Article 17.11 and Annex 17-C; KORUS, Article 13.19.

binding on an ISDS tribunal but even further the investor is deemed to have withdrawn its claim, and the ISDS proceedings will be discontinued.

6.3 Conclusions

Modern trade agreements encourage the liberalisation of cross-border trade in financial services but provide sufficient scope for regulatory interference in times of financial instability or threats thereof. Properly drafted, FTAs have the ability to assist in preserving the ability of governments to control capital flows and regulate for prudential reasons in times of financial and monetary duress. In addition to virtually mimicking or advancing upon the GATS model of providing for a regulatory carve-out for prudential measures in order to safeguard financial stability, one noteworthy innovation is to allow governments to insert themselves into the dispute settlement process via a binding joint declaration on investment disputes involving financial services. In this respect, governments are assured that an arbitral tribunal cannot ignore or even downplay measures taken to forestall or protect against legitimate risks to financial stability. Modern agreements, therefore, promote liberalisation of the financial services sector while at the same time recognising and protecting the long-standing right of governments to regulate in good faith for the sake of domestic, regional and international financial and monetary stability. With the addition of proper safeguards, FTAs neither constrain nor hamper governments in taking measures to promote financial and monetary stability or prevent financial crisis.

7

International Investment Agreements

Having clarified how capital movements are regulated at the multilateral level and explained how the multilateral framework translates to the bilateral and regional levels through FTAs, we now turn to the third level of regulation made available in an international law context – international investment agreements (IIAs).[1] IIAs are critical to capital movements and capital flows in that they create a specific legal framework with substantive provisions aimed at protecting and promoting cross-border investors and investment. With nearly three thousand signed IIAs, it is impossible to provide an exhaustive analysis of treaty practice. Like the previous chapter, this chapter refers extensively to the four representative comprehensive treaties – CPTPP, USMCA, RCEP and CETA. Where applicable, reference is made to other agreements, and in particular agreements negotiated by developing countries.

Most IIAs include standards such as national treatment, most favoured nation, fair and equitable treatment (FET) and safeguards against expropriation. These agreements also typically contain a clause ensuring that foreign investors should be able to enjoy the benefit of their investment at all times, which usually translates into provisions guaranteeing the free transfers of capital and profits by the investors. While the concept differs from the 'Payments and Transfers' term used in the previous chapter, the point is the same, and ultimately the idea of facilitating the flow of cross-border capital movements is found in services chapters of FTAs and in IIAs.

This chapter, however, finds that modern IIAs contain a wide range of safeguards and limitations which effectively allow host governments to put CFMs into place in circumstances of financial instability and financial duress. Moreover, the chapter details how arbitral tribunals have fairly narrowly interpreted state obligations such as the transfers clause and given substantial deference to host states when applying exceptions such as prudential measures.

---

[1] The term 'IIA' encompasses both investment chapters contained in comprehensive FTAs as well as freestanding BITs.

As will be demonstrated, treaties are drafted differently, and the language, terms and choices made in drafting the treaty can significantly affect obligations and outcomes. Through extensive coding, this chapter finds that modern treaties involving developed countries contain substantial obligations but also significantly more safeguards and exceptions than treaties negotiated between developing countries. Perhaps counterintuitively, the IIAs with fewer or even no safeguards and exceptions are always negotiated between (unlikely) developing countries. Such treaties do represent a significant risk to governments seeking to implement CFMs. But such risks need not exist, and this chapter demonstrates how they can be substantially mitigated through the use of targeted language, safeguards and exceptions.

7.1 Substantive Protection[2]

7.1.1 What Is an Investment?

IIAs normally apply to investors and investments of the other party to the agreement.[3] The definition of an investment is important, as it determines whether a person or entity is covered under the agreement and therefore whether that investor can bring a claim in ISDS. Simply stated, if there is no investment, there can be no such claim.

Most contemporary IIAs include portfolio investments in employing a broad asset-based definition of an 'investment'. Such is the case with Article 9.1 of the CPTPP, which defines an investment as 'every asset that an investor owns or controls, directly or indirectly, that has the characteristics of an investment, including such characteristics as the commitment of capital or other resources, the expectation of gain or profit, or the assumption of risk'. The article goes on to include a non-exhaustive list of forms that an investment may take, including:

(a) an enterprise;
(b) shares, stock and other forms of equity participation in an enterprise;
(c) bonds, debentures, other debt instruments and loans;
(d) futures, options and other derivatives;

---

[2] Parts of this section are drawn from Bryan Mercurio, 'Safeguarding Public Welfare? Intellectual Property Rights, Health and the Continuing Evolution of Treaty Drafting in International Investment Agreements' (2015) 6 *Journal of International Dispute Settlement* 252–76.
[3] See for instance CPTPP, Article 9.2; USMCA, Article 14.2; CETA, Article 8.2.

(e) turnkey, construction, management, production, concession, revenue-sharing and other similar contracts;
(f) intellectual property rights;
(g) licences, authorisations, permits and similar rights conferred pursuant to the Party's law; and
(h) other tangible or intangible, movable or immovable property, and related property rights, such as leases, mortgages, liens and pledges.

The USMCA (Article 14.1) provides for the same definition of an investment while RCEP (Article 10.1) and CETA (Article 8.1) provide for substantially similar definitions Furthermore, all of the treaties limit coverage to covered investments. Article 9.1 of the CPTPP and Article 4.1 of the USMCA define a covered investment as 'an investment in its territory of an investor of another Party in existence as of the date of entry into force of this Agreement for those Parties or established, acquired, or expanded thereafter'.

The CETA and RCEP offer more nuanced definitions, with the CETA (Article 8.1) covering investments (a) in its territory, (b) made in accordance with the applicable law at the time the investment is made, (c) directly or indirectly owned or controlled by an investor of the other Party and (d) existing on the date of entry into force of the Agreement, or made or acquired thereafter. Meanwhile, the RCEP (Article 10.1) defines a covered investment as 'an investment in its territory of an investor of another Party in existence as of the date of entry into force of this Agreement or established, acquired, or expanded thereafter, and which, where applicable, has been admitted by the host Party, subject to its relevant laws, regulations, and policies'. Three footnotes further clarify that for Malaysia and Thailand protection is only accorded to covered investments which, where applicable, have been specifically approved in writing for protection by their respective competent authorities in accordance with their respective laws, regulations and policies. For Cambodia, Indonesia and Vietnam, 'has been admitted' means 'has been specifically registered or approved in writing, as the case may be'. Finally, the term 'policies' refers to policies affecting an investment that are endorsed and announced by the government of a Party in a written form and made publicly available in a written form.

The inclusion of portfolio investment, including short-term debt and equity – the very type of 'hot money' that tends to be unstable and swiftly withdrawn in times of crisis – coupled with the free transfers clause (detailed below) could potentially serve as a restriction to the use of CFMs.

It should be noted, however, that some agreements exclude portfolio investment from the scope of the definition.[4]

In contrast to the more expansive asset-based definition of investment, India's Model BIT 2016 utilises an enterprise-based definition: 'investment means an enterprise in the Host State, constituted, organised and operated in compliance with the Law of the Host State and owned or controlled in good faith by an Investor: (i) in accordance with this Treaty; and (ii) that is at all times in compliance with the [certain] obligations … of this Treaty'.

Article 1.3 of the Morocco–Nigeria BIT provides an even narrower enterprise-based definition of investment which explicitly excludes portfolio investment:

> Investment means an enterprise within the territory of one State established, acquired, expanded or operated, in good faith, by an investor of the other State in accordance with law of the Party in whose territory the investment is made taken together with the asset of the enterprise which contribute sustainable development of that Party and has the characteristics of an investment involving a commitment of capital or other similar resources, pending profit, risk-taking and certain duration. An enterprise will possess the following assets:
>
> a) Shares, stocks, debentures and other instruments of the enterprise or another enterprise;
> b) A debt security of another enterprise;
> c) Loans to an enterprise;
> d) Movable or immovable property and other property rights such as mortgages, liens or pledges;
> e) Claims to money or to any performance under contract having a financial value;
> f) Copyrights and intellectual property rights such as patents, trademarks, industrial designs and trade names, to the extent they are recognized under the law of the Host State;
> g) Rights conferred by law or under contract, including licenses to cultivate, extract or exploit natural resources;
>
> For greater certainty, Investment does not include … Portfolio investments …

While often an overlooked aspect of IIAs, the definition of an investor and an investment can substantially shape the scope of potential liability of the substantive obligations of the underlying treaty.

---

[4] Article 45, EFTA–Mexico FTA (2000). Interestingly, the US–Canada FTA (1988) excluded portfolio investments but was superseded by Article 1139 of the NAFTA, which includes portfolio investment.

7.1.2 Substantive Obligations

7.1.2.1 Payments and Transfers

Customary international law does not require states to permit foreign investors to freely transfer funds into and out of a country. Such transfers are, of course, a 'crucial precondition' for making an investment and a 'key condition for the proper operation' of an investment.[5] Kolo and Walde state:

> the essence of making an investment is to make profits and distribute the same to its shareholders, who might reside in its home country or in several countries. Repatriation of funds might also be needed by the foreign investor for other purposes such as to service external loans, pay license fees and royalties, purchase raw materials and machinery for production and pay for other services. These are critical for the success of an investment.[6]

Transfers are thus not only of vital importance to investors but a core feature of investment treaties.[7] Unsurprisingly, therefore, provisions relating to the freedom of payments and transfers are a common feature of IIAs, as well as other multilateral and regional agreements.[8] The inclusion of a transfers clause can even be viewed as essential to the operation of an IIA, as without such a clause 'the requirement to pay compensation for the violation of other substantive treatment obligations [risks becoming]

---

[5] August Reinish and Christophe Schreuer, *International Protection of Investments* (Cambridge University Press 2020) 978; UNCTAD, *Bilateral Investment Treaties 1995–2006: Trends in Investment Treaty Rulemaking*, UNCTAD/ITE/IIT/2006/5 (United Nations 2007) 56.

[6] Abba Kolo and Thomas Wälde, 'Capital Transfer Restrictions under Modern Investment Treaties', in August Reinisch (ed), *Standards of Investment Protection* (Oxford University Press, 2007) 213–14.

[7] Article 4 of the first IIA, the Germany–Pakistan BIT (1959), contains a transfers clause.

[8] See Treaty on the Functioning of the European Union, Article 63(1) ('Within the framework of the provisions set out in this Chapter, all restrictions on the movement of capital between Member States and between Member States and third countries shall be prohibited'.); Code of Liberalisation of Capital Movements [OECD/C(61)96], adopted by the Council on 12th December, 1961, as amended, Article 1(a) OECD Code on Liberalisation of Capital Movements 1961 ('Members shall progressively abolish between one another … restrictions on movements of capital to the extent necessary for effective economic co-operation'.). Recall also that Article VIII, Section 2(a) of the IMF Articles of Agreement contains a general prohibition on restrictions to 'current international transactions', although Article VI, Section 3 permits 'necessary' restrictions on capital transfers so long as they do not unduly delay current transactions. On the divide between current and capital restrictions, see *Continental Casualty v Argentine Republic*, ARB/03/9, Award (ICSID 2008) para. 234.

nugatory, much like the lack of a dispute settlement clause'.[9] In drafting such clauses, however, states must balance investor interests with the legitimate right to control the inflow and outflow of capital.

Transfer provisions in IIAs are therefore not uniform, but the provision usually takes one of three forms: absolute freedom to transfer, transfers subject to the host state's law or guaranteed transfers subject to necessary measures taken in times of crisis.[10] Few modern treaties contain the absolute freedom to transfer – and even those that do actually provide for some form of exception (such as an essential security interest)[11] – or make transfers subject to the host state's laws.[12] The majority, therefore, provide for guaranteed transfers subject to necessary measures taken in times of crisis.

The USMCA is an example of a typical agreement. Article 4.9(1) of the USMCA provides that each Party shall permit all transfers related to an investment to be made freely – and to be made in a freely usable currency at the market rate of exchange prevailing at the time of transfer – and without delay into and out of its territory. The provision sets out that such transfers include (a) contributions to capital; (b) profits, dividends, interest, capital gains, royalty payments, management fees, technical assistance and other fees; (c) proceeds from the sale of all or any part of the covered investment or from the partial or complete liquidation of the covered investment; (d) payments made under a contract entered into by the investor, or the covered investment, including payments made pursuant to a loan agreement or employment contract and (e) payments made pursuant to Article 14.7 (Treatment in Case of Armed Conflict or Civil Strife) and Article 14.8 (Expropriation and Compensation).

Article 14.9(5) provides for exceptions whereby a Party 'may prevent or delay a transfer through the equitable, non-discriminatory, and good

---

[9] Micheal Waibel, 'BIT by BIT: The Silent Liberalisation of the Capital Account', in Christina Binder, Ursula Kriebaum, August Reinisch and Stephan Wittich (eds), *International Investment Law for the Twenty-first Century: Essays in Honour of Christoph Schreuer* (Oxford University Press 2009) 499.

[10] See generally Abba Kolo and Thomas Walde, 'Economic Crisis, Capital Transfer Restrictions and Investor Protection under Modern Investment Treaties' (2008) 3(2) *Capital Markets Law Journal* 154.

[11] See Energy Charter Treaty, Article 14 (transfers) and Article 24(3) (exception in the form of an essential security interest).

[12] In this regard, the state retains the discretion to modify its domestic laws and therefore investors do not have much protection under the clause. Some Chinese treaties make transfers subject to 'domestic laws and regulations'. See for instance China–Botswana BIT (2000), Article 6(1); China–Djibouti BIT (2000), Article 6(1). Such wording also appears in other treaties. See for instance Korea–Malaysia BIT (1988), Article 7(1).

faith application of its laws relating to: (a) bankruptcy, insolvency, or the protection of the rights of creditors; (b) issuing, trading, or dealing in securities or derivatives; (c) criminal or penal offenses; (d) financial reporting or record keeping of transfers when necessary to assist law enforcement or financial regulatory authorities; or (e) ensuring compliance with orders or judgments in judicial or administrative proceedings'.

The CPTPP (Article 9.9), CETA (Article 8.13) and RCEP (Article 10.9) each contain a substantially similar provision. The RCEP is unique, however, in that it directly links the free transfer clause with the IMF Articles.

> Nothing in this Chapter shall affect the rights and obligations of a Party as a member of the IMF under the IMF Articles of Agreement as may be amended, including the use of exchange actions which are in conformity with the IMF Articles of Agreement as may be amended, provided that the Party shall not impose restrictions on any capital transactions inconsistently with the obligations under this Chapter regarding such transactions, except under Article 17.15 (Measures to Safeguard the Balance of Payments) or on request of the IMF.

Other slight differences exist between and among treaties. Transfer clauses can explicitly cover only outbound transfers, contain an exhaustive list of the types of transfers covered, set out differing time periods to effectuate transfers and use different ways to establish the types of currencies and exchange rates used for the transfers.[13] IIAs differ more substantially in the use of exceptions to the transfers clause. While the exceptions listed above are common, another common exception is in the form of non-precluded measures (NPMs), which allow a party to take measures 'it considers necessary' to protect its 'essential security interests'. Such provisions are often 'self-judging', meaning a party can take measures it deems necessary to protect essential security interests, with the only caveat being that the measures be taken in good faith. The transfers clause is also subject to other exceptions, such as for BoP or prudential reasons. These and other exceptions will be further explored below.

7.1.2.2 National Treatment

National Treatment provisions are fairly standard and straightforward. The USMCA (Article 14.4), CPTPP (Article 9.4), CETA (Article 8.6) and RCEP (Article 10.3) all contain substantially similar provisions requiring a party to accord to investors and covered investments no less favourable treatment than that it accords, in 'like circumstances', to its own

---

[13] See Reinish and Schreuer (n 5) 981–86.

investors or investments with respect to the establishment, acquisition, expansion, management, conduct, operation and sale or other disposition of investments in its territory. All of the abovementioned treaties except for the CETA then clarify that whether treatment is accorded in 'like circumstances' depends on the totality of the circumstances, including whether the relevant treatment distinguishes between investors or investments on the basis of legitimate public welfare objectives.

It is important to note that all four agreements provide National Treatment in the 'establishment' of an investment and in so doing provide pre-entry market access rights for investors under the respective treaties. While the use of certain CFMs – including common controls such as taxes and limits on capital inflows and outflows, unremunerated reserve requirements and minimum stay requirements – could very well run counter to the National Treatment obligation for having a discriminatory impact on foreign investors, the risk is even greater in treaties that include pre-establishment rights. The inclusion of pre-establishment rights is certainly not the norm, but such rights are appearing in most modern treaties.

The IMF has stated that CFMs should not discriminate on the basis of residency but on currency,[14] but this may not be possible, as certain measures inherently discriminate between residents and non-residents. A possible way to escape liability, however, would be to assert that National Treatment is not relevant because cross-border and domestic capital flows are not 'like' because they are covered by different regulatory regimes in the host state.[15] In *Grand River Enterprises Six Nations Ltd. v USA*, the US recognised such a distinction based on differences in the applicable regulatory regimes.[16]

> ...simply being in the same economic sector or selling the same product is not sufficient to demonstrate 'like circumstances' under Article1102. Particularly in a highly regulated industry, a simple comparison between investments in the same business or economic sector, without additional analysis, may sweep in enterprises that are not in fact appropriate

---

[14] IMF, 'The Liberalization and Management of Capital Flows: An Institutional View' (14 November 2012).
[15] *United Parcel Service of America Inc. v Government of Canada*, UNCITRAL 46 ILM 922 (24 May 2007) paras. 117–18.
[16] *Grand River Enterprises Six Nations Ltd. v United States of America*, UNCITRAL (Rejoinder of United States) (13 May 2009) 62–65 (arguing the claimant was 'like' other tobacco product manufacturers that did not sign a Master Settlement Agreement (MSA) but not 'like' those tobacco product manufacturers that did sign the MSA).

comparators under a like circumstances analysis. Such analysis should also consider regulatory distinctions drawn within the industry, including distinctions drawn by the challenged measures at issue.[17]

The US, along with Canada, likewise stated in a declaration submitted during the Final Act of the Energy Charter Treaty Conference in 1994:

> Legitimate policy objectives may justify differential treatment of foreign Investors or their Investments in order to reflect a dissimilarity of relevant circumstances between those Investors and Investments and their domestic counterparts. For example, the objective of ensuring the integrity of a country's financial system would justify reasonable prudential measures with respect to foreign Investors or Investments, where such measures would be unnecessary to ensure the attainment of the same objectives insofar as domestic Investors or Investments are concerned. Those foreign Investors or their Investments would thus not be 'in similar circumstances' to domestic Investors or their Investments.[18]

The case is not open and shut, therefore, and it would be for the claimant to establish discrimination based on foreign origin and discriminatory impact.

7.1.2.3 Fair and Equitable Treatment

The guarantee of FET is a standard, if contentious, clause that appears in most IIAs. The typical definition of FET appears modest – 'investments of investors of either Contracting Party shall at all times be accorded fair and equitable treatment [...] in the territory of the other Contracting Party'[19] – yet numerous arbitral tribunals have revealed the complexity behind such a seemingly simplistic obligation.[20] Tribunals generally tend to avoid a precise

---

[17] Ibid. at para. 62 (footnotes omitted).
[18] Consolidated Energy Charter Treaty (17 December 1994), Article 10, 2080 U.N.T.S. 95.
[19] Article 2.2 of the Australia–Hong Kong BIT provides a typical example of the provision: 'Investments and returns of investors of each Contracting Party shall at all times be accorded fair and equitable treatment and shall enjoy full protection and security in the area of the other Contracting Party. Neither Contracting Party shall, without prejudice to its laws, in any way impair by unreasonable or discriminatory measures the management, maintenance, use, enjoyment or disposal of investments in its area of investors of the other Contracting Party'.
[20] See, for instance *Total S.A. v Argentine Republic*, ICSID Case No. ARB/04/01, Decision on Liability (27 December, 2010) para. 106. Considering the different ways in which FET may be incorporated into IIAs, the tribunal in *Sempra v Argentina* noted that FET is not a clear and precise standard and instead has evolved through case-by-case determinations. See *Sempra Energy International v Argentine Republic*, ICSID Case No. ARB/02/16, Award (28 September 2007) para. 296. See also *El Paso Energy International Company v Argentine Republic*, ICSID Case No. ARB/03/15, Award (31 October, 2011) para. 338.

standard and instead list examples of behaviour that violates the standard.²¹ For instance, the arbitral tribunal in *Waste Management v Mexico* held that conduct violating FET is defined as the following:

> Grossly unfair, unjust or idiosyncratic, is discriminatory and exposes the claimant to sectional or racial prejudice, or involves a lack of due process leading to an outcome which offends judicial propriety-as might be the case with a manifest failure of natural justice in judicial proceedings or a complete lack of transparency and candor in an administrative process. In applying this standard it is relevant that the treatment is in breach of representations made by the host State which were reasonably relied on by the claimant.²²

Likewise, the arbitral tribunal in *Thunderbird* stated that a violation of FET requires conduct which 'cannot be rationally supported by recourse to a legitimate and otherwise non-discriminatory public policy goal'.²³

Furthermore, tribunals have found that in order to meet the requirements of FET, the standard must be applied in a manner that balances the legitimate right of the host country government to exercise its authority in the public interest with the 'legitimate expectations' of the foreign investor.²⁴ In most cases, legitimate expectations has been viewed as regarding the relative fairness, stability and transparency of the local legal regime as opposed to explicit statements or promises made by the host state.

Standing independent from other obligations under the treaty, the scope of the provision can differ widely depending on the text of the provision, and whether it is linked to the minimum standard of treatment for aliens under customary international law. In this regard, the tribunal in *Spyridon Roussalis v Romania* noted that while FET is a standard feature in IIAs, the exact language of such undertakings is not uniform, and the generality of the FET standard beyond general principles (i.e. transparency,

---

[21] The tribunal in *Mondev v United States* simply observed that the minimum standard of treatment 'applies to a wide range of factual situations, whether in peace or in civil strife, and to conduct by a wide range of State organs and agencies'. See *Mondev International Ltd. v United States of America*, ICSID Case No. ARB(AF)/99/2, Award (11 October 2002) para. 95.

[22] *Waste Management, Inc. v United Mexican States*, ICSID Case No. ARB(AF)/00/3, Award, para. 98 (30 April 2004). For analysis of fair and equitable treatment, see Katia Yannaca-Small, 'Fair and Equitable Treatment Standard: Recent Developments', in August Reinisch (ed), *Standards of Investment Protection* (Oxford University Press 2008).

[23] See for instance *International Thunderbird Gaming Corporation v Mexico* (Award), Ad Hoc UNCITRAL Arbitral Tribunal (26 January 2006) para. 194.

[24] *Saluka Investments BV (Netherlands) v The Czech Republic*, UNCITRAL, Partial Award (17 March 2006) paras. 301–2.

good faith) distinguishes it from other specific obligations undertaken by the parties to a BIT.[25] With at least seven major textual variations of treaty drafting, it is clear from the jurisprudence that minimalist language will result in the most expansive obligations and thus impose a high threshold of protection on the state and in favour of investors.

Tying FET to the minimum standard of treatment for aliens under customary international law is one way to reduce the potential for an expansive interpretation. Most IIAs, however, simply provide for FET without any qualification, reference point or standard by which to determine the content of the standard.[26] This leaves the determination and interpretation unstated, and provides wide latitude to an arbitral tribunal to impose its views. On the other hand, IIAs which add clarity and definition to the standard guide the interpretation of the provision and in so doing have more control over the scope of the clause and provide for increased predictability to both investor and state.

Both the USMCA (Article 14.6) and the CPTPP (Article 9.6) require the Parties to 'accord to covered investments treatment in accordance with applicable customary international law principles, including fair and equitable treatment and full protection and security' before setting out that the customary international law minimum standard of treatment of aliens is the standard of treatment to be afforded to covered investments and that these concepts 'do not require treatment in addition to or beyond that which is required by that standard, and do not create additional substantive rights'. Instead, the treaties establish that FET 'includes the obligation not to deny justice in criminal, civil or administrative adjudicatory proceedings in accordance with the principle of due process embodied in the principal legal systems of the world'. Finally, the provisions clarify that breach of another provision of the Agreement, or of a separate international agreement, does not establish that there has been a breach of FET and that the mere fact that a Party takes or fails to take an action that may be inconsistent with an investor's expectations does not constitute a breach of the Article, even if there is loss or damage to the covered investment as a result.[27]

---

[25] *Spyridon Roussalis v Romania*, ICSID Case No. ARB/06/1, Award (1 December 2011) at 318.
[26] Despite the known threat, some governments continue to negotiate in this manner. See for instance China–ASEAN, Article 7.2(a).
[27] Article 10.5 of the RCEP contains a similar but more streamlined version of FET, which is tied to customary international law but does not contain the statement on a Party taking or failing to take action.

7.1 SUBSTANTIVE PROTECTION

The EU's recent IIAs further define and narrow the scope of FET by moving beyond the traditional language employed. More specifically, Article 8.10 (entitled 'Treatment of Investors and of Covered Agreements') of the CETA provides that 'a Party breaches the obligation of fair and equitable treatment ... where a measure or series of measures constitutes':

- Denial of justice in criminal, civil or administrative proceedings;
- Fundamental breach of due process, including a fundamental breach of transparency, in judicial and administrative proceedings;
- Manifest arbitrariness;
- Targeted discrimination on manifestly wrongful grounds, such as gender, race or religious belief;
- Abusive treatment of investors, such as coercion, duress and harassment; or
- A breach of any further elements of the fair and equitable treatment obligation adopted by the Parties in accordance with paragraph 3 of this Article.

Paragraph 3 then provides that the Parties shall regularly, or upon request of a Party, review the content of the obligation to provide fair and equitable treatment. The Committee on Services and Investment may develop recommendations in this regard and submit them to the CETA Trade Committee for decision.

Paragraph 4 then states that when applying the above fair and equitable treatment obligation, a tribunal 'may take into account whether a Party made a specific representation to an investor to induce a covered investment, that created a legitimate expectation, and upon which the investor relied in deciding to make or maintain the covered investment, but that the Party subsequently frustrated'. Paragraphs 6 and 7 then provide for greater certainty, respectively, that a breach of another provision of this Agreement, or of a separate international Agreement, does not establish that there has been a breach of this Article and the fact that a measure breaches domestic law does not, in and of itself, establish a breach of this Article.[28]

The innovations in this provision are striking, as instead of having FET serve as a minimum standard or an 'evolving concept' the Article attempts to set a 'precise and specific standard' of treatment with the inclusion of a closed list of six instances which give rise to a breach of FET. Moreover,

---

[28] For a similar, although slightly less detailed, provision see Article 9.4 of the EU–Singapore FTA.

while the provision includes the notion of an investor's 'legitimate expectations', it is limited to situations where the host state has made a specific representation which was relied up by the investor in making the investment.[29] Finally, it is also noteworthy to mention the explicit statement that a breach of another international agreement does not in and of itself constitute a beach of the FET obligation.[30]

The intent to limit the scope of FET is clear, and the provision is a major step in reclaiming policy space for public welfare measures. While claimants have not had much success in bringing FET claims against CFMSs enacted in the context of an economic crisis,[31] the possibility remains real, and language such as that employed in the CETA represents a real and purposeful innovation in treaty drafting.

7.1.2.4 Expropriation

The typical expropriation clause is based on the view that under customary international law, countries are allowed to expropriate foreign investors, provided four conditions are fulfilled. These conditions are set out in Article 9.8(1) of the CPTPP and Article 14.8(1) of the USMCA:

> No Party shall expropriate or nationalise a covered investment either directly or indirectly through measures equivalent to expropriation o nationalisation (expropriation), except:
>
> (a) for a public purpose;
> (b) in a non-discriminatory manner;

---

[29] In so doing, the CETA is taking a minority view on the proper interpretation of a legitimate expectation, as numerous arbitral tribunals have found it is not about explicit guarantees given to a particular investor but more so about the relative fairness, stability and transparency of the local legal regime. See for instance *International Thunderbird Gaming Corporation* (n 23) paras. 27 and 147; *Occidental Exploration and Production Co. v Ecuador*, London Court of International Arbitration Case No UN 3467, Award (1 July 2004); *CMS Gas Transmission Company v Argentina*, ICSID Case No. ARB/01/8, Award (12 May 2005); *CME Czech Republic BV v Czech Republic*, Ad Hoc UNCITRAL Arbitral Tribunal, Final Award and Separate Opinion (14 March 2003); *GAMI Investments, Inc. v Mexico*, NAFTA/UNCITRAL Tribunal, Final Award (15 November 2004); *Técnicas Medioambientales Tecmed S.A. v the United Mexican States*, ICSID Case No ARB(AF)/00/2, Award (29 May 2003); *MTD Equity Sdn. Bhd. and MTD Chile S. A. v Republic of Chile*, ICSID Case No. ARB/01/7, Award (25 May 2004). See contra, *Glamis Gold, Ltd. v. The United States of America* (Award), UNCITRAL Arbitral Tribunal (8 June 2009), at paras. 620, 766; *National Grid v Argentine Republic* (Award), Ad Hoc UNCITRAL Arbitral Tribunal (3 November 2008), at para. 173.

[30] A similar limitation now appears in numerous modern agreements. See for instance JAEPA, Article 14.5; KAFTA, Article 11.5, and Canada–China BIT, Article 4.

[31] See Jose E Alvarez and Gustavo Topalian, 'The Paradoxical Argentina Cases' (2012) 6(3) *World Arbitration and Mediation Review* 491.

(c) on payment of prompt, adequate and effective compensation in accordance with paragraphs 2, 3 and 4; and

(d) in accordance with due process of law.[32]

The provision further provides that compensation shall (a) be paid without delay; (b) be equivalent to the fair market value of the expropriated investment immediately before the expropriation took place (the date of expropriation); (c) not reflect any change in value occurring because the intended expropriation had become known earlier and (d) be fully realisable and freely transferable.[33] Article 8.12 of the CETA, Article 10.13 of the RCEP and countless other IIAs provide for the same or substantially similar wording to the same effect. Differences, when they exist, relate more to the degree of specificity with which the text deals with compensation and interpretively to the precise meaning and scope given to the concept of due process.

Protecting against direct and indirect expropriation, the clause attempts to be comprehensive in scope.[34] While undoubtedly helpful, the four factors do not resolve every issue. This is particularly true in the case of a measure challenged for being an indirect expropriation, as is almost certainly the case with a CFM. CFMs are unlikely to be viewed as an outright seizure. The line separating a legitimate regulatory measure and an indirect expropriation is sometimes difficult to detect; simply, there will be measures that reflect *prima facie* a lawful exercise of powers of governments but nevertheless may impact or affect foreign interests. Not all of these measures will be considered as tantamount to expropriation. For example, a state may subject foreign assets and their use to taxation, restrictions involving licenses and quotas or other measures which result in a devaluation of the value of the asset. While the facts of the case may

---

[32] On the historical development of the conditions, see August Reinisch, 'Legality of Expropriations', in August Reinisch (ed) *Standards of Investment Protection* (Oxford University Press 2008) 171–204; Rudolf Dolzer and Christoph Schreuer, *Principles of International Investment Law* (2nd ed., Oxford University Press 2012) 99–101; Surya Subedi, *International Investment Law* (2nd ed., Hart Publishing 2012) 79. Some consider these factors to be customary international law. See for instance OECD, '"Indirect Expropriation" and the "Right to Regulate" in International Investment Law', OECD Working Papers on International Investment (2004), 2004/04, 3.

[33] CPTPP, Article 9.8(2). Subparagraphs 3–4 discuss options whereby fair market value is denominated in a freely usable currency or not in a freely usable currency.

[34] A sub-set of indirect expropriation known as regulatory expropriation occurs where a measure has been taken for regulatory purposes but the impact is equivalent to expropriation. Regulatory expropriation may also be (but not necessarily is) a form of 'creeping expropriation', where it is not an individual act, but rather a series of measures that brings about the expropriatory effect. See for instance *Generation Ukraine v Ukraine* 44 ILM (2005) paras. 20.22, 20.26.

alter the outcome, in principle such measures are not unlawful and do not constitute indirect expropriation.[35]

Although a claim of indirect expropriation rarely finds favour with arbitral tribunals, the jurisprudence has not been very clear in delineating the line between a non-compensable regulatory measure and indirect expropriation. For this reason, the textual wording of the provision in the treaty at issue is of critical importance. Most modern agreements have identical or substantially similar phrasing. For example, Annex 14-B, paragraph 4 of the USMCA and Annex 9-B, paragraph 3 of the CPTPP define an indirect expropriation as an action or series of actions by a Party that has an effect equivalent to direct expropriation without formal transfer of title or outright seizure:

(a) The determination of whether an action or series of actions by a Party, in a specific fact situation, constitutes an indirect expropriation, requires a case-by-case, fact-based inquiry that considers, among other factors:
  (i) the economic impact of the government action, although the fact that an action or series of actions by a Party has an adverse effect on the economic value of an investment, standing alone, does not establish that an indirect expropriation has occurred,
  (ii) the extent to which the government action interferes with distinct, reasonable investment-backed expectations,19(CPTPP 36) and
  (iii) the character of the government action, including its object, context, and intent.
(b) Non-discriminatory regulatory actions by a Party that are designed and applied to protect legitimate public welfare objectives, such as health, safety and the environment, do not constitute indirect expropriations, except in rare circumstances.

Footnote 19/36 clarifies that 'whether an investor's investment-backed expectations are reasonable depends, to the extent relevant, on factors

---

[35] See *Quasar de Valores SICAV S.A. et al v the Russian Federation*, Final Arbitral Award, SCC Case No. V (024/2007) (20 July 2012) para. 45 ('Indirect expropriation, of course does not speak its name. It must be deduced from a pattern of conduct, observing its conception, implementation, and effects as such, even if the intention to expropriate is disavowed at every step. The fact that individual measures appear non to be well founded in law or to be discriminatory, or otherwise to lack bona fides, may be important elements of a finding that there has been the equivalent of an indirect expropriation, an expropriation by other means even though there be no need to determine whether the expropriation was unlawful'.)

such as whether the government provided the investor with binding written assurances and the nature and extent of governmental regulation or the potential for government regulation in the relevant sector'.

Such wording, often repeated in numerous agreements,[36] is undoubtedly helpful to governments instituting non-discriminatory measures in the pursuit of better public outcomes, as the language requires tribunals to weigh and balance the nature and potential impact of all three factors prior to making their determination. In this regard, neither firm government action nor economic impact will automatically outweigh the character of state action.

Arbitral tribunals have not deemed CFMs to be indirect expropriations. For instance, several tribunals held that Argentina's measures enacted during the 2001 financial crisis did not rise to the level of indirect expropriation but rather were regulatory measures of general application.[37] Similarly, in the Chobady Claim the US Foreign Claims Commission held that exchange restrictions taken in times of economic crisis did not eliminate ownership and were not confiscatory.[38] The Commission likewise stated in the Evanoff Claim that 'a prohibition against transfer of funds outside of a country is an exercise of sovereign authority which, though causing hardship to non-residents having currency on deposit within the country, may not be deemed a "taking" of their property'.[39] These decisions are in line with the above analysis, as the measures were temporary limitations on the repatriation of funds. A claimant would be more likely to succeed where *permanent* restrictions that would render investors incapable of commercial dealings prohibit a portfolio investor from repatriating capital or force the conversion of assets from a foreign currency into a domestic currency.[40]

---

[36] See also RCEP, Annex 10B. EU–Singapore FTA, Annex 9-A(2); US–CAFTA–DR, Annex 10C(4)(a); Canada–China BIT, Annex B.10, and with slightly different (and more narrow) wording, ASEAN Comprehensive Investment Agreement of 2009, Annex 2. See also Annex 8-A of the CETA, which is virtually identical to the USMCA/CPTPP but adds a fourth factor: the duration of the measure or series of measures of a Party.

[37] See *LG&E v Argentine Republic*, ICSID Case No. ARB/02/1, Decision on Liability (3 October 2006) para. 198; CMS Gas Transmission Company (n 29) para. 25; Total (n 20) para. 197.

[38] Josef Chobady, Claim No. HUNG – 20, Foreign Claims Settlement Commission of the US 187.

[39] George Evanoff, Claim No. Bul. 1, 005, Foreign Claims Settlement Commission of the US 2.

[40] See Annamaria Viterbo, *International Economic Law and Monetary Measures: Limitations to States' Sovereignty and Dispute Settlement* (Edward Elgar 2012) 273.

While only a handful of IIAs contain the treaty language reproduced above, the trend in doing so is clear. While the provision is not a panacea – it is somewhat vague and provides no direction to arbitrators as to how the factors should be weighed and balanced – the criteria and factors should serve as a clear indication to arbitrators determining whether a CFM amounts to an indirect expropriation requiring compensation.

7.2 Exceptions

7.2.1 Balance of Payments

A growing minority of IIAs contain a BoP exception. Those treaties that do contain a BoP exception differ in scope. For instance, some exceptions give a state almost complete authority to restrict transfers if carried out in accordance with IMF rules and applied equitably and the restrictions are applied in a non-discriminatory manner. An agreement with this type of exception is the Greece–Mexico BIT (2000), with Article 7(4) reading:

> In case of a serious balance of payments difficulties or the threat thereof, each Contracting Party may temporarily restrict transfers, provided that such a Contracting Party implements measures or a programme in accordance with the International Monetary Fund's standards. These restrictions would be imposed on an equitable, nondiscriminatory and in good faith basis.

Article 9(4) of the Australia–Mexico BIT (2005) likewise has the same effect, despite not explicitly mentioning the IMF:

> In case of serious balance of payments difficulties or the threat thereof, each Contracting Party may temporarily restrict transfers provided that such a Contracting Party implements measures or a programme in accordance with international standards. These restrictions shall be imposed on an equitable, non-discriminatory and in good faith basis.

It is common for IIAs to place more conditions on the restriction of transfers, including by adding a necessity and temporal requirement. For example, Article 16(1) Japan–Vietnam BIT (2003) provides:

1. A Contracting Party may adopt or maintain measures not conforming with its obligations under paragraph 1 of Article 2 relating to cross border capital transactions and Article 12: (a) in the event of serious balance-of-payments and external financial difficulties or threat thereof; or (b) in cases where, in exceptional circumstances, movements of capital cause or threaten to cause serious difficulties for macroeconomic management, in particular, monetary and exchange rate policies.

2. Measures referred to in paragraph 1 above: (a) shall be consistent with the Articles of Agreement of the International Monetary Fund so long as the Contracting Party taking the measures is a party to the said Articles; (b) shall not exceed those necessary to deal with the circumstances set out in paragraph 1 above; (c) shall be temporary and shall be eliminated as soon as conditions permit; and (d) shall be promptly notified to the other Contracting Party.
3. Nothing in this Agreement shall be regarded as altering the rights enjoyed and obligations undertaken by a Contracting Party as a party to the International Monetary Fund.

Less common are exceptions which concern the exercise of regulatory powers affecting the financial services industry. An example of which is Article 10(6) of the Canadian Model BIT (2021):

> a Party may prevent or limit transfers by a financial institution to, or for the benefit of, an affiliate of or person related to that institution, through the equitable, non-discriminatory and good faith application of a measure relating to maintenance of the safety, soundness, integrity or financial responsibility of financial institutions.[41]

The CPTPP, USMCA, RCEP and CETA all contain relatively similar BoP exceptions. For example, Article 28.5 of the CETA allows Members experiencing serious balance-of-payments or external financial difficulties, or threat thereof, to adopt or maintain restrictive measures with regard to capital movements or payments, including transfers, with the conditions being that the measures (a) do not treat a party less favourably than a third country in like situations, (b) are consistent with the Articles of Agreement of the International Monetary Fund (as applicable), (c) avoid unnecessary damage to the commercial, economic and financial interests of a party, (d) are temporary and phased out progressively as the difficulties improve.[42] The restrictions are limited in duration to 180 days, which in 'extremely exceptional circumstances' can be extended. The provision also provides for detailed consultations between

---

[41] Interestingly, Canada's Model BIT 2014 did not include a BoP exception, but its BIT with China (2012) includes the exception (Article 12).

[42] Article 28.4 of the CETA allows the EU, in exceptional circumstances, to impose safeguard measures for a period not exceeding 180 days on capital movements and payments, including transfers, 'that are strictly necessary' to address serious difficulties for the operation of the economic and monetary union. The safeguards shall not constitute a means of arbitrary or unjustifiable discrimination in respect of Canada or its investors compared to a third country or its investors.

the parties on the nature and extent of the difficulties, external economic and trading environment and the availability of alternative corrective measures and requires the parties to accept all findings of statistical and other facts presented by the IMF relating to foreign exchange, monetary reserves, balance-of-payments, and to base their conclusions on the assessment by the IMF of the balance-of-payments and the external financial situation of the Party concerned.

Article 17.15 of the RCEP allows restrictions in instances of serious balance of payments and external financial difficulties or under threat thereof, or where, in exceptional circumstances, payments or transfers relating to capital movements cause or threaten to cause serious difficulties for macroeconomic management, it may adopt or maintain restrictions on payments or transfers related to covered investments. Such measures must be consistent with the IMF Articles of Agreement as may be amended; avoid unnecessary damage to the commercial, economic, and financial interests of any other Party; be temporary and be phased out progressively as the situation improves (with no set temporal limitation); and be applied on a non-discriminatory basis such that no Party is treated less favourably than any other Party or a non-Party.

Article 29.3 of the CPTPP and Article 32.4 of the USMCA allows a Party to adopt or maintain restrictive measures for current account transactions in the event of serious balance of payments and external financial difficulties or threats thereof, and to do so with regard to payments or transfers relating to the movements of capital in the event of serious balance of payments and external financial difficulties or threats thereof; or if, in exceptional circumstances, payments or transfers relating to capital movements cause or threaten to cause serious difficulties for macroeconomic management. Such measures must be consistent with the IMF Articles and must not be discriminatory, cause unnecessary damage to other Parties' commercial, economic and financial interests, not exceed what is necessary to deal with the circumstances, not be inconsistent with the expropriation obligation in Chapter 2 (Investment) and in the case of restrictions on capital outflows, not interfere with an investor's ability to earn a market rate of return on any restricted assets in the Party's territory. The measures must also not be used to avoid necessary macroeconomic adjustment, must be temporary and be phased out progressively as the situation improves with a temporal limit of 18 months in the CPTPP (which can be extended in exceptional circumstances, and absent objections from more than half of the Parties) and 12 months in the USMCA (which in exceptional circumstances can be extended for a further 12 months).

It should be noted that a small minority of agreements go even further and offer almost a blanket exception in times of crisis. Such is the case with Article 43 of the European Economic Area (EEA):

> Where an EC Member State or an EFTA State is in difficulties, or is seriously threatened with difficulties, as regards its balance of payments either as a result of an overall disequilibrium in its balance of payments, or as a result of the type of currency at its disposal, and where such difficulties are liable in particular to jeopardize the functioning of this Agreement, the Contracting Party concerned may take protective measures.[43]

Thus, despite the EEA containing a provision on the free flow of capital, the EFTA Court ruled that given the conditions Iceland faced its measures restricting capital movements were not inconsistent with the Agreement.[44]

While the absence of a BoP exception in many IIAs has caused concern among activists, it is possible that states simply did 'not view limiting transfers as an appropriate measure to cope with foreign currency shortages'.[45] This sentiment is likely shifting, and although still not uniform, there is a trend among recent IIAs involving large, developed country parties to include a BoP exception.

7.2.2 Non-Precluded Measures and Essential Interests

Most IIAs contain overarching exceptions providing that a Party is 'not precluded' from taking measures 'it considers necessary' to protect its 'essential security interests'. For instance, under the heading of 'National Security', Article 28.6(b) provides that the agreement does not 'prevent a Party from taking an action that it considers necessary to protect its essential security interests'. A similar formulation is found in the RCEP (Article 17.13), CPTPP (Article 29.2) and USMCA (Article 32.2). Such provisions are often believed to be 'self-judging' – thereby allowing discretion to invoke such exception subject only to a generally applicable but unstated 'good faith' requirement – but arbitral tribunals have held the invocation is subject to review. As will be discussed below, Argentina invoked the NPM clause with limited success in response to claims filed following action it took in response to economic crisis in 2001.

---

[43] EEA Agreement, Article 43, para. 2.
[44] Request for an Advisory Opinion from the EFTA Court by Héraðsdómur Reykjavíkur received 14 February 2011 in the case of Pálmi Sigmarsson v Seðlabanki Íslands, E-3/11.
[45] Reinish and Schreuer, (n 5), 987.

Moreover, it should be stated that customary international law allows a state to take necessary measures to safeguard an 'essential interest' as a defence against allegations of treaty breach. This defence is narrower than a treaty-based exception, and it is questionable whether it applies to all substantive obligations as well as the existence of an economic crisis that would potentially justify the invocation of the defence.[46] As will be shown in the case law, the customary international law requirement of necessity is often (but not always) applied together with the NPM exception.

7.2.3 Prudential Measures

Modern comprehensive FTAs deal extensively with financial services in a separate chapter and link the prudential exception between that chapter and the investment chapter. For this reason, the analysis provided in Chapter 6 on the CPTPP, USMCA, RCEP and CETA applies to this chapter and does not need to be repeated. Instead, this section looks to a select group of recently negotiated BITs to outline the usual practice.

The drafting format for prudential exceptions in BITs follows closely those which were illustrated in Chapter 6. For example, Article 17.2 of the Canada–Hong Kong BIT (2016) contains a straightforward and typical provision that allows the Parties to adopt or maintain measures for prudential reasons, with the caveat that such measures shall not be used as a means of avoiding the Party's obligations under such provisions. The provision then provides a non-exhaustive list of illustrative examples:

(a) protecting investors, depositors, financial market participants, policy-holders, policy claimants, or persons to whom a fiduciary duty is owed by a financial institution;
(b) maintaining the safety, soundness, integrity or financial responsibility of financial institutions; and
(c) ensuring the integrity and stability of a Party's financial system.

What is somewhat striking is that it is not developed, but developing, countries which are now failing to provide for and protect prudential measures in BITs. For instance, there is no prudential exception in the most

---

[46] For discussion in the case law, see *CMS Gas Transmission Company* (n 29); *Sempra Energy International* (n 20).

recent BITs negotiated by leading developing countries such as China [Turkey (2015)] and India [Belarus (2018)], or indeed in any agreements negotiated by some developing countries that are less developed. India's Model BIT 2016 does not include the prudential exception, and only one of India's agreements negotiated since 2010 includes a prudential exception – India's agreements with Nepal (2011), Slovenia (2011), Lithuania (2011) and the UAE (2013) do not include the exception. But India's recent agreement with Brazil (2020) does include an exception for prudential measures.[47] Likewise, while Belarus has not included a prudential exception in any of its recently negotiated BITs with developing countries – Laos (2013), Azerbaijan (2013), Cambodia (2014), Sudan (2017), India (2018), Turkey (2018) and Uzbekistan (2019) – its agreement with Hungary (2019) contains a prudential exception. What must be stressed here is that India and Belarus are not the outliers among developing countries but simply representative. This is in sharp contrast to BITs negotiated by developed countries, which regularly include the prudential (and other) exceptions as a matter of course.

7.3 Tracking BIT Trends

After reviewing the substantive obligations and exceptions individually, it is useful to illustrate the trends relating to capital movement management by comparing treaty provisions from two different time periods of treaties. The recent period of BITs concluded in 2017–18 will be compared with those concluded ten years prior, in 2007–2008.[48]

The UNCTAD treaty database reveals that a total of seventy-five BITs were concluded in 2017–18, thirty-nine of which were publicly available in English as of January 2022. The vast majority of these agreements include provisions allowing for protective measures in case of financial governance difficulties. For instance, the two BITs signed by Brazil in 2018 with Suriname and Ethiopia both contain a free transfers provision (Article 10) which includes the usual built-in exceptions, including balance of payment difficulties, as well as a traditional NPM clause (Article 12) permitting CFM measures in cases involving financial instability, in line with

---

[47] Interestingly, while India's Model BIT 2003 did not include exceptions for financial stability, essential security interests, BoP difficulties or prudential measures, the Model BIT 2016 includes exceptions for financial stability, essential security interests and BoP difficulties, but still no prudential exception.
[48] This research was carried out with the assistance of Antoine P Martin and Maggie YuanYuan Zhang.

IMF policy. Note, however, that the drafters of these agreements have mixed the various concepts, which normally tend to be treated as separate and distinct components. For instance, the BoP exception is considered to be part of the Transfers provisions rather than as a prudential exception, while the prudential clause includes a financial stability exception. Neither of the agreements contains a specific dispute settlement provision. It is useful to reproduce the text of both articles:

Article 10 Transfers
3. Nothing in this Agreement shall be construed as to prevent a Party from adopting or maintaining temporary restrictive measures in respect of payments or transfers related to current account transactions in the event of serious difficulties in the balance of payments and external financial difficulties or threat thereof.

Article 12 Prudential Measures
1. Nothing in this Agreement shall be construed to prevent a Party from adopting or maintaining prudential measures, such as:
    a) the protection of investors, depositors, financial market participants, policyholders, policy-claimants, or persons to whom a fiduciary duty is owed by a financial institution;
    b) the maintenance of the safety, soundness, integrity or financial responsibility of financial institutions; and
    c) ensuring the integrity and stability of a Party's financial system.
2. Where such measures do not conform with the provisions of this Agreement, they shall not be used as a means of circumventing the commitments or obligations of the Party under this Agreement.

Similarly, the BIT between Colombia and the UAE provides for significant capital management possibilities. For example, Article 6 on Transfers permits safeguards for monetary reasons, provided the measures are consistent with IMF policy. A waiting period and consultation process further shield Colombia and the UAE from arbitration on these matters. In line with the Colombian Model BIT, the agreement also leaves room for distress management measures justified by financial stability preservation needs, which are included Article 1 of the treaty (scope of application).

The BIT signed by Israel and Japan in 2017 is similar, with Article 14 on Transfers providing for the traditional built-in exceptions while Article 16 allows temporary safeguard measures relating to balance of payment difficulties, monetary difficulties and financial stability as long as these measures are not discriminatory and remain consistent with IMF policy. Hong Kong's agreement with China (2017) likewise provides for built-in exceptions to the Transfers provision that refers to balance of payment and financial stability preservation while the article on 'financial prudence' preserves the integrity and stability of the financial and monetary systems. Similarly, Hong Kong's agreement with ASEAN (2017) provides for free transfers and exceptions and also permits temporary safeguard measures consistent with IMF policy in case of balance of payment or monetary difficulties.[49] This agreement, however, contains no reference to financial stability or prudential measures. The BIT signed by Rwanda and the UAE in 2017 follows the trend, even though it is less protective: Article 10 on transfers provides the usual provision and includes balance of payment as well as external and macroeconomic financial difficulty exceptions; however, Article 9 on the Right to Regulate mentions public health security or environment but does not include financial stability.[50] The real anomaly in the 2017–18 IIAs is the BIT signed by Cape Verde and Mauritius. While this agreement is very short, it provides guarantees on transfers of investment capital and returns (Article 7) but does not provide for general exceptions; nor does it contain exceptions applicable to financial distress.[51]

In order to determine whether these agreements coincide with a trend, they can be organised into five main indicators. The first indicator is whether the BIT contains a free transfers provision. The second indicator considers whether the BIT provides for a general exception to the free transfers rule, whether restrictive or comprehensive. The third indicator highlights whether the BIT provides for exceptions in circumstances involving monetary difficulties, in line with IMF policy. The fourth indicator assesses whether the BIT contains exceptions related to financial distress, whether in cases involving BOP difficulties or financial instability difficulties, or allowing for 'prudential' measures per se. The last indicator considers whether the BIT provides for a monetary policy exception and for financial instability difficulties.

The available treaties negotiated in 2017–18 are disparate in terms of drafting but similar in terms of content. Indeed, all thirty-nine available treaties include a provision on free capital transfers, with all but four (89.74 per cent) containing a form of exception to free transfers. All

---

[49] Hong Kong–ASEAN, Articles 12–13.
[50] Rwanda–United Arab Emirates BIT, Article 9.
[51] See Cape Verde–Mauritius BIT.

but five agreements (87.18 per cent) contain a form of monetary policy exception (in line with IMF policy), and all but three agreements (92.31 per cent) contain a form of financial distress exception (BoP, financial stability or prudential exception). That being said, only ten agreements (25.64 per cent) include exceptions for BoP, financial stability and prudential measures. Interestingly, eight of those agreements include at least one developed country as a Party, whereas the two exceptions both include Brazil as a Party (even more interesting is the fact that not all of the treaties Brazil concluded in 2017–18 contain all three exceptions). Twenty-five agreements contain a monetary policy exception in line with the IMF (64.10 per cent), and all but three of the agreements (92.31 per cent) contain at least one monetary policy exception and one financial distress exception.

For comparative purposes, we analysed the seventy-eight agreements available in English signed between 2007 and 2008. Interestingly, the statistics reveal a significantly different picture. Unsurprisingly, all the treaties signed during the period contain a free capital transfer clause; however, the span of available exceptions differs widely. Only 62.8 per cent of the treaties contains any form of an exception as part of the free capital flow clause while 59 per cent contain a form of monetary policy exception in line IMF policy. As far as financial distress exceptions are concerned, the ratio falls to only 34 per cent that contain one or more of a BOP, financial stability or prudential exception. Similarly, twenty of the agreements include a monetary policy exception in line with the IMF (25.65 per cent), and 29.5 per cent of the agreements contain at least one monetary policy exception and one financial distress exception.

While turning treaty provisions into statistics is a complex exercise, the above differences are stark and allow for two observations and conclusions to be drawn. The first observation is that reading and isolating the relevant provisions of FTAs is easier than those of BITs, as the former are more standardized while the latter writing tends to be dissimilar and unpredictable. In some cases, the objectives of certain provisions remain the same, but the terminology and placement differ. This is especially the case for exceptions clauses, with FTAs consistently referring to monetary policy, financial stability or the stability of the financial system. BITs use different language and seldom specifically refer to internal stability or macroeconomic difficulties.

Second, and most importantly, the older treaties do not provide nearly as many safeguards as the more modern agreements. This is especially the case of BITs negotiated between lower-income countries, where the agreements not only tend to be shorter but also tend to fall well short of the full suite of modern safeguards and exceptions. In contrast, treaties negotiated by experienced, sophisticated and traditional investor countries (many with Model BITs) were more likely to include exceptions to transfers and the full complement of financial distress exceptions. As a result, while in essence approximately 63 per cent of the treaties included generic exceptions allowing the host governments to impose CFMs, disparities between the treaties are significant, and less than 30 per cent allowed the regulators to take CFMs for both monetary and financial distress reasons.

This comparison reveals that older treaties are far more susceptible to investor claims regarding the imposition of CFMs than are their more modern counterparts. This contrasts with results of other studies which include a wider timeframe of studies and seem to refer to all post-2000 treaties as recent and thus conclude that treaties are 'increasingly restricting the policy space for regulating cross-border financial flows'.[52] Such studies also tend to find that treaties involving a developed country Party are more stringent than those negotiated by developing countries.[53] Those findings are in complete contrast to this study, which demonstrates a real and substantial change in treaty practice even between the years 2007–2008 and 2017–18. We find treaties involving a developed, traditional investor country are more comprehensive in nature, and include more exceptions and safeguards, than agreements negotiated between less developed countries that traditionally are recipients but not exporters of foreign investments.

This finding is further substantiated by a review of all treaties negotiated since 2015 and mapped by the UNCTAD Investment Policy Hub. In total, the database contains fifty mapped treaties, with five negotiated between developed countries, twenty-five containing at least one developed country and one developing country partner and twenty negotiated between developing countries. Here, we mapped how many of the treaties contain an essential security exception, general exception and prudential carve-out, and then we simply tabulated the number of exceptions contained in each treaty. The results are as follows:

---

[52] Kevin P Gallagher, Sarah Sklar and Rachel Thrasher, 'Quantifying the Policy Space for Regulating Capital Flows in Trade and Investment Treaties' (April 2019) G24 Working Paper, 23.
[53] Ibid.

Number of exceptions contained in the agreement	Treaties negotiated between developed countries	Treaties negotiated between at least one developed country and at least one developing country	Treaties negotiated between developing countries
None of the exceptions	0	3	11
One of the exceptions	0	2	1
Two of the exceptions	0	10	6
All three of the exceptions	5	10	2
Total number of treaties	5	25	20

The results of the treaties concluded in 2015 onwards are clear and again reveal that treaties negotiated by developed countries or including a developing country partner provide for far more exceptions than treaties negotiated between developing countries. Whereas 100 per cent of treaties between developed countries contain all three exceptions, only 10 per cent of treaties between developing countries do the same (both negotiated by Brazil), and 55 per cent of such treaties contain none of the exceptions. Agreements between developed and developing countries also were far more likely to contain two or three of the exceptions than were fully developing country agreements.

The findings of both the 2007–2008 to 2017–18 comparison and of all mapped post-2014 treaties demonstrate that the concern over modern agreements negotiated by the US, EU, Japan and the like is largely misplaced, and that attention should rather focus on agreements negotiated among developing countries. The failure of developing countries to negotiate exceptions into their IIAs limits governmental policy space to act in times of crisis and widens the scope of potential ISDS claims against a host state.

7.4 Investment Jurisprudence[54]

This section discusses relevant jurisprudence interpreting the transfers clause and other substantive obligations contained in IIAs. As previously discussed, critics often question whether exception clauses and NPMs

---

[54] Parts of this section draw heavily from Bryan Mercurio and Antoine Martin, 'Towards Convergence of Trade and Investment Law? A Right to Prudential Measures for the Preservation of Financial Stability' (2018) 51(3) *The International Lawyer* 553.

would in practice prove useful or be disregarded and rendered moot. This section therefore also reviews how the investment jurisprudence deals with these clauses in practice and reveals that contrary to the criticism, the investment tribunals have for the most part been sympathetic to such clauses. More specifically, arbitral tribunals have created a framework that favours general 'prudential freedom'. Interestingly, even tribunals that dismissed claims on jurisdictional grounds (and therefore did not discuss the issues in detail) made intriguing observations on the relevance of prudential regulations. The tribunals have not, however, been consistent in their reasoning. Thus, while issues relating to NPM, CFMs and financial stability have been considered by several investment tribunals, the tribunals have failed to create a robust and consistent set of case law capable of guiding the interpretation of investment treaties. Some of the tribunals did offer elements related to how prudential measures should be handled, but the jurisprudence in international investment law has never reached clear and coherent conclusions.

7.4.1 Transfers

Given the importance of the transfers clause and its relationship to CFMs, there is relatively little jurisprudence on the provision.[55] Many claims fail prior to the adjudication phase. This was the case in *Gruslin v Malaysia*, where a Belgian investor's argument that Malaysia's short-term controls during the Asian Financial Crisis breached the guarantee of transfer of capital under the Belgium–Luxembourg–Malaysia BIT was dismissed on jurisdictional grounds since the BIT restricted the definition of 'investment' to 'approved project(s)'.[56]

Much of the jurisprudence comes from the several cases filed against Argentina for its response to the financial crisis in 2001 in adopting restrictions on foreign transfers, including a prohibition to transfer foreign exchange abroad over certain nominal amounts without central bank authorisation. Even here, while some cases addressed Argentina's obligations under transfer clauses, most of the tribunals focused on potential

---

[55] In a case of regime conflict, the European Commission brought an action against Austria, Finland and Sweden, successfully arguing that BITs mandating the free transfer of capital are inconsistent with EU law in that under exceptional circumstances the European Council could require members to restrict capital outflow (Cases C-205/06, C-249/06 and C-118/07).

[56] *Gruslin v Malaysia*, ICSID Case No. ARB/99/3, Award (27 November 2000) para. 2.2.

violations of indirect expropriations or FET. For example, the tribunal in *Metalpar v Argentina* easily dismissed the claim of a breach of the transfers clause, as the restrictions only made the transfers dependent on central bank authorization, and the claimant did not ever seek to obtain the authorisation.[57]

The tribunal in *Continental Casualty v Argentina* analysed the transfers clause in more detail. In that dispute, the claimant asserted that an Argentine measure prohibited it from transferring $19 million in funds out of the country in prohibition of Argentina's obligation under the transfers clause (Article 5) of the Argentina–US BIT.[58] The tribunal rejected the claim, finding that the funds were not 'related to an investment' and thus not covered by Article 5 of the treaty.[59] More specially, the tribunal held:

> The transfer did not correspond to, nor was it required to satisfy any payment obligation of CNA, commercial, financial or other; nor would it involve the transfer of ownership of the funds involved to some different entity. It was clearly a legitimate operation from a business point of view, permissible under the convertibility regime of Argentina until the Corralito. This does not mean that it would fall within the 'transfers related to an investment' under Art. V. The fact that the BIT does not limit these transfers to those made by the foreign investor itself and that these transfers may be made by the local subsidiary, in favor of its parent company as well as of other entities (thus in case of payment of royalties, payments related to loans received etc.), does not mean that any trans-border movement of funds by such subsidiary is 'related to an investment'.[60]

It is also important to remember that the transfers clause protects the ability to transfer funds and not the value of assets per se. Many claims have failed for blurring the distinction. The tribunal in *Biwater Gauff v Tanzania* stated:

> Article 6 of the BIT is not a guarantee that investors will have funds to transfer. It rather guarantees that if investors have funds, they will be able to transfer them, subject to the conditions stated in Article 6. The free transfer principle is aimed at measures that would restrict the possibility to

---

[57] *Metalpar v Argentina*, Award, ICSID Case No. ARB/03/5, Award (6 June 2008) para. 179.
[58] *Continental Casualty v Argentina* (n 8) para. 124.
[59] Ibid., 241 ('The type of transfer at issue here does not fall into any of these categories, nor specifically does it represent the "proceeds from the sale or liquidation of all or any part of an investment". It was merely a change of type, location and currency of part of an investor's existing investment, namely a part of the freely disposable funds, held short term at its banks by CNA, in order to protect them from the impending devaluation, by transferring them to bank accounts outside Argentina'.). See also ibid., paras. 244–45.
[60] Ibid., para. 242.

transfer, such as currency control restrictions or other measures taken by the host State which effectively imprison the investors' funds, typically in the host State of the investment.[61]

When tribunals have found violations of the transfers clause, they have not been particularly diligent in explaining the reasons for the finding or elaborating upon the determinations. For instance, the tribunal in *Bernhard von Pezold and Others v Zimbabwe* found the host state violated the transfers clause of the Germany–Zimbabwe BIT and Switzerland–Zimbabwe BIT when it forced the claimants to be paid for tobacco in Zimbabwean dollars, when it forced the claimants to exchange sales proceeds in US currency for Zimbabwean dollars and for its failure to release US dollars earned through the sale of tobacco to enable the repayment of the claimants' loans to foreign creditors.[62] The tribunal did not, however, elaborate or explain its reasoning.[63]

Likewise, in *Achmea v Slovak Republic (Achmea I)*, after finding a 'ban on [the repatriation of] profits was inconsistent with Respondent's obligations' under Article 4 of the Netherlands–Slovakia BIT, the tribunal determined 'that the violation and the injury arising from the temporary adoption of the ban on profits are subsumed within the violation and the injury arising from the breach of the "fair and equitable treatment" obligation'.[64] While not all tribunals concur,[65] the tribunal in *AES Corporation and Tau Power B.V. v Kazakhstan* reached a similar determination in finding that:

> [The transfers clause is] a specific implementation of the general principle protected under the FET standard that an investor should have the right to earn and transfer reasonable returns of and on its investments. [The transfer of funds obligations] go further than the protection afforded under the FET by establishing more specific principles concerning the conditions for transfer of such returns and other capital.[66]

---

[61] *Biwater Gauff v Tanzania*, ICSID Case No. ARB/05/22, Award (24 July 2008) para. 735. See also *Duke Energy International v Peru*, ICSID Case No. ARB/03/28, Award (18 August 2008) paras. 260–66.
[62] *Bernhard von Pezold and Others v Zimbabwe*, ICSID Case No. ARB/10/15, Award (28 July 2015) paras. 607–9.
[63] See also *Valores Mundiales v Venezuela*, ICSID Case No. ARB/13/11, Award (25 July 2017) para. 639.
[64] *Achmea v Slovak Republic [I]*, UNCITRAL, PCA Case No. 2008-13, Award (7 December 2012) para. 286.
[65] *Valores Mundiales* (n 63) para. 636.
[66] *AES Corporation and Tau Power B.V. v Kazakhstan*, ICSID Case No. ARB/10/16, Award (1 November 2013) para. 425.

The final case worth highlighting is *Karkey Karadeniz v Pakistan*, where the tribunal took an expansive view of Article IV(1) of the Pakistan–Turkey BIT which provides that '[e]ach Party shall permit in good faith all transfers related to an investment to be made freely and without unreasonable delay into and out of its territory' and held that the provision covers not only funds but also physical/moveable property.[67] Hence, Pakistan's detention of a vessel violated the claimant's right to transfer assets related to its investment 'without unreasonable delay'.[68]

In several other proceedings, tribunals have either found that the state did not interfere with transfers[69] or simply rejected that the state behaviour amounted to a violation of the transfers clause.[70] The *OI European Group v Venezuela* case is worth mentioning, as the tribunal interpreted the meaning of the obligation to guarantee the transfer of funds 'with no restriction or undue delay' as not being an absolute guarantee that investors could repatriate their profits at all times or a right to the application of the official market exchange rate.[71] In short, the tribunal found that '[t]he introduction of exchange control systems is part of the economic and financial sovereignty of the States, and does not constitute an "undue restriction"'.[72]

7.4.2 Prudential Stability

Measures taken for prudential stability reasons have mainly been discussed in six publicly available cases filed against Argentina – *LG&E, CMS, Enron, Sempra, Continental Casualty* and *Urbaser*[73] – as well as in

---

[67] *Karkey Karadeniz Elektrik Uretim A.S. v Pakistan*, ICSID Case No. ARB/13/1, Award (22 August 2017) paras. 654–55.

[68] Ibid. para. 655. See contra *Rusoro v Venezuela*, ICSID Case No. ARB(AF)/12/5, Award (22 August 2016) paras. 574–75 (holding a limitation on the transfer of gold did not violate the transfers clause of the Canada–Venezuela BIT, as it is a commodity and not a currency).

[69] See for instance *White Industries v India*, UNCITRAL, Final Award (30 November 2011) para. 13.2.3; *MNSS B.V. and Recupero Credito Acciaio N.V. v Montenegro*, ICSID Case No. ARB(AF)/12/8, Award (4 May 2016), para. 366.

[70] See for instance *Vincent J. Ryan, Schooner Capital LLC, and Atlantic Investment Partners LLC v Poland*, ICSID Case No. ARB(AF)/11/3, Award (24 November 2015) para. 507.

[71] *OI European Group v Venezuela*, ICSID Case No. ARB/11/25, Award (10 March 2015), paras. 624–32.

[72] Ibid. para. 624.

[73] See *Continental Casualty v Argentina* (n 8); *Urbaser S.A. and Consorcio de Aguas Bilbao Bizkaia, Bilbao Biskaia Ur Partzuergoa v the Argentine Republic*, ICSID Case No. ARB/07/26, Award (8 December 2016); *Sempra Energy International* (n 20); *Enron Corporation and Ponderosa Assets, L.P. v Argentine Republic* (also known as: *Enron Creditors Recovery Corp. and Ponderosa Assets, L.P. v The Argentine Republic*), ICSID Case No. ARB/01/3, Award (22 May 2007); *LG&E Energy* (n 37); *CMS Gas Transmission Company* (n 29).

three annulment proceedings.[74] In the main, arbitral tribunals have identified two different ways of assessing whether Argentina's measures were justified based on economic duress in the country. Some tribunals have relied on the NPM clauses, which as discussed tend to be found in the majority of BITs, as a means to identify exceptions to treaty obligations in certain situations.

Alternatively, other tribunals have allowed the notion of 'necessity' under Customary International Law (as provided by Article 25 of the ILC draft articles on Responsibility of States for Internationally Wrongful Acts) to prevail over NPM provisions. Interestingly, however, while the jurisprudence coming from the investment cases lacks coherence, it points in the same direction as that of the WTO decision in *Argentina–Financial Services* (as discussed in Chapter 5).

7.4.2.1 Non-Precluded Measures

In two cases, the *LG&E* and *Continental Casualty*, the tribunals gave weight to the NPM treaty clauses which they considered as *lex specialis* exempting the State from its treaty obligations.[75] NPM clauses commonly ensure that treaty obligations shall not preclude the application by either Party of measures necessary for the preservation of investors and other financial actors, for the maintenance of public order or for the protection of essential security interests.

The relevant provision in both disputes, Article XI of the Argentina–US BIT, reads as follows: 'This Treaty shall not preclude the application by either Party of measures necessary for the maintenance of public order, the fulfilment of its obligations with respect to the maintenance or restoration of international peace or security, or the Protection of its own essential security interests'.[76] Article 1410 of the NAFTA fulfilled the same goals as the above mentioned BIT but provided more space to the host by providing for financial stability and financial market-related exceptions. More specifically, the Article provided that: 'nothing [...] shall be

---

[74] *Enron Corporation and Ponderosa Assets, L.P. v Argentine Republic* (also known as: *Enron Creditors Recovery Corp. and Ponderosa Assets, L.P. v The Argentine Republic*), ICSID Case No. ARB/01/3, Annulment Proceeding (30 July 2010); *Sempra Energy Int'l v Argentine Republic*, ICSID Case No. ARB/02/16, Annulment Proceeding (29 June 2010); *CMS Gas Transmission Co. v Argentine Republic*, ICSID Case No. ARB/01/8, Annulment Proceeding (25 September 2007).

[75] *Continental Casualty v Argentina* (n 8) paras. 163–68; *LG&E Energy* (n 37) paras. 92–99.

[76] Treaty between United States of America and the Argentine Republic Concerning the Reciprocal Encouragement and Protection of Investment, US–Argentina, entered into force 20 October 1994, 31 I.L.M. 124, Article XI.

construed to prevent a Party from adopting or maintaining reasonable measures for prudential reasons, such as:

(a) the protection of investors, depositors, financial market participants, policyholders, policy claimants, or persons to whom a fiduciary duty is owed by a financial institution or cross-border financial service provider;
(b) the maintenance of the safety, soundness, integrity or financial responsibility of financial institutions or cross-border financial service providers; and
(c) ensuring the integrity and stability of a Party's financial system.'

While NPM clauses would seem to preclude the wrongfulness of an action deemed in breach of the applicable treaty, drafting differences between and among the various treaties make it difficult to authoritatively assert how the clauses operate and/or would be interpreted in a dispute.

Recognising the possibility of an exception under NPM clauses,[77] the tribunal in *LG&E* held that given the aggregate devastating economic, political and social conditions, the domestic regulations taken by Argentina could qualify as 'necessary and legitimate measures' capable of precluding wrongfulness.[78] The tribunal in *Continental Casualty*, similarly, concluded that 'a severe economic crisis [could] thus qualify under Art. XI as affecting an essential security interest' of the state despite the absence of a 'total collapse' of the system and justify an exception because, overall, 'there is no point in having such protection if there is nothing left to protect'.[79]

7.4.2.2 Necessity under Customary International Law

The tribunals in *CMS*, *Sempra* and *Enron* adopted a different approach. While noticing the existence of the NPM clause, they ignored the treaty clause and instead dealt with wrongfulness preclusion on a different ground, rather considering that necessity as provided under Article 25 of the ILC draft articles on Responsibility of States for Internationally Wrongful Acts could justify an exemption to existing commitments under Customary International Law (CIL). As a reminder, Article 25 reads as follows:

---

[77] It should be noted here that while the LG&E tribunal built its argumentation focusing on a NPM logic, it also confirmed its reasoning by applying the customary international law test to the case, as a mere formality. See *LG&E Energy* (n 37) paras. 245–49.
[78] Ibid. para. 240.
[79] *Continental Casualty v Argentina* (n 8) paras. 174–80.

Article 25. Necessity

1. Necessity may not be invoked by a State as a ground for precluding the wrongfulness of an act not in conformity with an international obligation of that State unless the act: (a) is the only way for the State to safeguard an essential interest against a grave and imminent peril; and (b) does not seriously impair an essential interest of the State or States towards which the obligation exists, or of the international community as a whole.
2. In any case, necessity may not be invoked by a State as a ground for precluding wrongfulness if: (a) the international obligation in question excludes the possibility of invoking necessity; or (b) the State has contributed to the situation of necessity.[80]

In other words, while the previous section considered the possibility of lifting state responsibility for treaty breaches on the basis of a treaty exception and in particular circumstances related to public order and, in certain cases, financial stability, Article 25 ILC provides an additional source of exemption grounded on Customary International Law aimed at preserving the 'essential interest' of a state 'against a grave and imminent peril'.[81]

In practice, this approach led to complex and questionable considerations because it required a review of numerous issues such as whether the situation faced by Argentina (a) threatened its essential interests,[82] (b) represented a grave and imminent peril,[83] (c) was the only way available to settle the issue,[84] (d) had not been created by Argentina itself[85] and (e) was temporary.[86] The *CMS*, *Enron* and *Sempra* decisions, overall, rejected the argument that an economic crisis could compromise a state's existence as being 'not convincing',[87] and in *CMS* the tribunal rejected a finding of

---

[80] Responsibility of States for Internationally Wrongful Acts, U.N. 53rd Sess., Art. 25, U.N. Doc. A/56/10 (2001).
[81] Ibid.
[82] See *Sempra Energy International* (n 20) para. 374; *Enron* (n 73) para. 332; *LG&E Energy* (n 37) para. 251; *CMS Gas Transmission Company* (n 29) para. 359.
[83] See *Sempra Energy International* (n 20) paras 329–32; *Enron* (n 73) para. 306; *LG&E Energy* (n 37) paras. 253–57; *CMS Gas Transmission Company* (n 29) paras. 322, 354–56.
[84] See *Sempra Energy International* (n 20) para. 351; *Enron* (n 73) para. 309; *LG&E Energy* (n 37) para. 257; *CMS Gas Transmission Company* (n 29) para. 323, 355–56.
[85] See *Sempra Energy International* (n 20) para. 374; *Enron* (n 73) para. 332; *LG&E Energy* (n 37) para. 251; *CMS Gas Transmission Company* (n 29) para. 359.
[86] See *Sempra Energy International* (n 20) paras. 255–56; *Enron* (n 73) paras. 219–24; *LG&E Energy* (n 37) para. 251; *CMS Gas Transmission Company* (n 29) para. 382.
[87] See *Sempra Energy International* (n 20) paras. 348–49; *Enron* (n 73) para. 306; *CMS Gas Transmission Company* (n 29) paras. 319–22, 354–58.

Customary International Law–grounded necessity because the 'constitutional order was not on the verge of collapse'.[88]

In the end, these three decisions were subsequently annulled, with the Annulment proceedings in both *Sempra* and *CMS* concluding that NPM provisions indeed allowed for measures that deviate from treaty obligations without compensation being due,[89] while the *Enron* Annulment Committee questioned the tribunal's reasoning before concluding that it had no jurisdiction to make its own findings on the matter.[90]

Hence, while some tribunals have ignored the very idea of clauses precluding wrongfulness, all three annulment proceedings provided analogous reasoning in suggesting that, contrarily to the reasoning formulated in the respective awards, NPM treaty provisions had to be considered as a source of exception *per se*, while NPM provisions and Customary international Law exceptions could *not* be considered as equals or in a similar fashion.

In this regard, the *CMS* Annulment Committee emphasised that NPM and CIL exceptions had 'different operation and content' and stated that NPM treaty clauses could not be analysed and applied in light of CIL clauses, which must be interpreted separately.[91] Hence, it concluded that the tribunal had failed to analyse the NPM clause:

> 123. The problem is, however, that the Tribunal stopped there and did not provide any further reasoning at all in respect of its decision under Article XI...[92]
> 124. Along those lines, the Tribunal evidently considered that Article XI was to be interpreted in the light of the customary international law concerning the state of necessity and that, if the conditions fixed

---

[88] *CMS Gas Transmission Company* (n 29) para. 322. See also William W. Burke-White and Andreas von Staden, 'Investment Protection in Extraordinary Times: The Interpretation and Application of Non-Precluded Measures Provisions in Bilateral Investment Treaties' (2008) 48 *Virginia Journal of International Law* 307.

[89] *Sempra Annulment Decision* (n 74) para. 115. See also *CMS Annulment Decision* (n 74) para. 133–35.

[90] *Enron Annulment Decision* (n 74) para. 408 ('Having annulled these findings of the Tribunal, the Committee cannot go further and make its own findings as to whether or not Argentina is entitled to rely on the principle of necessity under customary international law or on Article XI of the BIT, or as to whether or not Argentina is responsible for breaches of its obligations vis-à-vis the Claimants under the fair and equitable treatment clause and umbrella clause of the BIT. These questions could only be determined by a tribunal, in the event that either party were to request resubmission pursuant to Article 52(6) of the ICSID Convention'.).

[91] *CMS Annulment Decision* (n 74).

[92] Ibid, para. 123.

under that law were not met, Argentina's defense under Article XI was likewise to be rejected…[93]

131. Those two texts having a different operation and content, it was necessary for the Tribunal to take a position on their relationship and to decide whether they were both applicable in the present case. The Tribunal did not enter into such an analysis, simply assuming that Article XI and Article 25 are on the same footing.

132. In doing so the Tribunal made another error of law. One could wonder whether state of necessity in customary international law goes to the issue of wrongfulness or that of responsibility. But in any case, the excuse based on customary international law could only be subsidiary to the exclusion based on Article XI.[94]

133. …Article XI and Article 25 thus construed would cover the same field and the Tribunal should have applied Article XI as the *lex specialis* governing the matter and not Article 25.

134. …Only if it concluded that there was conduct not in conformity with the Treaty would it have had to consider whether Argentina's responsibility could be precluded in whole or in part under customary international law.[95]

The *Enron* and *Sempra* Annulment Committees formulated similar reasoning and reached the same conclusion. The *Enron* Committee refused to take a position on whether Article XI of the treaty could equate to CIL exceptions but suggested that in practice both preclusion sources had to be considered and analysed separately.[96] The *Sempra* Committee[97] similarly insisted that a treaty's *lex specialis* (the NPM clause) would have to be applied first, before even considering the possibility of a CIL exception, and explicitly rejected the idea that CIL exceptions could prevail over treaty exceptions. In fact, the Committee went so far as to explain that while a CIL exception was meant to make a wrongful act non-compensable, a treaty exception was rather intended to make the same type of act lawful from the beginning:

196. In the opinion of the Committee, the reasoning of these passages compels the conclusion that the Tribunal did not deem itself to be required – or even entitled – to consider the applicability of Article XI, both because this provision did not deal with the legal elements necessary for the legitimate invocation of a state of necessity and

---

[93] Ibid, para. 124.
[94] Ibid. paras. 131–32.
[95] Ibid. para. 134.
[96] Ibid. paras. 394–405.
[97] *Sempra Annulment Decision* (n 74).

because the Tribunal found that the Argentine economic crisis did not meet the customary international law requirements as set out in Article 25 of the ILC Articles.

197. [...] It does not follow, however, that customary law (*in casu*, Article 25 of the ILC Articles) establishes a peremptory 'definition of necessity and the conditions for its operation'. While some norms of customary law are peremptory (*jus cogens*), others are not, and States may contract otherwise [...]

198. [...] Article XI differs in material respects from Article 25 [...]

199. It is apparent from this comparison that Article 25 does not offer a guide to <u>interpretation</u> of the terms used in Article XI. The most that can be said is that certain words or expressions are the same or similar.

200. More importantly, Article 25 is concerned with the invocation by a State Party of necessity 'as a ground for precluding the wrongfulness of an act not in conformity with an international obligation of that State'. Article 25 presupposes that an act has been committed that is incompatible with the State's international obligations and is therefore 'wrongful'. Article XI, on the other hand, provides that 'This Treaty shall not preclude' certain measures so that, where Article XI applies, the taking of such measures is not incompatible with the State's international obligations and is not therefore 'wrongful'. Article 25 and Article XI therefore deal with quite different situations. Article 25 cannot therefore be assumed to 'define necessity and the conditions for its operation' for the purpose of interpreting Article XI, still less to do so as a mandatory norm of international law.

As a result, while the *CMS*, *Enron* and *Sempra* tribunals considered that no necessity could excuse Argentina's financial crisis–related measures *and* suggested that there was possibly little difference between treaty and CIL exceptions, the respective Annulment Committees both came to very different conclusions.

Implicitly (depending on the case), the Committees also accepted the notion that states ought to have leeway in their decision-making powers. The Committee in the *Enron* Annulment stated clearly that while tribunals ought to consider whether the authorities *could* have relied on alternative measures, it is not for a tribunal to decide whether the authorities *should* have opted of one reason over another. In so doing, they explicitly and repeatedly questioned who would be capable of deciding what course of action is suitable for the State.[98]

---

[98] See *Enron Annulment Decision* (n 74) paras. 309, 360–78, 392–93.

It is worth stressing again that another point of agreement among the Committees is that treaty and CIL exceptions are different and cannot be set on equal footing. That being the case, the Committees have not applied common and consistent reasoning or formulated clear guidelines in this regard. While the Committee in *Sempra* rather clearly confirmed the CMS conclusion that treaty and CIL are different, the *Enron* Committee refused to take a position on this point and annulled the award due to the tribunal's failure to adequately discuss the relevant issues.

The above points are important, as they suggest that despite several cases (and their respective annulments), there is so far no clear rule as to how to rely on and apply treaty and CIL exceptions. Interestingly, the recent tribunal in *Urbaser v Argentina* confirms this particular conclusion, although as will be explained below, it does so by only considering one of the two sources of exception.

In December 2016, the tribunal in *Urbaser v Argentina* also dealt with the issue of necessity,[99] but the award made no mention of NPM clauses and essentially focused on the Customary Law–based and necessity-based argument. Thus, without providing any legal analysis, the award rather matter-of-factly acknowledged that a state of necessity can have priority over investment considerations before concluding that Argentina did not have a choice in taking its measures.[100]

More specifically, the tribunal first focused on Section 2 of Article 25 ILC and commented on the idea that necessity exceptions cannot be invoked where the state is responsible for the duress situation at stake. In this regard, the tribunal found no proof that Argentina could be held responsible for the alleged state of emergency. Perhaps more interesting, the tribunal insisted that a finding of responsibility would require the demonstration 'that the Government must have known that such crisis and emergency must have been the outcome of its economic and financial policy'.[101]

The tribunal next considered Section 1 of Article 25 ILC and discussed whether Argentina had alternative means of acting. To the tribunal, the issue of regulatory alternatives depended on two perspectives, 'the wide one, taking into account the needs of Argentina and its population

---

[99] *Urbaser* (n 73).
[100] Ibid. paras 683–730.
[101] Ibid. para. 711.

nation-wide, and the narrower one of the situation of investors engaged in performing contracts protected by the international obligations arising out of one of the many BITs'.[102] Hence, the tribunal considered that the claimant ought to have offered 'at least a serious indication as to the nature of other measures that had been available to the Government at that time'[103] and concluded that its argument was 'too short' in that it failed to 'resolve the [hosts'] conflict between the obligation to guarantee the Concessionaire's right under the Concession and the access of the poor and vulnerable population to water when this cannot be ensured otherwise than by failing to comply with the host State's obligations toward the Concessionaire'.[104] As a result, the tribunal concluded that Argentina had indeed faced 'a situation of state of necessity as sufficient support for the emergency measures when promulgated in January 2002'[105] and emphasised that, overall, contract renegotiation would have been the only alternative method.[106]

7.4.3 Additional Case Law

Several other investment awards deserve mention, even though the insights they provide are far more limited than the cases highlighted in the previous sub-section. In the main, these awards did not proceed due to jurisdictional issues and thus failed to fully discuss and interpret the prudential measure.

Moreover, while these cases have been described as relating to prudential measures,[107] most only briefly mention or do not even contain the term 'prudential measure'. For instance, the word 'prudential' appears only once in *KT Asia Investment Group*, in a factual manner as part of a descriptive section of the award and without any analysis of the concept.[108] Likewise, in *Renée Rose Levy*, the phrase 'prudential regulator' is mentioned once and without any analysis of prudential measures being

---

[102] Ibid. para. 716.
[103] Ibid. para. 717.
[104] Ibid. para. 720.
[105] Ibid. para. 718.
[106] Ibid. paras. 730–32.
[107] See for instance Andrew Mitchell, Jennifer Hawkins and Neha Mishra, 'Dear Prudence: Allowances under International Trade and Investment Law for Prudential Regulation in the Financial Services Sector' (2016) 19 *Journal of International Economic Law* 787.
[108] See *KT Asia Investment Group B.V. v Kazakhstan*, ICSID Case No. ARB/09/8, Award (17 October 2013).

taken.[109] Another example is *Ping An Life Insurance*, which directly relates to financial matters, but the tribunal does not make mention of financial crisis or prudential measures.[110]

Having said this, such cases provide further evidence of the trend towards regulatory freedom in regards to prudential measures. For instance, while the word 'prudential' does not appear in *Poštová Banka*, the decision nonetheless emphasises that – economic crisis or not – a 'sovereign debt is an instrument of government monetary and economic policy and its impact at the local and international levels makes it an important tool for the handling of social and economic policies of a State'.[111] In other words, while the tribunal did not elaborate on the ability of host states to take prudential measures in order to safeguard financial stability, it nonetheless noted the importance of preserving room for financial, economic and monetary policy.

While making no mention of prudential measures, the *Renée Rose Levy* tribunal did make two important statements concerning a host state's actions in times of financial crisis. First, the tribunal emphasised that 'it [is] logical to assume that State authorities would take measures to maintain the stability of the financial system, as mandated by Peruvian law and, to that end, promulgate Emergency Decrees'.[112] Second, the tribunal recognised the important role to be played by financial authorities in times of financial crises and stated that the relevant governmental authority 'should contribute to the stability of the financial system, for which purpose it has discretionary powers, and that no bank has the power to require [it] to act in a certain way in order to disprove rumors'.[113]

Another example in this regard is the *Saluka* Award, where the investor claimed that its legitimate expectations had been frustrated by the introduction of more stringent prudential rules on banks.[114] On the one hand, the tribunal emphasised 'that the increased stringency of the CNB's prudential rules contributed to the distress suffered by the Czech banking system by forcing the banks to increase provisioning'. As a result, 'it became

---

[109] See *Renée Rose Levy de Levi v Republic of Peru*, ICSID Case No. ARB/10/17, Award (26 February 2014).
[110] See *Ping An Life Insurance Company, Limited and Ping An Insurance (Group) Company, Limited v The Government of Belgium*, ICSID Case No. ARB/12/29, Award (30 April 2015).
[111] *Poštová banka, a.s. and ISTROKAPITAL SE v Hellenic Republic*, ICSID Case No. ARB/13/8, Award (9 April 2015) para. 324.
[112] Renee (n 109) para. 323.
[113] Ibid. para. 335.
[114] *Saluka Investments* (n 24) para. 354.

even more difficult for the banks to meet the regulatory capital requirements than it had been before due to the bad loan problem'.[115] On the other hand, it nonetheless insisted that 'tightening the regulatory regime' had to be seen as part of a larger European Accession process[116] and concluded that the host's financial policy was not a breach of the treaty standards.[117]

Another relevant case is *Fireman's Fund Insurance*, which had the potential to provide important interpretive guidance but did not engage in any legal reasoning on the issue. The case was the first brought under Chapter 14 (cross-border investment in Financial Services) of the NAFTA following a financial crisis in Mexico (and a 96 per cent reduction in the value of the Mexican peso) in the mid-1990s.[118] In defending a claim concerning the loss of investment in financial products, Mexico emphasised that the 'sophisticated investor … made a risky investment in a bank at a time that there was a very serious financial crisis in Mexico'[119] and argued 'that the measures in question are "reasonable measures for prudential reasons" within the meaning of Article 1410 (Exceptions) of the NAFTA'.[120] The tribunal did not engage in, discuss or contribute to the NPM versus customary international law exceptions debate. Instead, the tribunal simply held that before considering an exception a measure must be found to be inconsistent with a provision of the NAFTA and concluded that in the case at stake 'the condition precedent for invocation of the Prudential Measures Exception, a finding of expropriation, ha[d] not been fulfilled'.[121] Hence, it found that it had no ground for proceeding with a further analysis of the prudential exception and left the issue untouched.

---

[115] Ibid. para. 356.

[116] A particularity of the *Saluka* case lies in the fact that the Czech government justified its financial regulatory measures by the fact that the country had signed a pre-accession agreement with the European Commission committing it to bring its regulatory regime into line with the norms in the European Union. In 1999 a 'Twinning Programme' for banking supervision had been launched to adjust the Czech regulatory methodology and the practical implementation of banking supervision to European Union standards. See ibid. para. 357.

[117] Ibid. para. 500 ('The Tribunal does not find, however, that the Respondent has violated its "fair and equitable treatment" obligation by a failure to ensure a predictable and transparent framework for Saluka's investment. Neither was the increase of the provisioning burden for nonperforming loans unpredictable for Saluka/Nomura, nor could Saluka/Nomura legitimately expect that the Czech Republic would fix the legal shortcomings regarding the protection of creditor's rights and the enforcement of loan security within a timescale of help to Nomura.').

[118] See *Fireman's Fund Ins. Co. v the United Mexican States*, ICSID Case No. ARB(AF)/02/1, Award (17 July 2006).

[119] Ibid. para. 116.

[120] Ibid. para. 156.

[121] Ibid. para. 165.

7.5 Conclusions

This chapter leads to two significant conclusions. First, while modern BITs provide for a range of obligations on host states, they also provide for a significant degree of leeway when it comes to implementing CFMs. While most treaties contain a free transfer clause, modern treaties allow parties to make use of NPMs, BoP, essential security, financial stability and prudential exceptions which enable governments to exercise a form of restraint over capital movements. Importantly, the findings of this chapter indicate that it is far more likely that agreements negotiated between developing countries lack sufficient safeguards, whereas agreements which contain a developed country Party are more likely to include a more detailed and wider range of exceptions.

The second conclusion is that in practice investment tribunals are – despite a degree of inconsistency and complexity – progressively recognising that host governments have the means at their disposal under international law to ensure that financial regulatory needs will not systematically lead to the payment of compensation to foreign investors. The case law considered in this chapter demonstrates that tribunals have been cautious to delineate the boundaries of the transfers clause and to make clear that NPMs and other exceptions will be interpreted broadly and enforced.

What is certain, however, is that while the tribunals have identified two methods of allowing a certain degree of regulatory freedom to the host states in times of financial duress, their analysis on prudential measures has been found wanting in two main regards. First, and most obviously, the tribunals have failed to determine which of the interpretive methods ought to prevail over the other, or more precisely when and to what extent one should prevail over the alternative approach. Second, the tribunals failed to provide robust guidelines capable of equipping states (and future tribunals) with a reliable methodological precedent. Thus, while the tribunals provided a direction towards prudential regulatory freedom, the precise legal mechanisms for framing and processing such freedom remains unclear. Regardless, the point to be made here is that there is a trend in the investment tribunal case law pointing towards a general ability of host states to take on measures for prudential reasons. But again, an arbitral tribunal must work with the treaty language with which it is presented, and it is incumbent on governments to negotiate agreements that preserve policy space to implement CFMs should they desire to do so at some point in the future and in particular in times of financial crisis.

8

Conclusions

This book began by introducing the contentious debates on financial liberalisation which have taken place throughout the past two decades, explaining how increased capital volatility created by the 'stop and go' nature of financial cycles led to shocks across the globe and emphasising that progressive liberalisation of cross-border capital flows could not only create wealth and increase investor returns but also increased risks of crises and periods of instability. The book proceeded to discuss how and why commentators and governments increasingly called for a 'brake' mechanism in the form of restrictions or controls on capital flows and explained how such measures have progressively become part of the global financial policy toolbox. Establishing that CFMs are an important element of financial and monetary policy provided the necessary background to enable sufficient discussion and evaluation of whether and to what extent the IMF should monitor CFMs, and the compatibility of CFMs with the various strains of international economic law. This analysis led to the following six observations and concluding remarks.

8.1 The IMF Has Regulation Authority over Capital Controls

Without any international organisation or framework to oversee or regulate cross-border capital flows, it is the view of this author that given the increased importance of capital flows to the global economy, the IMF *had* to assert its authority over capital movements to avoid a legal lacuna and breakdown of the entire system. This being the case, the Articles of Agreement did not provide the Fund with a mandate over capital movements. Thus, the Fund's role in the regulation of the capital account and financial stability matters comes despite the lack of a specifically designed framework or clear mandate to do so.

Nevertheless, over the course of several decades, the Fund increasingly provided itself with the legal mandate over capital movements to act as a *de facto* financial authority. More specifically, and as detailed in Chapter 3, the Fund grounded its shift in focus from a purely monetary institution into a global financial institution on the text and wording of the Articles of Agreement and used an 'Article IV byroad' which allowed it to interpret its constitutive instrument in such a manner so as to escape the historical distinction between 'capital movements' and 'current international transactions'. The *ex post* legitimisation of the mandate expansion was established in several Decisions (most notably in 1977, 2007 and 2012) and was ultimately codified and further embedded in the Institutional View.

Chapter 4 explored the legality of the IMF's shift in mandate over time through *de facto* legal doctrines rather than through the consent of the members. The conclusion is that the Fund can legally monitor and discipline capital movements. This conclusion was reached after evaluating the theory of legal personality of international organisations and the basic principles behind the development of a mandate, most notably the implied powers doctrine. Under the implied powers doctrine, the Fund gains the ability to rely on the intent of its founders to justify mandate evolutions in line with the original purposes of the organisation – since the primary goal of the Fund is to ensure monetary stability, and it is well established that monetary stability can be impacted by unpredictable capital flows, an expansion of the mandate to encompass capital movements into its monetary supervision mandate is legally rational.

The mandate expansion also passes testing under soft law. The IMF did not radically shift its mandate in a short period of time, but rather the expansion of mandate occurred through consistent actions taken and legal documents established over the course of decades. Members never voiced objection to the Fund's expansion into the capital account and, in fact, on a number of occasions called on the Fund to do more to regulate capital flows in a manner that provides stability and predictability to the international financial system. Such calls reinforce the notion that the Fund's evolution is in line with the spirit of the Articles and its role in maintaining stability and predictability. Thus, the constituent doctrine of 'separate will' or '*volonté distincte*' which allows an organisation to act independently – that is, without the express or implied consent of members – also applies to the IMF's mandate expansion as it ensured the Fund maintained relevancy in an ever-changing world.

8.2 The WTO Is Not an Impediment to the Implementation of CFMs

Some commentators have expressed concern that the GATS could effectively prohibit Members from utilising CFMs in times of financial crisis or threat thereof.[1] To others, the WTO is 'the wrong tree to bark up' since the limitations against CFMs under GATS 'are only derived from voluntary commitments on market access adopted by countries [...] And even then, notwithstanding any provision of the GATS ... WTO Members preserve policy space to take measures for prudential reasons or to ensure the integrity and stability of the financial system'.[2] Indeed, the GATS does not prohibit the use of CFMs; rather, limitations to the use of CFMs apply only when a Member has taken liberalisation commitments in the relevant sectors. Moreover, the GATS contains exceptions for BoP difficulties and when IMF policy calls for specific measures going in that direction. In addition, the Annex on Financial Services allows Members to take measures for prudential reasons in order to preserve the integrity and stability of the financial service sector.

After careful analysis of the obligations and exceptions contained in the GATS Agreement (Chapter 5), it is difficult to see how the agreement is a threat to the use of CFMs taken in times of financial instability or in accordance with an IMF package. While there are some limited uncertainties with the BoP clause, and the exception to satisfy a request from the IMF appears unworkable, the prudential exception can operate to effectively allow for legitimate CFMs. The Appellate Body's interpretation of the prudential exception in *Argentina–Financial Services* should serve to provide additional comfort to those that had previously expressed concern. Moreover, the decision should finally end the concern that the second sentence of paragraph 2(a) of the Annex on Financial Services stating that non-conforming measures 'shall not be used as a means of avoiding the Members' commitments or obligations under the agreement' is self-cancelling and therefore worthless.[3] These arguments were always polemical, speculative and rather unconvincing, as reading the provision with state regulatory needs in mind inevitably leads to an alternative and more rational interpretation. Far from being self-cancelling, the wording clearly suggests that in special circumstances measures which would

---

[1] See generally Kevin Gallager and Leonardo Stanley, 'Capital Account Regulations and the Trading System: A "Compatibility Review"' (Pardee Center for the Study of Longer-Range Development, Boston University 2013), and in particular Annamaria Viterbo, 'How to Make the GATS a Code of Conduct for Capital Controls', 9.

[2] Hector R. Torres, 'Capital Controls Can Smoothen Trade Tensions', in Gallagher and Stanley (n 1) 41. See also Deborah Siegel, 'Using Free Trade Agreements to Control Capital Account Restrictions' (2003–2004) 10 *ILSA Journal of International and Comparative Law* 297, 302.

[3] See for instance Todd Tucker, 'The Looming GATS Conflict with Capital Controls', in Gallagher and Stanley (n 1) 32.

normally be inconsistent with WTO commitments that have been undertaken are allowable for prudential reasons, provided that the prudential clause is not used as a mere excuse to initiate protectionist measures and escape the general obligations under the agreement.[4]

8.3 Modern FTAs and IIAs Are Not an Impediment to the Implementation of CFMs, but …

As a general rule, FTAs and IIAs do not result in an unlimited and unrestricted flow of capital across borders. While they tend to facilitate payments and transfers on a broad scale, they also leave room for a range of exceptions, subject to certain conditions such as being reasonable, equitable and non-discriminatory, or ensuring that the measures do not amount to disguised restrictions. In doing so, the agreements allow governments to send an important signal to investors that they are trade- and investment-friendly while also willing to preserve a certain margin of space in which to manoeuvre.

As far as FTAs and IIAs are concerned, the big picture is similar, but FTAs are more comprehensive than IIAs, as they cover more ground. That being the case, when FTAs create obligations relating to capital movements, they almost always provide for a host of exceptions. For instance, FTAs providing for general capital account liberalisation that ensures capital convertibility also have monetary policy exceptions. Provisions on payments and transfers contained in FTAs and IIAs operate in a similar fashion – payments and transfers guarantee free capital flows to facilitate trade in goods as well as the development of financial services and in the case of investment allow repatriation of capital and profits, yet they also provide for built-in exceptions which thus would allow CFMs to coexist. Additional limitations are also typically included in most FTAs. For example, a variety of general exceptions tend to shield domestic regulators in circumstances where the BoP is threatened, or when prudential motivations, including the integrity and the stability of the signatories' financial system, are involved. On the investment side, modern IIAs increasingly include specific mechanisms aimed at shielding host authorities from arbitration claims, including NPMs, BoP, essential security, financial

---

[4] See Antoine P Martin and Bryan Mercurio, 'Liberalization Commitments, Financial Stability Safeguards and Capital Controls: Practice Evolutions from GATS to TPP and Mega-Regional Trade Agreements' (2019) 9(1) *Trade, Law and Development* 71, 86.

stability and prudential exceptions. While in the early 2000s the liberalization in FTAs and BITs may not have 'appear[ed] to have any general principles other than increased openness',[5] the same cannot be said today, as most states are acutely aware that the liberalisation of capital flows should be balanced with appropriate safeguards and exceptions.

We cannot forget, however, that significant disparities exist from one agreement to another. For example, while provisions referring to BoP exceptions are found in most agreements, there are differences in the drafting and effect depending on the signatories involved. For instance, the Korea–EU FTA provides for a comprehensive provision cumulating financial stability safeguards, monetary policy space and BoP exceptions. But many US FTAs – including KORUS – make no mention of a BoP exception. The exact wording and scope of the prudential exception also differ between and among agreements.

The lack of consistency and an overarching framework has led some commentators to question the system's ability to control financial flows. Among the criticisms is the idea that 'many FTAs and [IIAs] may be significantly incompatible with the ability of nations to deploy [CFMs]'[6] and that FTAs and IIAs are 'seen to be very restrictive'.[7] The analysis in this monograph cautions against broad-brushed attacks on instruments of international economic law. Thus, while the Pardee Report is correct in stating that 'many FTAs and BITs do not have a balance of payments safeguard and/or a prudential carve out',[8] many more do contain an increasing number of safeguards, exceptions and exclusions. Contrary to earlier research and popular belief, this is particularly the case with modern agreements negotiated by developed countries such as the CPTPP, USMCA, RCEP and CETA. Such agreements do not constrain or hamper governments in taking measures to promote financial and monetary stability or prevent financial crisis. On the other hand, agreements negotiated between developing countries still tend to be shorter and provide for far fewer safeguards, exceptions and exclusions and therefore potentially limit government policy space.

---

[5] Michael Waibel, 'BIT by BIT: The Silent Liberalization of the Capital Account', in Christina Binder, Ursula Kriebaum, August Reinisch and Stephan Wittich (eds), *International Investment Law for the 21st Century: Essays in Honour of Christoph Schreuer* (Oxford University Press 2009) 498.

[6] Executive Summary, Gallagher and Stanley (n 1) 6.

[7] Kevin P Gallagher, *Ruling Capital: Emerging Markets and the Reregulation of Cross-Border Finance* (Cornell University Press 2015) 6.

[8] Executive Summary, Gallagher and Stanley (n 1) 7.

8.4 Investment Tribunals and WTO Dispute Settlement Panels Have Interpreted the Prudential Exception Broadly, Fairly and Reasonably

There is growing consensus both in trade and investment jurisprudence towards a right to regulate for prudential reasons and in order to preserve financial stability. The prudential exception has been deemed to be functional and to provide States with regulatory room in the face of financial crisis in investment tribunals and at the WTO. The recent jurisprudence in both fora also provides several valuable and instructive lessons as to the effectiveness of prudential provisions. Among those lessons is the distinction the Panel in *Argentina–Financial Services* made between the commonly used term 'prudential measure' and the preferred understanding that the subject matter must refer to measures that are being taken 'for prudential reasons'. The distinction between a 'prudential measure' and a measure taken 'for prudential reasons' may at first appear illusory, but the Panel spent some time explaining the divergence in meaning and effect of the difference in meaning, and this distinction will likely survive and be used in future disputes.

Another related lesson is the focus of both the investment and trade disputes on the circumstances in which the measures have been designed – that is, whether the measures operate in line with the exceptional goal they serve or whether the mechanisms put into place generate a certain degree of unfairness detrimental to the legitimately pursued goal. In this regard, the tribunals have shown a high degree of deference to the host government while at the same time applying the prudential provisions as a good faith or anti-abuse mechanism in a manner similar to the general exception clauses of GATT and the GATS (less the need for a necessity test).

The third lesson is that the tribunals have gone some way in clarifying the context in which exceptions may legitimately occur. While the investment tribunals have not been hesitant to engage in second-guessing policy decisions of host governments, it is noteworthy that those decisions that rejected the notion of preserving economic stability were annulled. Meanwhile, the *LG&E* tribunal held that exceptions could be justified by aggregate devastating economic, political and social conditions. Similarly, the Panel in *Argentina–Financial Services* concluded that measures could be taken for 'preventive or precautionary reasons' so as to prevent risk, injury or danger that does not necessarily have to be imminent and that Members should be granted a certain dose of freedom when assessing the necessity to act. Although the jurisprudence between the investment and trade spheres is not in complete harmony – for instance, the time limitation criteria listed by investment tribunals has not been confirmed by a WTO Panel – the decisions do pave the way for the emergence of a definitive standard, regardless of whether the standards in trade and investment law differ.

The fourth lesson is that prudential exception provisions are not uniformly drafted in most investment and trade agreements, and thus the interpretation of each provision will not necessarily correspond to the interpretation of another provision with even slightly different wording. This is critical to some issues, including when determining whether the provision contains a temporal limitation. In essence, a rather large question regarding the prudential carve-out is whether such measures have to be temporary in nature. In contrast with the findings of investment arbitral tribunals, *Argentina–Financial Services* suggests that governments facing the threat of financial instability could take long-term regulatory measures and remain in compliance with paragraph 2(a) of the Annex, provided that the measures are indeed taken for prudential reasons and without intent to escape existing trade obligations. Here, treaty language may determine the outcome on a case-by-case basis.

The fifth lesson is that while there is an emerging jurisprudence relating to prudential measures, it is important to remember that the tribunals have relied upon different assessment methods in reaching their determinations. The investment tribunals considered whether states could regulate on the grounds of both customary law exceptions and *lex specialis* provisions (NPM) specifically drafted to offer carve-out opportunities in times of duress. In contrast, the WTO tribunal assessed whether a prudential measure could qualify as a general exception to GATS commitments (under Article XIV) and whether the carve-out clause contained in its *lex specialis* Annex on Financial Services could qualify a measure as a valid exception to existing commitments. In the end – and most importantly – the conclusions of both the investment and trade tribunals largely converge in terms of direction but perhaps tend to diverge in terms of logic. The tribunals share a common reliance on a two-step procedure involving the identification of a special objective and establishment of a cause and effect relationship (to ensure that regulatory measures avoid arbitrariness and unjustifiable discrimination and do not constitute disguised restrictions on existing obligations). A divergence, however, occurs, as the depth of the logic provided by the WTO Appellate Body is much more significant than that of investment tribunals which have tended to focus on and make factual assessments without spending much time on the legal analysis. The classic example here is the *Urbaser* case, which while relying on a customary international law approach to justify the use of a prudential measure (due to the lack of NPM clause in the applicable treaty) provided no analysis for the decision or on the legal consequences (or lack thereof) of the absence of an NPM clause in the treaty.

A final lesson is that both the trade and investment tribunals have recognised a right of States/Members to take measures deemed necessary to preserve their essential interests against a threat of instability – that is, before the emergence of a crisis renders action too late and moot – notwithstanding existing commitments, and as long as certain requirements are observed. This is in an important point because although the idea has long been defended in the doctrinal debates, until now it lacked the jurisprudence to substantiate the position and counter critics offering a different viewpoint.

8.5 A CFM Taken in Accordance with IMF Recommendations or Guidance Is Unlikely to Conflict with Modern Trade and Investment Agreements

Another claim which needs to be directly addressed is whether a CFM taken in accordance with IMF recommendations or guidance could create conflicts with obligations undertaken in a trade or investment agreement. The answer to this question can be complex, again, as agreements vary widely in regard to both obligations and exceptions.

In various agreements, indeed, we have seen that CFMs would not be inconsistent with the substantive obligations so long as certain criteria are observed. Here, it is worth recounting that GATS specifically points to coordination with the IMF in several places. For instance, Article XI(2) on payments and transfers states that:

> Nothing in this Agreement shall affect the rights and obligations of the members of the International Monetary Fund under the Articles of Agreement of the Fund, including the use of exchange actions which are in conformity with the Articles of Agreement, provided that a Member shall not impose restrictions on any capital transactions inconsistently with its specific commitments regarding such transactions, except under Article XII or at the request of the Fund.

It is further worth highlighting that Article XII(5)(e) on BoP provides:

> [A]ll findings of statistical and other facts presented by the International Monetary Fund relating to foreign exchange, monetary reserves and balance of payments, shall be accepted and conclusions shall be based on the assessment by the Fund of the balance-of payments and the external financial situation of the consulting Member.

The plain reading of these provisions demonstrates that Members can take measures deemed to conform with IMF policy without violating their commitments in the GATS. Some commentators, however, suggest that articles such as these would not provide valid defenses to GATS obligations. Viterbo, in particular, writes that while GATS Article XI(2) 'contains an "ex ante coordination clause" which prevents conflict between the GATS and the IMF treaties to arise in the first place [...] Since the IMF has never exerted its right to request the introduction of capital controls, the exception set forth by GATS Article XI:2 would remain without effect'.[9] It is not clear, however, why these provisions would remain without any effect. Certainly, just because the IMF has not triggered the provisions does not mean that Members are deprived of a right to regulate for financial stability purposes. The phrasing of the provisions instead suggests that 'a Member shall not impose restrictions on any capital transactions inconsistently with its specific commitments regarding such transactions, except under Article XII or at the request of the Fund'. The 'request' part of the provision may indeed be illusory because in practice, a borrower 'voluntarily' reaches an agreement with the IMF, and the Fund never 'requests' that the country initiate CFMs. Nonetheless, a Member would still be entitled to impose restrictions consistent with their specific commitments, as well as restrictions 'in the event of serious balance-of-payments and external financial difficulties or threat thereof' in accordance with Article XII.

Similar provisions can be found in FTAs and IIAs, where exceptions depend on the absence of discrimination, on the temporary nature of the incriminated measure and on the consistency of the measure with IMF policy. These suggest that where an agreement provides for such a provision and provided that the measure is non-discriminatory and temporary, its consistency with IMF policy would provide a valid defence to a claim of inconsistency with a provision of the treaty. In addition, as illustrated in Chapters 6 and 7, some modern FTAs and IIAs negotiated by leading developed countries now include a range of exceptions and safeguards as well as a special mechanism to deal with claims questioning measures taken in circumstances of economic turmoil – meaning where financial stability is involved – which provides a committee with the authority to recognise the validity of the measures and essentially reject a claim brought to arbitration on such grounds.

That being said, such provisions are not found in every trade and investment agreement, and some IIAs provide for little to no exceptions and

[9] Annamaria Viterbo, 'How to Make the GATS a Code of Conduct for Capital Controls', in Gallagher and Stanley (n 1) 15.

safeguards. This could be problematic, as IMF policies would not provide a valid justification in an ISDS dispute. That being said, another layer of protection could possibly apply via customary international law. As a reminder, Article 31(2)(c) of the Vienna Convention on the Law of Treaties provides that, as a general rule, treaty interpretation may take into account '[a]ny relevant rules of international law applicable in the relations between the parties'. Hence, considering that the policy and mandate of the IMF are shifting towards recognising the necessity of CFMs, it would be coherent to suggest that a measure taken to preserve financial stability would be considered as legitimate – provided that a measure is not discriminatory according to the various standards of international investment law.

8.6 Potential Convergence between WTO and International Investment Law

While there has not been a high degree of uniformity in the investment jurisprudence on prudential measures, several arbitral tribunals have nonetheless paved the way towards recognising a right to regulate for the preservation of financial stability. In this regard, three important aspects are worth emphasising.

First, and from a practical point of view, the investment case law – and in particular the Annulment Proceedings – have provided host states with a certain degree of latitude when regulating for the preservation of economic and financial stability, despite the existence of clear obligations contained in the treaty. At the same time, the awards have failed to clarify whether the overall state of an economy could constitute an acceptable essential interest susceptible to justifying necessity or even whether an economic crisis would constitute a sufficient peril justifying the taking of special measures. The Annulment Committees have, however, for the most part agreed that two distinct exceptions exist which are capable of precluding wrongfulness in specific situations, unlike the initial awards which barely considered the issues.

Notable in this regard is the award in *Continental Casualty*, which stated that a tribunal's 'objective assessment' on regulatory matters 'must contain a significant margin of appreciation for the State applying the particular measure: a time of grave crisis is not the time for nice judgments, particularly when examined by others with the disadvantage of hindsight'.[10] Similarly,

---

[10] *Continental Casualty Company v Argentine Republic*, ARB/03/9, Award (ICSID 2008), para. 181.

while the *Urbaser* award lacked legal analysis it did significantly highlight the importance of differentiating between a wide perspective 'taking into account the needs of Argentina and its population nation-wide' and a 'narrower ... situation of investors engaged in performing contracts protected by the international obligations arising out of one of the many BITs'.[11] Thus, while commentators have asserted that 'to date, [the relevant case law] provide[s] little direct guidance on the interpretation [of] prudential exceptions',[12] this case law nevertheless points very clearly towards regulatory freedom in times of financial duress and thus contains important indicative value despite the absence of direct discussion and decisions on prudential matters per se.

The second point worth emphasising is that the findings of investment tribunals are converging with those of the WTO Appellate Body in *Argentina–Financial Services*. Although the arbitral findings are complex and not entirely consistent, the tribunals have found consensus and agree with the WTO Appellate Body that governments have the right to retain the ability to regulate in times of economic turmoil and instability.

The third observation is that while *Argentina–Financial Services* provides extensive analysis of treaty-based exceptions, the investment tribunals have failed to reach consensus on the proper interpretation. While some tribunals have emphasised the relevance of NPM clauses towards wrongfulness preclusion and would therefore seem to be in line with the WTO jurisprudence, others discussed the opportunity of exceptions grounded in customary international law, particularly in the absence of NPM provisions in the applicable treaties. Hence, the investment jurisprudence to date leaves us uncertain about whether customary international law exceptions might make the treaty-based NPM exception moot and without legal effect. Simply put, the ease with which the *Urbaser* tribunal ignored the NPM argument (and the lack of an NPM clause in the relevant treaty) and entirely focused on customary international law suggests that – if future tribunals followed the path – prudential measures could be dealt with under investment law as a matter of customary international law and without the need for a more specific treaty provision.[13]

***

---

[11] *Urbaser S.A. v Argentine Republic*, ARB/07/26, Award (ICSID 2016), para. 716.

[12] See Andrew Mitchell, Jennifer Hawkins and Neha Mishra, 'Dear Prudence: Allowances under International Trade and Investment Law for Prudential Regulation in the Financial Services Sector' (2016) 19 *Journal of International Economic Law* 787, 800.

[13] To this extent, it is also worth noting that while investment tribunals have so far considered the possibility of justifying measures taken for prudential reasons by making reference to necessity, some commentators have highlighted the idea of relying on 'Force majeure' as a

The main conclusion coming from this analysis is that the risk of international economic law instruments constraining governments from using CFMs as part of their policy toolkit has been overstated. Not only are modern treaties being drafted in such a manner so as to restrict investor protections and governmental obligations through targeted treaty language and the use of safeguards and exceptions, but both investment tribunals and the WTO panel/Appellate Body have demonstrated awareness and appreciation of broader societal interests and in the main avoided interpreting the relevant treaties in a narrow and constricting manner. The main risk lies with FTAs and IIAs that do not incorporate modern drafting techniques which limit or condition State obligations and provide for a wide range of safeguards and exclusions to ensure that legitimate CFMs do not run afoul of treaty obligations. In this regard, I agree with the IMF that 'the limited flexibility afforded by some [trade and investment agreements] in respect to liberalization obligations may create challenges for the management of capital flows',[14] and call upon governments not only to be mindful of the issues discussed in this book when negotiating new agreements but also to seek to revise older agreements to provide for more and better protections as a safeguard should they desire or need to employ CFMs in the face of financial turmoil and crisis.

---

relevant tool for use by States. Gourgourinis, in particular, notes that in various cases falling under the jurisdiction of the Court of Justice of the EFTA and of the Permanent Court of International Justice, financial crisis – particularly the recent Greek crisis – could be considered as force majeure and preclude wrongfulness. Thus, the margin of appreciation doctrine might in the future be considered by investment tribunals either through necessity or force majeure, with the latter perhaps providing a more flexible exception in that the role played by the host state in creating the crisis would not be given the same weight. For more details on the force majeure discussion, see Anastasios Gourgourinis, 'Financial Crisis as Force Majeure under International Law and EU Law: Defending Emergency Measures, à l'européenne in Investment Arbitration under intra-EU BITs', in Christian J Tams, Stephan W Schill and Rainer Hofmann (eds), *International Investment Law and the Global Financial Architecture* (Edward Elgar, 2017) 311–13.

[14] IMF, 'Liberalizing Capital Flows and Managing Outflows' (13 March 2012).

BIBLIOGRAPHY

Books and Chapters

Abdelal R, *Capital Rules: The Construction of Global Finance* (Harvard University Press, 2007).

Alfaro L, *Global Capital and National Institutions: Crisis and Choice in the International Financial Architecture* (World Scientific, 2010).

Amann E, Azzoni C and Baer W, *The Oxford Handbook of the Brazilian Economy* (Oxford University Press, 2018).

Baba C and Kokenyne A, *Effectiveness of Capital Controls in Selected Emerging Markets in the 2000s* (International Monetary Fund, 2011).

Bakker A, *The Liberalization of Capital Movements in Europe* (Kluwer Academic Publishers, 1996).

Blustein P, *The Chastening: Inside the Crisis That Rocked the Global Financial System and Humbled the IMF* (PublicAffairs, 2001).

Bradlow D, 'Rapidly Changing Functions and Slowly Evolving Structures: The Troubling Case of the IMF', *Proceedings of the ASIL Annual Meeting* (Cambridge University Press, 2000).

Brummer C, *Soft Law and the Global Financial System: Rule Making in the 21st Century* (Cambridge University Press, 2015).

Cantore C, '"Parallel Convergences" in Free Trade Agreements on Financial Services: Select Issues', in Rhea Tamara Hoffmann and Markus Krajewski (eds), *Coherence and Divergence in Services Trade Law: European Yearbook of International Economic Law* (Springer, 2020).

Cantore C, *The Prudential Carve-Out for Financial Services: Rationale and Practice in the GATS and Preferential Trade Agreements* (Cambridge University Press, 2018).

Chwieroth J, *Capital Ideas: The IMF and the Rise of Financial Liberalization* (Princeton University Press, 2009).

Dell'Ariccia G and others, *Reaping the Benefits of Financial Globalization* (International Monetary Fund, 2008).

Dolzer R and Schreuer C, *Principles of International Investment Law* (2nd ed, Oxford University Press, 2012).

Eichengreen B, *Toward a New International Financial Architecture: A Practical Post-Asia Agenda* (Institute for International Economics, 1999).

Gallagher K, 'Policy Space to Prevent and Mitigate Financial Crises in Trade and Investment Agreements', in *G-24 Discussion Paper Series Research papers for the Intergovernmental Group of Twenty-Four on International Monetary Affairs and Development* (United Nations Conference on Trade and Development, 2010).

Gallagher K, *Ruling Capital: Emerging Markets and the Reregulation of Cross-Border Finance* (Cornell University Press, 2015).

Gautier P, 'The Reparation for Injuries Case Revisited: The Personality of the European Union', in Erika de Wet and Kathrin Maria Scherr (eds), *Max Planck Yearbook of United Nations Law*, vol 4 (Kluwer Law International, 2000).

Goodman J and Pauly L, 'The Obsolescence of Capital Controls? Economic Management in an Age of Global Markets', in Jeffry A. Frieden and David A. Lake (eds), *International Political Economy: Perspectives on Global Power and Wealth* (4th ed, Routledge, 2000).

Gourgourinis A, 'Financial Crisis as Force Majeure under International Law and EU Law: Defending Emergency Measures, à l'européenne in Investment Arbitration under intra-EU BITs', in Christian J. Tams, Stephan W. Schill and Rainer Hofmann (eds), *International Investment Law and the Global Financial Architecture* (Edward Elgar, 2017).

Grivoyannis E (ed), *The New Brazilian Economy: Dynamic Transitions into the Future* (Palgrave Macmillan, 2016).

Hart J and Spero J, *The Politics of International Economic Relations* (6th ed, Routledge, 2013).

Hieronymi O, 'From "Global Finance" to the Crisis of Globalization', in Otto Hieronymi (ed) *Globalization and the Reform of the International Banking and Monetary System* (Palgrave Macmillan, 2009).

Jeanne O, Subramanian A and Williamson J, *Who Needs to Open the Capital Account* (Peterson Institute, 2012).

Joyce J, *The IMF and Global Financial Crises: Phoenix Rising?* (Cambridge University Press, 2012).

Kaul I, Grunberg I and Stern M, 'Defining Global Public Goods', in Inge Kaul, Isabelle Grunberg and Marc Stern (eds) *Global Public Goods: International Cooperation in the 21st Century* (Oxford University Press, 1999).

Key S, *The Doha Round and Financial Services Negotiations* (AEI Press, 2003).

Klabbers J, *An Introduction to International Institutional Law* (Cambridge University Press, 2002).

Kolo A and Wälde T, 'Capital Transfer Restrictions under Modern Investment Treaties', in August Reinisch (ed), *Standards of Investment Protection* (Oxford University Press, 2007) 213.

Lester S, Mercurio B and Davies A, *World Trade Law: Text, Materials and Commentary* (3rd ed, Bloomsbury, 2018).

Mahoney J and Thelen K, 'A Theory of Gradual Institutional Change', in James Mahoney and Kathleen Thelen (eds), *Explaining Institutional Change: Ambiguity, Agency, and Power*, vol 1 (Cambridge University Press, 2010).
Melvin M, *International Money & Finance* (7th ed, Pearson/Addison-Wesley, 2004).
Mundell R, *International Economics* (Macmillan, 1968).
Polak J, 'The Changing Nature of IMF Conditionality', in *Essay in International Finance* (Princeton University Press, 1991).
Reinhart C and Smith R, 'Too Much of a Good Thing: The Macroeconomic Effects of Taxing Capital Inflows', in Reuven Glick (ed) *Managing Capital Flows and Exchange Rates: Perspectives from the Pacific Basin* (Cambridge University Press, 2011).
Reinisch A, 'Legality of Expropriations', in August Reinisch (ed), *Standards of Investment Protection* (Oxford University Press, 2008).
Reinish A and Schreuer C, *International Protection of Investments* (Cambridge University Press, 2020).
Rodrik D, *The Globalization Paradox: Democracy and the Future of the World Economy* (W. W. Norton & Company, 2011).
Sarooshi D, *International Organizations and Their Exercise of Sovereign Powers* (Oxford University Press, 2005).
Siegel D, 'Capital Account Restrictions, Trade Agreements, and the IMF', in Kevin Gallager and Leonardo Stanley (eds), *'Capital Account Regulations and the Trading System: A "Compatibility Review"'* (Pardee Center for the Study of Longer-Range Development, Boston University, 2013).
Stiglitz J, *Globalization and Its Discontents* (W. W. Norton and Company, 2002).
Subedi S, *International Investment Law* (2nd ed, Hart Publishing, 2012).
Tirole J, *Financial Crises, Liquidity, and the International Monetary System* (Princeton University Press, 2002).
UNCTAD, Bilateral Investment Treaties, 1995–2006: Trends in Investment Treaty Rulemaking, UNCTAD/ITE/IIT/2006/5 (United Nations, 2007).
Viterbo A, *International Economic Law and Monetary Measures: Limitations to States' Sovereignty and Dispute Settlement* (Edward Elgar, 2012).
Waibel M, 'BIT by BIT: The Silent Liberalisation of the Capital Account', in Christina Binder, Ursula Kriebaum, August Reinisch and Stephan Wittich (eds), *International Investment Law for the Twenty-First Century: Essays in Honour of Christoph Schreuer* (Oxford University Press, 2009)
Wallace R and others, *International Law* (8th ed, Sweet & Maxwell, 2016).
White N, *The Law of International Organisations: Second Edition* (2nd ed, Manchester University Press, 2005).
Wolf M, *Why Globalization Works* (Yale University Press, 2004).
Yannaca-Small K, 'Fair and Equitable Treatment Standard: Recent Developments', in August Reinisch (ed), *Standards of Investment Protection* (Oxford University Press, 2008).
Zimmermann C, *A Contemporary Concept of Monetary Sovereignty* (Oxford University Press, 2014).

Journal Articles

Arestis P and Glickman M, 'Financial Crisis in Southeast Asia: Dispelling Illusion the Minskyan Way' (2002) 26(2) *Cambridge Journal of Economics* 237.

Alvarez J and Topalian G, 'The Paradoxical Argentina Cases' (2012) 6(3) *World Arbitration and Mediation Review* 491.

Baldursson F and Portes R, 'Capital Controls and the Resolution of Failed Cross-Border Banks: The Case of Iceland' (2014) 9(1) *Capital Markets Law Journal* 40.

Barbee I and Lester S, 'Financial Services in the TTIP: Making the Prudential Exception Work' (2014) 45(4) *Georgetown Journal of International Law* 953.

Blundell-Wignall A and Roulet C, 'Macro-Prudential Policy, Bank Systemic Risk and Capital Controls' (2014) 2013/2 *OECD Journal: Financial Market Trends* 7.

Bradlow D and Grossman C, 'Limited Mandates and Intertwined Problems: A New Challenge for the World Bank and the IMF' (1995) 17(3) *Human Rights Quarterly* 411.

Broomfield E, 'Reconciling IMF Rules and International Investment Agreements: An Innovative Derogation for Capital Controls' (2012) Columbia FDI Perspectives.

Chari A and Henry P, 'Risk Sharing and Asset Prices: Evidence from a Natural Experiment' (2004) 59(3) *The Journal of Finance* 1295.

Chwieroth J, 'Controlling Capital: The International Monetary Fund and Transformative Incremental Change from within International Organisations' (2014) 19(3) *New Political Economy* 445.

Chwieroth J, 'Managing and Transforming Policy Stigmas in International Finance: Emerging Markets and Controlling Capital Inflows after the Crisis' (2015) 22(1) *Review of International Political Economy* 44.

Chwieroth J, 'Normative Change from Within: The International Monetary Fund's Approach to Capital Account Liberalization' (2008) 52(1) *International Studies Quarterly* 129.

Claessens S, 'Portfolio Capital Flows: Hot or Cold?' (1995) 9(1) *The World Bank Economic Review* 172.

Costinot A, Lorenzoni G and Werning I, 'A Theory of Capital Controls as Dynamic Terms-of-Trade Manipulation' (2014) 122(1) *Journal of Political Economy* 77.

Cottier T and Krajewski M 'What Role for Non-Discrimination and Prudential Standards in International Law?' (2010) 13(3) *Journal of International Economic Law* 817.

Crotty J and Epstein G, 'In Defence of Capital Controls' (1996) 32 *Socialist Register* 118.

Feibelman A, 'The IMF and Regulation of Cross-Border Capital Flows' (2015) 15(2) *Chicago Journal of International Law* 409.

Fu J and Mercurio B, 'Do Beijing's Capital Controls Restrict Hong Kong? Reality or Illusion' (2021) 9(1) *Chinese Journal of Comparative Law* 109.

Gabor D, '(De)Financialization and Crisis in Eastern Europe' (2010) 14(3–4) *Competition & Change* 248.

Gabor D, 'Paradigm Shift? A Critique of the IMF's New Approach to Capital Controls' (2012) 48(6) *Journal of Development Studies* 714.

Gallagher K and Ocampo J, 'IMF's New View on Capital Controls' (2013) 48(12) *Economic and Political Weekly* 10.

Gallagher K and Tian Y, 'Regulating Capital Flows in Emerging Markets: The IMF and the Global Financial Crisis' (2017) 7(2) *Review of Development Finance* 95.

Gari G, 'GATS Disciplines on Capital Transfers and Short-Term Capital Inflows: Time for Change?' (2014) 17(2) *Journal of International Economic Law* 399.

Grabel I, 'The Rebranding of Capital Controls in an Era of Productive Incoherence' (2015) 22(1) *Review of International Political Economy* 7.

Grilli V and Milesi-Ferretti G M, 'Economic Effects and Structural Determinants of Capital Controls' (1995) 42(3) *IMF Economic Review* 517.

Kolo A and Walde T, 'Economic Crisis, Capital Transfer Restrictions and Investor Protection under Modern Investment Treaties' (2008) 3(2) *Capital Markets Law Journal* 154.

Korinek A, 'The New Economics of Prudential Capital Controls: A Research Agenda' (2011) 59(3) *IMF Economic Review* 523.

Krongkaew M, 'Capital Flows and Economic Crisis in Thailand' (1999) 37(4) *The Developing Economies* 395.

Lupo-Pasini F, 'Movement of Capital and Trade in Services: Distinguishing Myth from Reality Regarding the GATS and the Liberalization of the Capital Account' (2012) 15(2) *Journal of International Economic Law* 581.

MacFarlane P, 'The IMF's Reassessment of Capital Controls after the 2008 Financial Crisis: Heresy or Orthodoxy?'(2015)' 19 *UCLA Journal of International Law and Foreign Affairs* 167.

Marchetti J and Mavroidis P, 'The Genesis of the GATS (General Agreement on Trade in Services)' (2011) 22(3) *European Journal International Law* 689.

Martin A, 'Coordinating Modern Cross-Border Financial Services: No Global Policy, No Global Legal Framework, but Some Regional Opportunities' (2016) 50(3) *International Law* 467.

Martin A and Mercurio B, 'The IMF and Its Shifting Mandate towards Capital Movements and Capital Controls: A Legal Perspective' (2017) 44(3) *Legal Issues in Economic Integration* 211.

Martin A and Mercurio B 'The IMF Mandate on Capital Controls: Legal Analysis of the Article IV Byroad and the Institutional View of 2012' (2017) 34(3) *Arizona Journal of International and Comparative Law* 529.

Martin A and Mercurio B, 'Liberalization Commitments, Financial Stability Safeguards and Capital Controls: Practice Evolutions from GATS to TPP and Mega-Regional Trade Agreements' (2019) 9(1) *Trade, Law and Development* 71.

Martin A and Mercurio B, 'Towards Convergence of Trade and Investment Law? A Right to Prudential Measures for the Preservation of Financial Stability' (2018) 51(3) *The International Lawyer* 553.

Meester B, 'The Global Financial Crisis and Global Support for Banks: What Role for the GATS?' (2010) 13(1) *Journal of International Economic Law* 27.

Mercurio B, 'Safeguarding Public Welfare? Intellectual Property Rights, Health and the Continuing Evolution of Treaty Drafting in International Investment Agreements' (2015) 6(2) *Journal of International Dispute Settlement* 252.

Mercurio B, Buckley R and Fu J, 'The Legitimacy of Controlling Capital Flows Under International Economic Law during a Retreat from Globalization' (2021) 70(1) *International and Comparative Law Quarterly* 59.

Mitchell A, Hawkins J and Mishra N, 'Dear Prudence: Allowances under International Trade and Investment Law for Prudential Regulation in the Financial Services Sector' (2016) 19(4) *Journal of International Economic Law* 787.

Moschella M, 'The Institutional Roots of Incremental Ideational Change: The IMF and Capital Controls after the Global Financial Crisis' (2015) 17(3) *The British Journal of Politics and International Relations* 442.

Naim M, 'Washington Consensus or Washington Confusion?' (Spring, 2000) 118 *Foreign Policy* 87.

Neely C, 'An Introduction to Capital Controls' (1999) 81 *Federal Reserve Bank of St. Louis Review* 14.

Ostry J and others, 'Capital Controls: When and Why?' (2011) 59(3) *IMF Economic Review* 562.

Pak-Hung M, 'Impossible Trinity, Capital Flow Market and Financial Stability' (2009) 62(4) *Kyklos* 611.

Reinhart C and Rogoff K, 'The Aftermath of Financial Crises' (2009) 99(2) *American Economic Review* 466.

Rodrik D, 'Goodbye Washington Consensus, Hello Washington Confusion? A Review of the World Bank's Economic Growth in the 1990s: Learning from a Decade of Reform' (2006) 44(4) *Journal of Economic Literature* 973.

Sarooshi D, 'The Essentially Contested Nature of the Concept of Sovereignty: Implications for the Exercise by International Organizations of Delegated Powers of Government' (2003) 25(4) *Michigan Journal of International Law* 1107.

Sauvé P, 'Towards a Plurilateral Trade in Services Agreement (TISA): Challenges and Prospects' (2014) 5(1) *Journal of International Commerce, Economics and Policy* 1.

Schmidt V, 'Discursive Institutionalism: The Explanatory Power of Ideas and Discourse' (2008) 11 *Annual Review of Political Science* 303.

Siegel D, 'Using Free Trade Agreements to Control Capital Account Restrictions' (2003-04) 10 *ILSA Journal of International and Comparative Law* 297.

Sigurgeirsdottir S and Wade R, 'From Control by Capital to Control of Capital: Iceland's Boom and Bust, and the IMF's Unorthodox Rescue Package (2015) 22(1) *Review of International Political Economy* 103.

Singh A, 'Capital Account Liberalization, Free Long-Term Capital Flows, Financial Crises and Economic Development' (2003) 29(2) *Eastern Economic Journal* 191.

Stiglitz J, 'Capital Market Liberalization, Economic Growth, and Instability' (2000) 28(6) *World Development* 1075.

Stiglitz J, 'The World Bank at the Millennium' (1999) 109 *The Economic Journal* 577.
Wade R and Veneroso F, 'The Gathering World Slump and the Battle over Capital Controls' (1998) *New Left Review* 231.
Watanabe R, 'Foreign Exchange and Capital Movement Controls in Taiwan' (1997) 16(1) *UCLA Pacific Basin Law Journal* 1.
Weller C, 'Financial Crises after Financial Liberalisation: Exceptional Circumstances or Structural Weakness?' (2001) 38(1) *The Journal of Development Studies* 98.
Williams D, 'Policy Perspectives on the Use of Capital Controls in Emerging Market Nations: Lessons from the Asian Financial Crisis and a Look at the International Legal Regime' (2001–2002) 70(2) *Fordham Law Review* 561.
Williamson J, 'Democracy and the "Washington Consensus"' (1993) 21(8) *World Development* 1329.
Williamson J. 'A Short History of the Washington Consensus' (2009) 15(1) *Law and Business Review of the Americas* 7.

Online Articles, Newspapers, and Reports

Alfaro L, Chari A and Kanczuk F, *'The Real Effects of Capital Controls: Financial Constraints, Exporters, and Firm Investment'* (Harvard Business School, 2014) Working Paper No. 15-016.
Clements B and Kamil H, *'Are Capital Controls Effective in the Twenty-First Century? The Recent Experience of Colombia'* (International Monetary Fund, 2009) IMF Working Paper No. 09/30 https://papers.ssrn.com/abstract=1356459.
European Central Bank and others, *'Monetary Policy Spillovers, Capital Controls and Exchange Rate Flexibility, and the Financial Channel of Exchange Rates'* (2019) 2019 Federal Reserve Bank of Dallas, Globalization Institute Working Papers www.dallasfed.org/~/media/documents/institute/wpapers/2019/0363.pdf.
Fratzscher M, *'Capital Controls and Foreign Exchange Policy'* (Social Science Research Network, 2012) ECB Working Paper No. 1415 2 https://papers.ssrn.com/abstract=1991084.
G20, 'Communiqué of the Meeting of Finance Ministers and Central Bank Governors' (2010) www.g20.utoronto.ca/2010/g20finance101023.html.
Gabor D, *'Paradigm Shift? A Critique of the IMF's New Approach to Capital Controls'* (Bristol Business School, University of West England, 2011) Working Paper from Department of Accounting, Economics and Finance.
Gallagher K and others, 'Capital Account Regulations and the Trading System: A Compatibility Review' in Pardee Center Task Force Report (Boston University, 2013).
Gallagher K, Sklar S and Thrasher R, 'Quantifying the Policy Space for Regulating Capital Flows in Trade and Investment Treaties' G24 Working Paper (April 2019).
GATT Group of Negotiations on Services, Working Group on Financial Services Including Insurance: Communication from the European Communities, MTN. GNS/FIN/W/1 (10 July 1990).

GATT Group of Negotiations on Services, Working Group on Financial Services Including Insurance: Communication from the United States, MTN.GNS/FIN/W/2 (12 July 1990).

GATT Group of Negotiations on Services, Working Group on Financial Services Including Insurance: Note on the Meeting of 12–13 July 1990, MTN.GNS/FIN/2 (10 August 1990).

GATT Trade Negotiations Committee, Communication from Canada, Japan, Sweden and Switzerland, MTN.TNC/W/50 (3 December 1990).

GATT Trade Negotiations Committee, Communication from Canada, Japan, Sweden and Switzerland: Addendum, MTN.TNC/W/50/Add.2 (15 October 1991).

Giles C, 'Kuroda Calls for China to Tighten Capital Controls' (*Financial Times*, 23 January 2016) www.ft.com/content/03395bdc-c1c4-11e5-808f-8231cd71622e.

Gochoco-Bautista M and Rhee C, 'Capital Controls: A Pragmatic Proposal' (2013) No. 337 ADB Economics Working Paper Series 4.

Graciela L, '*International Capital Flows, Financial Stability and Growth*' (United Nations, Department of Economic and Social Affairs, 2005) DESA Working Paper ST/ESA/2005/DWP/10 www.un-ilibrary.org/economic-and-social-development/international-capital-flows-financial-stability-and-growth_6f7080e3-en.

Habermeier K, Kokenyne A and Baba C, 'The Effectiveness of Capital Controls and Prudential Policies in Managing Large Inflows' IMF Staff Discussion Notes No. 11/14 (5 August 2011).

ICJ, Effects of Awards of Compensation made by the UN Administrative Tribunal, ICJ Report (1956) 61.

IEO IMF, 'IMF's Approach to Capital Account Liberalization 2005' (International Monetary Fund) www.imf.org/en/Publications/Independent-Evaluation-Office-Reports/Issues/2016/12/31/IEO-Evaluation-Report-on-the-IMF-s-Approach-to-Capital-Account-Liberalization-2005-18289.

IEO IMF, *IMF Response to the Financial and Economic Crisis* (International Monetary Fund 2015) www.imf.org/en/Publications/Independent-Evaluation-Office-Reports/Issues/2016/12/31/The-IMF-and-the-Crises-in-Greece-Ireland-and-Portugal-An-IEO-Assessment-42404.

IEO IMF, '*The IMF's Approach to Capital Account Liberalization: Revisiting the 2005 IEO Evaluation*' (International Monetary Fund, 2015) 10 https://ieo.imf.org/en/our-work/Evaluations/Updates/The-IMFs-Approach-to-Capital-Account-Liberalization.

IMF, 'Annual Report on Exchange Arrangements and Exchange Restrictions 2014' (International Monetary Fund, 2014) www.imf.org/external/pubs/nft/2014/areaers/ar2014.pdf.

IMF, 'Annual Report on Exchange Arrangements and Exchange Restrictions' (International Monetary Fund, 2012) www.imf.org/external/pubs/nft/2012/eaer/ar2012.pdf.

IMF, '*Article IV of the Fund's Articles of Agreement: An Overview of the Legal Framework*' (International Monetary Fund, 2006) Policy Paper 10 www.imf

.org/en/Publications/Policy-Papers/Issues/2016/12/31/Article-IV-of-the-Funds-Articles-of-Agreement-An-Overview-of-the-Legal-Framework-PP3883.

IMF, 'Article IV of the Fund's Articles of Agreement: An Overview of the Legal Framework' (International Monetary Fund 2006) Policy Paper 27 www.imf.org/en/Publications/Policy-Papers/Issues/2016/12/31/Article-IV-of-the-Funds-Articles-of-Agreement-An-Overview-of-the-Legal-Framework-PP3883.

IMF, 'Capital Account Convertibility and the Role of the Fund: Review of Experience and Consideration of a Possible Amendment of the Articles' (International Monetary Fund, 1997) SM/97/32.

IMF, 'Communiqué of the International Monetary and Financial Committee of the Board of Governors of the International Monetary Fund, Press Release No. 09/347' (4 October 2009) www.imf.org/en/News/Articles/2015/09/14/01/49/pr09347.

IMF, 'Communiqué of the Twenty-Fourth Meeting of the IMFC: Collective Action for Global Recovery, Chaired by Mr. Tharman Shanmugaratnam, Deputy Prime Minister of Singapore and Minister for Finance' (IMF 2011) IMF Press Release No. 11/348 www.imf.org/en/News/Articles/2015/09/28/04/51/cm092411.

IMF, 'Executive Board Discusses the Fund's Role Regarding Cross-Border Capital Flows' (IMF 2011) Public Information Notice No. 11/1 www.imf.org/en/News/Articles/2015/09/28/04/53/pn1101.

IMF, 'Financial Sector Assessment Program (FSSA)' (7 October 2019) www.imf.org/external/np/fsap/fssa.aspx.

IMF, '*The Fund's Role Regarding Cross-Border Capital Flows*' (International Monetary Fund, 2010) 22 www.imf.org/en/Publications/Policy-Papers/Issues/2016/12/31/The-Fund-s-Role-Regarding-Cross-Border-Capital-Flows-PP4516.

IMF, 'IMF Executive Board Adopts New Decision on Bilateral Surveillance Over Members' Policies' (International Monetary Fund, 2007) Public Information Notice No. 07/69 www.imf.org/en/News/Articles/2015/09/28/04/53/pn0769.

IMF, 'IMF Executive Board Discusses the Multilateral Aspects of Policies Affecting Capital Flows' (International Monetary Fund, 2011) Public Information Notice No. 11/143 www.imf.org/en/News/Articles/2015/09/28/04/53/pn11143.

IMF, 'IMF Executive Board Discusses Recent Experiences in Managing Capital Inflows' (2011) Public Information Notice No. 11/42 www.imf.org/en/News/Articles/2015/09/28/04/53/pn1142.

IMF, '*The Liberalization and Management of Capital Flows: An Institutional View*' (International Monetary Fund, 2012) www.imf.org/external/np/pp/eng/2012/111412.pdf.

IMF, '*Liberalizing Capital Flows and Managing Outflows*' (International Monetary Fund, 2012) www.imf.org/external/np/pp/eng/2012/031312.pdf.

IMF, '*Making the Global Economy Work for All*' (International Monetary Fund, 2008) Annual Report of the Executive Board www.imf.org/en/Publications/AREB/Issues/2016/12/31/Annual-Report-of-the-Executive-Board-for-the-Financial-Year-Ended-April-30-2008.

IMF, 'Meeting New Challenges to Stability and Building a Safer System' (International Monetary Fund, 2010).
IMF, 'Modernizing the Legal Framework for Surveillance – An Integrated Surveillance Decision' (International Monetary Fund, 2012) Policy Paper 7–8 www.imf.org/en/Publications/Policy-Papers/Issues/2016/12/31/Modernizing-the-Legal-Framework-for-Surveillance-An-Integrated-Surveillance-Decision-PP4673.
IMF, 'Pursuing Equitable and Balanced Growth' (International Monetary Fund, 2011) www.imf.org/en/Publications/AREB/Issues/2016/12/31/Pursuing-Equitable-and-Balanced-Growth.
IMF, 'Pursuing Equitable and Balanced Growth' (International Monetary Fund, 2011) www.imf.org/en/Publications/AREB/Issues/2016/12/31/Pursuing-Equitable-and-Balanced-Growth.
IMF, 'Reference Note on Trade in Financial Services' Prepared by the Strategy, Policy, and Review and Legal Departments (9 July 2010) www.elibrary.imf.org/view/journals/007/2010/056/article-A001-en.xml.
IMF, 'The Relationship between the Multilateral Agreement on Investment and the International Monetary Fund' (DAFFE/MAI/RD(96)35, 2 September 1996).
IMF, 'Resolving the Crisis Legacy and Meeting New Challenges to Financial Stability', in *Global Financial Stability Report, April 2010: Meeting New Challenges to Stability and Building a Safer System* (International Monetary Fund, 2010) www.elibrary.imf.org/view/IMF082/10503-9781589069169/10503-9781589069169/C1.xml?redirect=true.
IMF, 'Seminar on IMF Conditionality' (10 July 2001) www.imf.org/en/News/Seminars/Conferences/2016/12/31/Seminar-on-IMF-Conditionality.
IMF Global Financial Stability Report 3. www.imf.org/en/Publications/GFSR/Issues/2016/12/31/Meeting-New-Challenges-to-Stability-and-Building-a-Safer-System.
Jeanne Olivier, Arvind Subramanian and John Williamson, *Who Needs to Open the Capital Account* (Peterson Institute 2012).
Johnston R and Tamirisa N, 'Why Do Countries Use Capital Controls?' (International Monetary Fund, 1998) IMF Working Paper No. 98/181.
Krugman P, 'Saving Asia: It's Time to Get Radical the IMF Plan Not Only Has Failed to Revive Asia's Troubled Economies but Has Worsened the Situation. It's Now Time for Some Painful Medicine' (*Fortune Magazine*, 7 September 1998) https://archive.fortune.com/magazines/fortune/fortune_archive/1998/09/07/247884/index.htm.
Kokeyne A and others, 'Global Liquidity Expansion: Effects on Receiving Economies and Policy Response Options' (International Monetary Fund 2010) IMF Global Financial Stability Report.
Kose M and others, 'Financial Globalization: A Reappraisal' (2009) 56 (1) *IMF Staff Papers* 8.

Lei K, *Financial Services in the Current WTO Framework: Monetary Authority of Macao* (2006), http://docplayer.net/5989501-Financial-services-in-the-current-wto-framework.html.

Minsky H, 'The Financial Instability Hypothesis' (1992) The Jerome Levy Economics Institute Working Paper.

OECD, '*Foreign Direct Investment for Development: Maximising Benefits, Minimising Costs*' (OECD 2002) www.oecd.org/investment/investmentfordevelopment/1959815.pdf.

OECD,' "*Indirect Expropriation" and the "Right to Regulate" in International Investment Law*"', OECD Working Papers on International Investment, 2004/04 (2004) 3.

Qureshi M and others, '*Managing Capital Inflows: The Role of Capital Controls and Prudential Policies*' (National Bureau of Economic Research, 2011) Working Paper No. 17363 www.nber.org/papers/w17363.

Reparation for Injuries Suffered in the Service of the United Nations, Advisory Opinion, ICJ Reports (1949) 178.

Sarooshi D, '*Some Preliminary Remarks on the Conferral by States of Powers to International Organizations*' (NYU School of Law, 2003) Jean Monnet Working Paper 4/03 7.

Schuknecht L, 'A Simple Trade Policy Perspective on Capital Controls' (WTO, 1998) WTO Staff Working Paper No. ERAD-98.

Tucker T and Wallach L, '*To Promote Economic Stability, Nations Must Free Themselves from WTO Financial Deregulation Dictates*' Public Citizen (October 2009) www.citizen.org/sites/default/files/introductiontowtoderegulation.pdf.

U.N. Conference on Trade and Development, Policy Space to Prevent and Mitigate Financial Crises in Trade and Investment Agreements, UNCTAD/GDS/MDP/G24/2010/1 (May 2010), 8.

UNGA, '*The Commission of Experts of the President of the UN General Assembly on Reforms of the International Monetary and Financial System*' (United Nations, 2009) www.un.org/en/ga/president/63/pdf/calendar/20090325-economiccrisis-commission.pdf.

Viterbo A, 'How to Make the GATS a Code of Conduct for Capital Controls', in Kevin Gallagher and Leonardo Stanley (eds), *Capital Account Regulations and the Trading System: A 'Compatibility Review'* (Pardee Center for the Study of Longer-Range Development, Boston University 2013).

Williamson J, Jeanne O and Subramanian A, 'International Rules for Capital Controls' (VoxEU.org, 11 June 2012) https://voxeu.org/article/international-rules-capital-controls.

WTO, 'Overview of the 1995 and 1997 Negotiations on Financial Services' www.wto.org/english/tratop_e/serv_e/finance_e/finance_fiback_e.htm.

WTO Secretariat Background Note 'Exceptions and Balance of Payments Safeguards' (WT/WGTI/W/137, 2002).

INDEX

Alfaro, Laura, 13, 35–37
Argentina - Financial Services dispute (WTO). *See also* GATS application to capital controls/CFMs; prudential measures exceptions
  implications, 120–21, 186–87, 190
  investment jurisprudence, convergence with, 194–95
  on prudential cause requirement, 117–19, 189
  on prevention role of prudential measures, 116–17, 189
  summary, 112–16
  on temporal aspects of prudential measures, 119–20
Argentine financial crisis
  investment jurisprudence arising from, 157, 169–70, 172–80, 190–91
  liberal economics questioned after, xv, 3
Article IV of the Fund's Articles of Agreement - An Overview of the Legal Framework (IMF, 2006), 61–64, 72, 85
Articles of Association of IMF. *See* IMF Articles of Association
Asian financial crisis
  capital controls reappraised after, xvii, 25, 34–35, 61
  IMF policies criticized, 23–24, 89
  investment jurisprudence arising from, 169
  liberal economics questioned after, xv, 3, 14–17
attributed powers doctrine, 78–79, 83

balance of payment difficulties exceptions
  of FTAs (free trade agreements), 132–34, 188
  of GATS, 103–6, 186, 191–92
  of IIAs (international investment agreements), 158–61, 163–64
Barbee, Inu, 111–12
bilateral investment treaties. *See* IIAs (international investment agreements)
bilateral trade agreements. *See* FTAs (free trade agreements)
Bradlow, Daniel D., 88, 89
Bretton Woods system, xix, xx, 8–9, 88
Broomfield, Elizabeth, xxi
Brummer, Chris, xix, 19

Canada-EU CETA. *See* CETA (Comprehensive Economic and Trade Agreement between EU and Canada)
Cantore, Carlo M., 122, 139
capital account liberalization
  capital flows concept, 4–6, 29
  economic growth, uncertain relationship with, xviii, 18–19, 56
  financial crises, reappraisal after, xix–xx, 3–4, 14–18, 25–26, 34–36, 61
  IMF supervision of. *See* IMF, capital flows supervision
  sequencing doctrine limiting, 20–22
  trade liberalization, asymmetry with, 18–20
  under FTAs, 125–26, *See also* FTAs (free trade agreements)

capital controls/CFMs, xv–xvi
  alternatives to, 39
  arguments against, 30–33
  arguments in favour, 33–37
  CFMs definition, 26–29
  in China. *See* China, capital controls
  complementary and temporary
    use recommendations, 38–39,
    65–66, 71–72
  conflicts with liberalization
    objectives, xxii–xxiii, 94–95
  currency manipulation concern, 33,
    36–37, 40, 42
  effectiveness debated, 37–38
  financial crises, reappraisal after,
    xix–xx, 3–4, 14–18, 25–26,
    34–36, 61
  FTAs application. *See* FTAs (free
    trade agreements)
  G20 on, xxii, 65, 68–69, 86, 93
  GATS application. *See* GATS
    application to capital controls/
    CFMs
  IEL framework. *See* international
    economic law framework for
    capital controls/CFMs
  IIAs application. *See* IIAs
    (international investment
    agreements)
  IMF supervision of. *See* IMF, capital
    controls/CFMs supervision
    (*de facto*)
  policymaking dilemma, 41–43
  types, 10
capital flows concept, 4–6, 29
CETA (Comprehensive Economic and
  Trade Agreement between EU
  and Canada)
  balance of payments difficulties
    exception, 159–60
  on current and capital account
    liberalization, 125
  expropriation protections, 155
  FET (fair and equitable treatment)
    standard, 153–54
  government authority/procurement
    exclusion clauses, 131–32
  'investment' definition, 144

  national security exception, 161
  national treatment provision,
    148–49
  on payments and transfers, 127, 129,
    130, 148
  prudential measures exceptions,
    137–38, 140–41, 162
CFMs (capital flow management
  measures). *See* capital controls/
  CFMs
China, capital controls
  capital outflows restriction aim,
    28–29
  currency manipulation using, 33,
    40, 42
  IMF's response, xvi–xvii
Clements, Benedict, 37
Comprehensive and Progressive
  Agreement for Trans-
  Pacific Partnership. *See*
  CPTPP (Comprehensive and
  Progressive Agreement for
  Trans-Pacific Partnership)
Comprehensive Economic and
  Trade Agreement between
  EU and Canada. *See* CETA
  (Comprehensive Economic and
  Trade Agreement between EU
  and Canada)
Cottier, Thomas, 111
CPTPP (Comprehensive and
  Progressive Agreement for
  Trans-Pacific Partnership)
  balance of payment difficulties
    exception, 133, 160–61
  expropriation protections,
    154–57
  FET (fair and equitable treatment)
    standard, 152–53
  government authority/procurement
    exclusion clauses, 131, 132
  'investment' definition, 143–44
  on market access, 129–30
  national security exception, 161
  national treatment provision,
    148–49
  on new financial services provision,
    130

on payments and transfers, 126–28, 148
prudential measures exception,
  136–37, 162
cross-border capital flows. *See* capital
  account liberalization
currency manipulation using capital
  controls, 33–37, 40, 42

*Decision on Bilateral Surveillance Over
  Members' Policies* (IMF, 2007),
  64–67, 69, 72, 74–75
*Decision on Surveillance over Exchange
  Rate Policies* (IMF, 1977), 59–61,
  63, 72, 75, 87
developing countries
  BITs (bilateral investment treaties)
    of, 143, 162–63, 167–68
  capital controls/CFMs, value for,
    xx, 38
  liberal economic model, adoption
    of, 10, 12
  Mundell-Fleming model,
    application to, 41–42

economic crises. *See* Argentine financial
  crisis; Asian financial crisis;
  GFC (Global Financial Crisis)
EEA (European Economic Area)
  Agreement, 161
essential interests exceptions in IIAs,
  161–62, 172–80, 191
EU-Canada CETA. *See* CETA
  (Comprehensive Economic and
  Trade Agreement between EU
  and Canada)
express powers doctrine, 78–79, 83
expropriation protections of IIAs,
  154–58

Feibelman, Abel, 50, 70, 72
FET (fair and equitable treatment)
  standard of IIAs, 150–54, 171–72
financial crises. *See* Argentine
  financial crisis; Asian financial
  crisis; GFC (Global Financial
  Crisis)
Financial Sector Assessment
  Programmes (IMF), 57–58

Financial Services Annex of GATS
  generally, 55, 98, 100, 102
  prudential measures exception,
    108–12
  WTO rulings interpreting. *See
    Argentina - Financial Services*
    dispute (WTO)
financial services industry, 18–19, 55
force majeure doctrine, 194
Fratzscher, Marcel, 30
FTAs (free trade agreements)
  balance of payment difficulties
    exceptions, 132–34, 188
  capital controls/CFMs application,
    conclusions on, 187–93
  current and capital account
    liberalization provisions,
    125–26
  GATS on, 123–24
  generally, 122–23, 141
  government authority/procurement
    exclusion clauses, 131–32
  investment dispute provisions,
    140–41
  MFN, market access and national
    treatment provisions, 124,
    130–32, 135–36
  monetary policy exclusions, 140
  payment and transfer provisions,
    126–30
  prudential measures exceptions,
    134–40, 190
  typical FTA provisions, 124–25

G20 on capital controls/CFMs, xxii, 65,
  68–69, 86, 93
Gabor, Daniela, 17, 20, 37
Gallagher, Kevin P.
  *Capital Account Regulations and the
    Trading System* (Pardee Report,
    2013), 94, 110, 188
  on capital inflows and economic
    crises, 35–36, 39
  on global coordination of capital
    flow management, 45, 90,
    93
  on IMF's *Institutional View*, 46
Gari, Gabriel, 107

GATS application to capital controls/CFMs
　balance of payment difficulties exception, 103–6, 186, 191–92
　conclusions on, 185–87, 191–92
　FTAs under GATS, 123–24, *See also* FTAs (free trade agreements)
　IMF request satisfaction exception, 106–8, 186
　introduction to study, 97–98
　MFN, market access and national treatment provisions, 98–103, 108, 114
　payments and transfers provision, 191–92
　potential conflicts with other obligations, 94–95
　prudential measures exception, 108–12
　WTO rulings interpreting. See *Argentina - Financial Services* dispute (WTO)
Gautier, Philippe, 80
Geithner, Timothy, 112
General Agreement on Trade in Services (WTO). *See* GATS application to capital controls/CFMs
GFC (Global Financial Crisis)
　IMF's *Institutional View* formulated after, 65–70
　liberal economics and capital controls reappraised after, xv, xix, 3, 16, 17, 25–26, 35
Gochoco-Bautista, Maria Socorro, xx–xxi, 17, 33, 36, 40, 50, 72
Gourgourinis, Anastasios, 194
Grabel, Ilene, xix, 14

Hart, Jeffrey A., 6–7
Hieronymi, Otto, xix, xx, 60
Hong Kong Declaration (IMF, 1977), 59–61, 63, 72, 75, 87

IIAs (international investment agreements)
　balance of payment difficulties exceptions, 158–61, 163–64
　capital controls/CFMs application, conclusions on, 187–93
　expropriation protections, 154–58
　FET (fair and equitable treatment) standards, 150–54, 171–72
　generally, xxi, 142–43, 183
　'investment' definitions, 143–46
　investment jurisprudence. *See* investment jurisprudence
　national treatment provisions, 142, 148–50
　NPM (non-precluded measures) and necessity exceptions, 161–62, 172–80, 191
　payment and transfer provisions, 146–48, 169–72
　prudential measures exceptions, 162–64, 180–83, 190
　trends in BITs (bilateral investment treaties), 163–68
IMF Articles of Association
　Article I Purposes, 7–8, 51–52, 82, 83, 87
　Article IV Obligations Regarding Exchange Arrangements, 52–53, 57, 60, 62–63, 73, 82–83, 87–88
　Article VI Capital Transfers, 52, 60, 83, 106–7
　Article VIII General Obligations of Members, 52, 57
　Article XII Organization and Management, 82
IMF, capital controls/CFMs supervision *(de facto)*
　Articles of Association, mandate under, 50–56
　'Article IV byroad' strategy, 59–65, 73–74, 86–88, 184–85
　CFMs, IMF definition, 26–27
　Chinese controls, response to, xvi–xvii
　conclusions on, 184–85, 191–93
　as global financial institution, 56–59
　Institutional View. See *Institutional View* (IMF, 2012)
　Integrated Surveillance Decision (2012), mandate under, 72–74

INDEX

legitimacy concerns, 45–47, 76–77
mandate shifts, international law
  theory on, 77–81, 185
theory applied to IMF, 81–84
volonté distincte (separate will)
  doctrine application, 84–91, 185
IMF, capital flows supervision
capital controls/CFMs, concerns
  about, 30–32, 38
initiatives, xxi–xxii, 12–14
'integrated approach' of *Institutional View*, 70–71
mandate for, 6–9, 49–52, 55–56
policies criticized, 21–25, 45–46, 89
IMF request satisfaction exception
  (GATS), 106–8, 186
implied powers doctrine, 78–81, 83–84, 185
'impossible trinity' (Mundell-Fleming model), 41–42
indirect expropriation, 155–58
inherent powers doctrine, 81, 83
Institutional View (IMF, 2012)
background to, 65–70
on conflicts with liberalization
  objectives, xxii–xxiii, 94–95, 149
significance, xvii–xviii, xxiv, 46–47, 50, 71–75
Integrated Surveillance Decision (IMF, 2012), 72–74
International Bank for Reconstruction and Development (World Bank), 7, 89–90
international economic law framework for capital controls/CFMs
coherence lacking, xx–xxiii
conclusions on, 184–95
consequences of incoherence
conflicts with liberalization
  objectives, xxii–xxiii, 94–95
currency manipulation, 33, 36–37, 40, 42
snowball effects, 43
FTAs application. *See* FTAs (free trade agreements)
GATS application. *See* GATS application to capital controls/CFMs

IIAs application. *See* IIAs
  (international investment agreements)
IMF as *de facto* supervisor. *See*
  IMF, capital controls/CFMs
  supervision *(de facto)*
legal analysis lacking, 93–94
international investment agreements.
  See IIAs (international
  investment agreements)
International Monetary Fund. *See* IMF
  entries
international organizations, mandate
  shifts, 77–81, 185
'investment' definitions in IIAs, 143–46
investment jurisprudence. *See also*
  IIAs (international investment
  agreements)
FET (fair and equitable treatment)
  standards interpreted, 150–53, 171–72
force majeure doctrine application, 194
FTA (free trade agreement)
  provisions on, 140–41
generally, 168–69, 183, 189–91, 193–95
on indirect expropriation, 156–58
NPM (non-precluded measures)
  and necessity exceptions
  interpreted, 172–80, 191
payment and transfer provisions
  interpreted, 169–72
prudential measures exceptions
  interpreted, 138–40, 180–83, 190

Jeanne, Olivier, 17, 20, 32–35, 38–39
Joyce, Joseph P., 13–14, 21, 22, 24, 46, 60–61

Kamil, Herman, 37
Key, Sydney J., 111
Keynes, John Maynard, 8, 41, 54
Kolo, Abba, 146
Korinek, Anton, 28, 90
Krajewski, Markus, 111
Krugman, Paul, xvii, 16
Kuroda, Haruhiko, xvi–xvii

Lagarde, Christine, xvi–xvii
legal framework for capital controls/
    CFMs. *See* international
    economic law framework for
    capital controls/CFMs
legal personality of international
    organizations, 77–82, 185
Lester, Simon, 111–12
liberal economic model
    capital controls/CFMs, conflicts
        with, xxii–xxiii, 94–95
    cross-border capital flows. *See*
        capital account liberalization
    and financial services industry,
        18–19, 55
    validity questioned, xv, xvii
    Washington Consensus, 10–12, 56, 60
Liberalization and Management of
    Capital Flows - An Institutional
    View. See *Institutional View*
    (IMF, 2012)
long-term capital flows, 5, 6

mandate shifts by international
    organizations, 77–81, 185
market access provisions
    of FTAs (free trade agreements),
        124–25, 129–30
    of GATS, 98–101, 103, 108
MFN (most-favoured-nation)
    provisions
    of FTAs (free trade agreements), 124,
        131–32, 136
    of GATS, 98, 114
    of IIAs (international investment
        agreements), 142
Mo Pak-Hung, 41–42
monetary policy exclusions of FTAs,
    140
Moschella, Manuela, 13, 90–91
Mundell-Fleming model ('impossible
    trinity'), 41–42

NAFTA (North American Free Trade
    Agreement), 134–35, 138–40,
    182–83, *See also* USMCA (United
    States-Mexico-Canada)
    Agreement

national security exceptions in IIAs,
    161–62, 172–80, 191
national treatment provisions
    of FTAs (free trade agreements), 124,
        130–32, 135–36
    of GATS, 98–99, 101–3
    of IIAs (international investment
        agreements), 142, 148–50
necessity exceptions in IIAs, 161–62,
    172–80, 191
Neely, Christopher J., 17–18, 38
Nixon, Richard, 9
NPM (non-precluded measures)
    exceptions in IIAs, 161–62,
    172–80, 191

Ocampo, Jose Antonio, 39, 90

payment and transfer provisions
    of FTAs (free trade agreements),
        126–30
    of GATS, 191–92
    of IIAs (international investment
        agreements), 146–48, 169–72
protectionist use of capital controls/
    CFMs, 33, 36–37, 40, 42
prudential measures exceptions
    of FTAs (free trade agreements),
        134–40, 190
    of GATS, 108–12
        WTO rulings interpreting. *See*
        Argentina - Financial Services
        dispute (WTO)
    of IIAs (international investment
        agreements), 162–64, 180–83,
        190

Qureshi, Mahvash S., 28, 37, 38

rachet clauses, 124–25
RCEP (Regional Comprehensive
    Economic Partnership)
    Agreement
    balance of payment difficulties
        exception, 133–34, 160
    expropriation protections, 155
    'investment' definition, 144
    national security exception, 161

national treatment provision, 148–49
on payments and transfers, 127–29, 148
prudential measures exception, 137, 162
regional trade agreements. *See* FTAs (free trade agreements)
regulatory expropriation, 155
Rhee, Changyong, xx–xxi, 33, 36, 40, 50, 72

Sarooshi, Dan, 81
Sauvé, Pierre, 98
separate will *(volonté distincte)* doctrine, 84–91, 185
sequencing doctrine, 20–22
short-term capital flows, 5–6
Siegel, Deborah, 50, 60, 72
Soto, Hernando de, 12
Spero, Joan Edelman, 6–7
standstill clauses, 124
Stanley, Leonardo, 94, 110, 188
Stiglitz, Joseph, 23, 45–46, 89–90
Subramanian, Arvind, 34–35, 38–39

Tirole, Jean, xix, 20
Torres, Hector R., 186
trade and capital flows asymmetry, 18–20
transfer provisions. *See* payment and transfer provisions
Tucker, Todd, 110

United Nations, xxii, 79–80
USMCA (United States-Mexico-Canada) Agreement. *See also* NAFTA (North American Free Trade Agreement)

balance of payments difficulties exception, 132–33, 160–61
expropriation protections, 154–57
FET (fair and equitable treatment) standard, 152–53
government procurement of financial services exclusion clause, 132
'investment' definition, 144
national security exception, 161
national treatment provision, 148–49
on payments and transfers, 127, 128, 147–48
prudential measures exception, 137, 162

Viterbo, Annamaria, 110, 192
volonté distincte (separate will) doctrine, 84–91, 185

Wade, Robert, 15, 89
Waibel, Michael, 146–47, 188
Wälde, Thomas, 146
Wallace, Rebecca M.M., 77
Washington Consensus, 10–12, 56, 60
White, Nigel D., 79–80, 85
Williamson, John, 10–12, 34–35, 38–39
World Bank (International Bank for Reconstruction and Development), 7, 89–90
WTO (World Trade Organization), xxi, 20, 55, 82, *See also* GATS application to capital controls/CFMs

Xi Jinping, xvi–xvii

For EU product safety concerns, contact us at Calle de José Abascal, 56–1°, 28003 Madrid, Spain or eugpsr@cambridge.org.

www.ingramcontent.com/pod-product-compliance
Ingram Content Group UK Ltd.
Pitfield, Milton Keynes, MK11 3LW, UK
UKHW022246220326
469255UK00019B/387